ICHI BAN OUTFIT

TITLE: ICHI BAN OUTFIT
AUTHOR: E. GERALD PIRES
PUBLISHER: ELDERBERRY PRESS, LLC
1393 OLD HOMESTEAD ROAD, SECOND FLR
OAKLAND OR 97462
PUBLICIST: D.W.ST.JOHN TEL:541.459.6043
PUB DATE: 2/15/03
ALL RIGHTS CONTACT: D.W.ST.JOHN
INITIAL PRINT RUN: 20,000
RETAILERS: B&N, BORDERS, WALDENS
WHOLESALERS: B&T, INGRAMS, SPRING
ARBOR
DISTRIBUTORS: PARTNERS WEST
MEDIA EXPOSURE: RADIO, TV INTERVIEW R
PRINT MEDIA: ADS IN PW, THE WASHINGTON
IMES
BOOK TOUR: 11 CITY WEST COAST
ISBN:1930859392 212p. hardcover, $29.95 retai

ICHI
BAN
OUTFIT

E. GERALD PIRES

Elderberry Press

Elderberry Press

1393 Old Homestead Drive, Second floor
Oakland, Oregon 97462—9506.
E-MAIL: editor@elderberrypress.com
TEL/FAX: 541.459.6043

All Elderberry books are available from your favorite bookstore,
amazon.com, or from our 24 hour order line: 1.800.431.1579

Library of Congress Control Number: 2002109541
Publisher's Catalog—in—Publication Data
Ichi Ban Ou'fit/E. Gerald Pires
ISBN 1-930859-39-2
1. Japan.
2. SCARWAF.
3. U.S. Army.
4. Military History.
5. 474th Signal Aviation Construction Company.
I. Title

This book was written, printed and bound in the United States of America.

For all of the Officers and Men who served with the
474th Signal Aviation Construction Company

But especially for
Richard L. Wakefield
who brought us together again

CONTENTS

Introduction: A Very Unique Unit..............................9
Chapter I   Camp Stoneman, California...........................13
Chapter II   Going To War......................................18
Chapter III   First Impressions.................................27
Chapter IV   474th Signal Aviation Construction Company..34
Chapter V   Misawa...46
Chapter VI   Shiroi...59
Chapter VII   Ashiya I...65
Chapter VIII   Kashii...83
Chapter IX   Ashiya II..92
Chapter X   Showa I..103
Chapter XI   Fujiyama...113
Chapter XII   Showa II...133
Chapter XIII   Nikko..146
Chapter XIV   Showa III..156
Chapter XV   The Official End.................................165
Chapter XVI   Itazuke..175
Chapter XVII   "Figmo" At Fuchu.................................186
Chapter XVIII   The Final End....................................191
Chapter XIX   The Aftermath....................................197

Appendix I   More Men of the 474th , 1954.....................202
Appendix II   Full Roster as of November 1, 2001...............205

INTRODUCTION

Introduction
A Very Unique Unit
Col. John W. Leddon, Jr. (USA Ret.)

The 474th Signal Aviation Construction Company was one of the most unique units ever in the United States Army. The fact that it was one of a very limited number of Army units to be assigned to the United States Air Force, in accordance with a program known as Special Category Army with Air Force (SCARWAF) made it unique in that aspect alone. However, it was the great variety of construction projects, the wide dispersion of those projects and the conditions under which they were completed, that set the 474th Signal apart.

The program entitled SCARWAF was only in effect during the period 1949 to 1956. The majority of the units were Aviation Engineer, whose mission it was to construct air bases and perform related supply and maintenance functions. A number of Ordnance, Medical and Signal units were also assigned to the Air Force under this program. Although the term SCARWAF was not employed until 1949, certain units, as mentioned above, had been attached to the Air Force since it was established as a separate Service in 1947.

Officially designated the 474th Signal Heavy Construction Company (Aviation) (Colored), the unit was activated on the Island of Guam on 30 August 1946 with an authorized strength of 7 officers and 149 enlisted men. Although assigned as part of the United States Army Forces, Pacific, it was activated by the Commander-in-Chief, United States Air Force, Pacific and further assigned to the Twentieth Air Force.

After going through a series of redesignations and reorganizations, the 474th was reassigned, effective 22 October 1950, to the Far East Air Material Command, Fuchu, Japan to support the Far East Air Force during the Korean conflict. In response to this reassignment the Company departed Guam on 14 October 1950 and arrived in Japan on 18 October. By this date, the designation (Heavy) and (Colored) had been dropped as the unit was capable of all levels of construction and was fully integrated.

The 474th established itself outside the city of Tachikawa on a former Japanese airfield at Showa Mae. This sub-base was known then as FEAMCOM Area B and it was from this home station that the construction teams traveled throughout the Far East to complete their tasks. The workload increased until there was rarely more than half the Company in the barracks at Showa Air Base at any one time. When at home station, training continued, equipment was maintained, and preparations made to move out again.

On 25 May 1951, the name was finally changed to the 474th Signal Aviation Construction Company, with an authorized strength of 6 officers and 213 enlisted men. Thus named and organized, the Company performed the many varied construction, maintenance and repair projects for which it gained a reputation as a highly reliable organization composed of skilled construction soldiers.

Construction of antenna fields became the most common assignment but construction of steel structures, upon which Air Force technicians installed electronic gear, was also routine. These antenna fields often contained wooden, spliced poles and steel towers ranging up to 110 feet. At the same time the usual work of a Signal Construction Company was also completed. Wiring an alarm system in a bomb storage area in Korea, as well as an underground cable system on Iwo Jima, made hazardous by volcanic fumes, and building an overhead power line on that island, are examples of the variety of the projects completed by the 474th. On several small islands off the coast of Japan and Korea, in extreme weather conditions, the competence and determination of the construction crews were evident as they completed their projects skillfully and on time. Throughout Japan major antenna fields were constructed or rebuilt at places such as Sasebo, Ashiya, Sendia, Fukuoka, Misawa, and elsewhere.

The primary, almost exclusive method of travel was by air, though often the trucks and other heavy equipment were moved by rail and water. Some teams would be gone for several weeks, others for a few days.

The other side of this excellent outfit was the discipline of these construction teams while away from the home station. Unfavorable reports were very rare while complimentary reports concerning the behavior of the troops and their efficiency on the job, were regularly received. Members of the 474th were known for their pride, sharp appearance and soldierly bearing.

The 474th Signal Aviation Construction Company was awarded the Meritorious Unit Citation for exceptionally meritorious conduct in outstanding performance of service to the United Nations Forces during the Korean conflict. The red campaign streamer, with the white letters KO-REA, was tied to the company guidon by Major General Paul E. Ruestow, Commander Far East Air Logistic Force, during a parade on Tachikawa Air Base on 26 September 1953. In part the citation reads, "…personnel of this Company made an outstanding contribution to the accomplishment of the Far East Air Force mission through their construction, repair, rehabilitation and maintenance of communications systems throughout the theater…" The citation ends, "Through their collective diligence and determination in discharging urgent responsibilities imposed by combat operations and through their outstanding resourcefulness, devotion to the best interests of the military service, the personnel of the 474th Signal Aviation Construction Company greatly enhanced the effectiveness of communications systems in the Far East theater, and reflected great credit upon themselves, the Far East Air Forces and the United States Air Force."

The 16th Communication Construction Squadron, USAF, was moved from stateside to Showa Air Base during the last two months of 1953 to replace the 474th which was officially inactivated on 18 January 1954 in Japan. A highly specialized unit had completed its mission and passed into history. Now it exists only in the memory of its veterans.

During the peak years of 1952 and 1953, the unit became very confident of themselves and was a proud, cocky outfit. They exhibited this attitude by wearing their bright orange scarves and spit shined boots, whenever appropriate to do so. "We are good and we know we are good," is the way one sergeant put it. The Company Commander was once asked by an officer of another unit, "What do you feed those guys?" This attitude still prevails at the yearly reunions of this truly unique organization.

CHAPTER I

Camp Stoneman, California

I t wasn't because of a matter of preference that I was pacing back and forth across the brick platform in front of the Pittsburg, California train station that night in October, 1952.

Preferences didn't count then. I was next to the lowest form of animal life on Earth – an Army Private just out of field wire school.

Still, eleven others and I had been the envy of our wire class when orders came down assigning us to the Air Force for project SCARWAF (Special Category Army Reassigned With Air Force). None of us knew what we were getting into, but most of us were given the opportunity to volunteer for this duty. I volunteered because I already had a friend taking flight training in the Air Force. However, the same orders read, "destination EVIL" which sounded ominous in itself. As the loneliness and chill and dampness of the station pressed down upon us, I became convinced that the code word was descriptive. We all expected to be in Korea very soon and none of us had ever been outside our Country before.

I was kicking myself for leaving home in Jacksonville, Illinois a day early. I could have had another day to explore the cliffs along the Illinois River, and to enjoy the crisp air and sunshine. The color of the foliage that autumn was as beautiful as I had ever remembered it to be. I hated to leave.

When I tried to get my duffel bag out of the baggage room, the fellow in there said it would be delivered to Camp Stoneman. I decided then that I had better go on into camp.

There were quite a number of Army and Air Force men that had been on the same train. We waited about twenty minutes before a military bus pulled in behind the station to pick us up. We rode through Pittsburg to Camp Stoneman, which was located on the other side of town.

The bus driver let us out in front of a shed-like building. We went inside and registered on some cards so that they would know that we were on the base. It was the 2349th Personnel Processing Group.

When we got outside again, the bus was gone, but an open truck was waiting to take us to another place. The Army got off at the first stop and the Air Force at the next. I went with the last group since I had been assigned to them.

However, I had no more than stepped through the door when a sergeant saw my Army uniform and said that I was in the wrong place. He described at great length how to get to the right place. After a considerable amount of walking, I arrived at the "right place". Glancing at my orders, a fellow at the "right place" informed me that I was at the wrong place and that I should return to the other place to get my records checked.

With no small amount of luck, I found my way back to the original place, but by this time I was at the end of a long line waiting for records check. Those Air Force boys apparently hadn't heard of SCARWAF. I was able to escape from there with no more injury than a small pox vaccination.

From there, some Air Force boys and I walked several blocks to the flight "O" orderly room to report in. They took an impression from our dog tags, assigned us to a barracks and a bunk, and sent us to the supply room for bedding. All of the barracks in the flight were filled, so we carried the stuff almost out to the main gate. We found our barracks at the bottom of a slope on the other side of the fenced off WAC's barracks. Before we got moved to the flight area, we had already developed a dread of having to salute WAC officers.

Lights were out by this time so we had to feel around in the darkness to find an empty bunk. After the bunk was made, I went to take a shower. I was surprised to discover how much softer the water was compared to the water at Fort Riley, Kansas. It seemed as though I would never get all the soap washed off.

I didn't wake up in time for the 5:00 o'clock breakfast next morning. Our only requirement was to be at the two formations held at 0700 hours and 1200 hours. If we didn't catch a detail then, nor have any processing to do, we were off duty and could do as we liked.

Unfortunately, I had missed evening chow that first day, too, so I was really hungry. As I walked back to the barracks, I spotted an outdoor snack bar and thought my problem was solved.

I asked the girl behind the counter to fix me a couple of hot dogs. She made no more movement than a frog would have if I had asked it to do the same thing. I asked again and then she replied, "Don't you have fatigues on?"

After receiving my assurances that I did have fatigues on, she stated, "I can't serve you in fatigues."

That seemed to be the end of it, so I turned away disgusted. It wouldn't have been worthwhile to change clothes to eat a couple of hot dogs if my barracks had been next door let alone a mile down the road.

As I walked past a table where two airmen were eating, one of them asked, "What did you want, Buddy?" I told him and he went up and bought them for me. I didn't miss any more meals at that camp, for I revolted at the thought of contributing to that girl's salary.

The next morning at 0445 hours, as I groped my way out of the barracks toward the flight area for chow, I bumped into Vincent C. Priola (Chicago, Ill.) and Richard P. Scott (Cicero, Ill.). Richard had become a good friend and was the only man in our unit with a civilian pilot's license. They had arrived during the night and had taken bunks upstairs. They were in the process of missing chow, as the formation they were waiting on had already left by way of the front door. We created our own formation and hurried on down to eat.

We had a lot of time on our hands before and during processing, so we eventually looked up everyone we knew that had been scattered to other flights. Some of them were: Eugene J. Bartasavage and Harold G Bullo, both from Detroit, Mich.; Jack E. Erickson (Chicago, Ill.); Gordon J. Gebbens (Grand Rapids, Mich.); Richard H. Haberkamp (Roselle, Ill.); Richard D. Hovorka (Tabor, S.Dak.); Kenneth W. Jones (Carbondale, Ill.); Stanley J. Kozenko (Chicago, Ill.); and Arthur C. Thearling (Wyandotte, Mich.).

Processing began upon arrival at Camp Stoneman with the record's check. Then there was an interval of a day or so until the enlisted man's (EM's) group number was called for more processing. The group number was based upon the day the EM arrived in camp.

The last part of the processing consisted of an orientation, various lectures, and a clothing shakedown. In the shakedown we had to dump our clothing out of our duffel bags and have them checked. If any article was missing, it had to be purchased.

During the lectures we were given a description of each Pacific Island

and the countries of the Far East. We were told something of their geography and resources, their inhabitants and customs, how to act, and what to expect. Still, no one knew where he would be sent.

Though each event was comprehensive, they seldom lasted more than an hour and a half each. After each event was over, someone at the exit would rubber-stamp a card for us to show that we had attended everything. These cards had to be turned in with each event stamped before we could ship out.

After the processing was completed, we were subject to catching details and pulling K.P. again. The details weren't hard, and with so many men in the area, there was better than a 50-50 chance of not getting one. Even K.P. in the consolidated mess hall wasn't as hard as I expected. The food was good as well as sufficient.

Time began to hang pretty heavy on our hands after the second week at Stoneman. Scott, Priola, and I went into San Francisco one weekend to see the sights and to break the monotony of waiting; but we were restless anyway.

We had seen several shipments leave and were getting anxious to go too. By Wednesday of the third week, the camp seemed almost full to bursting, but still the troops were pouring in. It was on that day that our names came out on shipping orders.

Priola, Scott, and I checked with the other flights and all twelve of us wiremen were shipping together. The orders read, "destination Japan", but a sergeant in charge said that wiremen could expect to be sent to Korea from there. We couldn't be sure, and didn't care then.

After dark Thursday, all the men scheduled to be in the shipment fell out for a shot record check. They lined us up in a column of ducks (double file), and we marched up to the immunization center. There we received the remainder of shots that the record indicated we needed.

Next day, we received our pay records and turned in our bedding. The rest of the day we packed and repacked our duffel bags until we could get all of our belongings in them. We were limited to what we could carry on the ship. Only the duffel bag and a small handbag could be carried. Anything else had to go as hold baggage.

In the evening, I called my folks in Jacksonville, Ill. The telephone exchange was crowded with others calling home, too. Everything about a troop movement is supposed to be secret, so there wasn't much to say; but it was nice to hear home voices once again.

Since we had turned in our bedding to save time, we had to sleep on the bare mattress that last night. It was cold, so I threw my overcoat over me. It didn't cover my feet, so I eventually had to dig the field jacket out of the duffel bag. The jacket wouldn't stay over my feet, so I had to stick them into the sleeves before I got warm enough to go to sleep.

CHAPTER II

Going To War

We didn't get much rest that last night. The company runner came through the barracks at 0100 hours to wake us. As soon as we got our clothes on we rushed outside to get in the chow line for breakfast.

Following chow, there was a formation in the flight area for roll call and last minute instructions. From there we carried our duffel bags and other gear about three blocks to the troop movement area. A single file of men, straining with their bags stretched along one side of the road the whole distance. In the darkness one could sense the feeling of urgency and stifled excitement in the men. The troop movement area was a large firebreak that was illuminated by floodlights. Although we were there by 0330 hours, troops from other flights had already arrived. As soon as all flights were accounted for, we were placed in a ship line number formation, *i.e.*, the order our names appeared on the shipping roster.

It was cold waiting there for the buses to take us down to the docks. Some of the men laid their duffel bags down and slept on them. Others smoked and talked quietly. There was a good deal of talk about being seasick accompanied by various ways of preventing and curing it.

The buses arrived and the men began to file into them and to be carried away. The sky was turning gray with the first light of dawn by the time my turn came. We crowded into the bus and held the bags on our laps.

A large river ferry was tied to the dock. All of the lower deck was packed with airmen. Apparently, they expected to take everyone in one trip. I didn't see at the time how it would be possible; but it was done.

Not too much later, all the troops were packed in, and the ferry began to move. The water was so choppy it made me feel woozy. Dinner cured that feeling, however. It came in a paper sack, and consisted of a ham sandwich, cookies, and an apple.

It took approximately four hours for the ferry to arrive at a certain dock, which was to be our port of embarkation. The entire dock was covered by a warehouse-type structure. The ferry docked at the end of it, and after the records were taken off, we filed into the building.

Red Cross workers served us some fruit juice and a cookie, then we climbed aboard the USNS General M.C. Meigs which was alongside the dock. The ship was named after Major General Montgomery Cunningham Meigs.

I considered myself very lucky. The lower compartments of the ship were filled first, and by the time I came aboard, only the top compartments were empty. I immediately chose a top rack near an air vent and threw my duffel bag on it. Life jackets and pillows were already on the racks.

Priola took the top rack across the narrow aisle from me. Kozenko had the rack next to him and Scott had one at the foot of Priola's rack. "Rack" was a very descriptive Navy term for those bunks. Very simply, they were a pipe framework of rectangular shape with heavy canvas tied across them. There were four of the racks, one on top of another, on each side of two heavy-duty vertical supporting pipes. Several hundred men could crowd into each compartment using these uncomfortable space savers. We were given a blanket and a pillowcase to use on our first night on board. No mattresses were provided, but somehow we didn't miss them.

As soon as some of the confusion subsided, I changed into my fatigue uniform, put on my field jacket, and went up on deck. A fog was coming in. I could no longer see the Golden Gate Bridge, but could make out Alcatraz Island very faintly.

Two freshly painted tugs pushed us away from the dock and out into the bay around 1600 hours. A band played on the dock, but there were too many troops on the rail for me to get close enough to see anything on the dock. Everyone was crowding and pushing for one last look at the people below. It was a strange sensation. We had no feeling that we were moving, but the dock and shore was becoming smaller as we moved further away.

The tugs left us sitting out in the fog with absolutely nothing to see.

Visibility had become zero. Some of the troops had wandered below, as a mist had begun to fall and it was becoming cold again.

Between 1600 and 1700 hours, we had several practice boat drills and a fire drill. These were to acquaint us with the procedure to follow in case of an emergency. The boat drill was in the event that we had to abandon ship.

We heard the ship's engines start up. I went back on deck as soon as I felt the ship moving. I was determined to see the Golden Gate Bridge as we passed under it. The dampness made it seem very cold. My teeth were chattering uncontrollably. Practically everyone else had gone below.

Although I had been gazing very intently, after what seemed like ages, I began to fear that the ship had passed under the bridge and I hadn't seen it because of the fog. It came as a surprise when it suddenly came into view. The bridge wasn't where I had expected to see it. It was almost overhead. I could see the yellow fog lights and a dark silhouette through the swirling fog. It was huge from this perspective. The foghorns on the bridge and on the Meigs called their farewells a few times, and we were on the open sea.

Second Lt. Edward Benward held an orientation in our compartment before supper. He was an engineer, I believe. He explained the schedule to be followed while on the ship, and the special duties of our compartment. We were to police the heads. "Head" is the Navy term for their toilets. "Does everyone know our destination?' Benward asked. There were many that shouted no, and some that knew, wanted to hear it officially.

"Yokohama", was the reply. The orientation ended with everyone asking questions and talking at once. The Lieutenant said he didn't know much more about it than anyone else but he had heard that men going to the Fifth Air Force would be in Japan only two days before going to Korea. We wiremen supposed that he was referring to us.

After supper a couple of fellows produced guitars from someplace among their baggage and began to play and sing. They sat on the duffel bags stacked over the cargo hatch cover in our compartment. Shortly, there was a whole mob of men sitting on the bags listening. Some sergeants ran them all off to keep them from crushing anything valuable that might be in the bags.

Since we were issued only one blanket for the first night on the ship, I took off my boots and socks and pushed my feet into the sleeves of my field jacket again. The blanket was rather short and my feet stuck out at the bottom. With the exception of my shirt, I slept with my clothes on to keep warm. Next day we drew an additional blanket and a pillowcase.

I awoke the next morning with a hangover due to the ship's rolling and tossing. I was groggy and slightly dizzy. It was in this condition that I went to breakfast. Two little sausages burnt black, toast and jelly, and a boiled egg was on the menu. I tasted a bite of sausage and a little toast, and decided that it was sufficient for my appetite.

My stomach made a few efforts to get rid of that sausage; but I covered my mouth and kept swallowing, thus holding it down. As I did this, I walked over to a porthole to look at the sunrise. A fellow eating near the porthole looked pretty worried and took a good grip on his tray as he saw me approaching with that misbehaving sausage. I looked at the sunrise, conquered the sausage, and turned to the airman and said, "Beautiful sunrise, isn't it?"

An expression of immense relief came over his face, and he stammered with the profuseness of his agreement.

The troop galley was located mid-ship and one deck below the main deck. Narrow metal tables were suspended waist high much in the same way the racks were hung. The troops ate standing up. There was just room enough for a man to walk between the tables when men were standing at each side eating.

With the exception of most of the breakfasts, where they consistently served repulsive looking green boiled eggs, the chow was very good. We had fruit at least once a day and plenty of fresh meat and vegetables. We had ice cream several times during the voyage.

We had it pretty good, but the officers had it better. They had cabin quarters above the main deck, a lounge, they sat down to eat at a table with a clean tablecloth on it, and their food appeared more palatable. The officers on the Meigs certainly had nothing to complain about on that trip.

Kitchen police were picked for a permanent detail before the ship left San Francisco. The men on K.P. had compartments on the C-deck, or far down in the hold of the ship. They worked every other day.

Never have I seen a group of men work with such noise and enthusiasm as they did. The galley was a bedlam with their shouting, "Let's go!" or "Hot stuff!" They shouted to one another, clanged pans, and in general seemed to be enjoying themselves. I didn't see how they could be, for they really worked hard. Some carried heavy garbage cans up the steep narrow stairs to the main deck, while others mopped, washed pans and trays, or worked on the serving line. All would be wringing wet with perspiration.

The K.P.'s whom I asked about the cause for such noise, explained that they were off duty just as soon as their work was done after each meal, so they just naturally hurried and made noise. At any rate, their enthusiasm made everyone feel better.

During the day all radios were to be turned in to the office for safe-keeping. They were not to be used on the ship.

Toward evening, the sea became rougher. The surface of the water seemed to be large glass hills. We seemed to be heading into these rollers, and as one would pass under us, the ship would rear up and then dive down the other side only to meet another wave that would toss the bow up again. Each time the ship dived down the side of one of the rollers, the fantail would be out of the water, and the vibration at the rear of the ship due to the propellers spinning in the air was tremendous.

I got up dizzy and sick the next morning. I went down to breakfast, but couldn't eat a thing. At 0800 hours, the squad that I was in went down for head detail. We had to clean the ship's latrines.

The head was a mess. There was water all over the floor that had splashed out of the wash basins and showers. The wash basins and stools were filthy, and apparently, some of the boys who got sick during the night had used them instead of the large cans place around for that purpose.

These latrines were located on each deck and right over the propeller shafts. It was hot and noisy in all of them, but especially so on the lower decks. The ship was tossing around so much that we had to hold on to something to stand up in there.

We started work, but it wasn't long before one of the fellows began heaving. Several more got sick, and then my face began to heat up and the perspiration popped out. I threw cold water on my face and swallowed fast and soon felt better. However, a few minutes later the same symptoms occurred and I began to heave. Immediately afterward I felt fine, but it wasn't long before the pressure built up and I was sick again.

For the next two or three days, I was miserable. Nothing would stay on my stomach, and I kept getting weaker. Only when I was out lying on the open deck or in my rack was I comfortable.

On the second day of my seasickness, I didn't even try to eat supper. Soon afterward, Richard Scott brought up some fresh milk in a paper carton. Next, Arthur Thearling showed up with an orange. I had just started eating the orange, when Vincent Priola arrived bearing a large ham sandwich and two cookies. They seemed determined to cure me. I ate almost everything and was surprised at how good it tasted. I managed to keep it down, too.

Next day, I felt better and much stronger. The Pacific had settled down and the weather was warm. Two albatross that glided along behind the ship had replaced the gulls that had deserted us before dawn of the first day. Everytime the ship's garbage was thrown overboard they would drop down and pick up a meal. Now and then another albatross would join our flock. They must have come from the ships we saw passing in the opposite direction on the horizon.

While I was the sickest, I received a lot of advice on how to cure seasickness. The first piece of advice on everyone's mind seemed to be to keep eating. In my condition it sounded foolish, but I later found it to be good advice. Once, as I lay sunning myself on the crowded deck, I discovered Harold Bullo beside me. After some conversation had passed between us, he pulled some broken up bread crusts from his pocket and began nibbling on them. They were enough to turn one's stomach, but he offered me a few to cure my seasickness. Foolishly, I didn't accept any. I was sick enough.

Then Bullo told me how he had thrown up the peaches he had eaten for dessert as he came up the stairs from the galley. He said that he caught them in his mouth, chewed them again, and swallowed them. Then he exclaimed, "Boy, did they taste good the second time!"

Actually the men were very careful and considerate where they got sick. I never saw anyone throw up down in the galley, and it was infrequent that anyone threw up in the companionways. Regardless of how sick they were, the men usually made it to the rail or to the latrine or to one of the many cans placed around for that purpose.

After those first few days, we had some wonderful weather. The deck was always crowded with men watching the ocean, standing around smoking and talking, playing cards, writing letters, or just sleeping.

Whenever I could find the space on the deck, I assumed a horizontal position on a bulkhead and dozed or day dreamed. It was a nice place to be then. The sun was warm; the breeze was gentle and carried a fresh salty smell; the cumulus clouds were white against the very blue sky; and around us was the ever new and changing sea. It was a wonderful time and place for dreaming of the things one would do when he got back, but somehow the ideas didn't always come in the right proportions.

Little things often seemed too important, or really important things too small, and the plans wouldn't fit together logically. In the back of everyone's mind was, "Maybe I won't get back", but no one could really believe that it could happen to him. Still we did a lot of thinking, wondering, and dreaming.

At 1000 hours someone would put some records on a player and play them over the ship's loud speaker system. There was a song about an Indian that had a tricky chorus, and everyone on deck would join in. Then there were some beautiful sentimental ballads by Doris Day. She took everyone home in memory.

It was so crowded, but so very lonely. I looked at the faces of the men about me: the fellows playing cards, the guys listening to another making wisecracks (anything was good for a laugh), the boy sleeping, others reading paperback novels. Sitting against the opposite bulkhead was a boy with tears in his eyes. He was surrounded—but completely alone. I was half startled to see a tear run down his cheek. Then another followed before he wiped them away and hastily glanced around to see if anyone was looking.

There were a lot of letters written during those twelve days at sea, but I expect that many were never mailed. Many of the men whiled away the hours by cleaning their equipment over and over again. Some of them put beautiful finishes on their boots.

One evening when we were all particularly hungry, Priola sat on his rack describing how delicious Italian food is. We still believed that we were going to Korea, so he said that if we all stayed together and could find a stove over there, he would have his wife send the ingredients, and he would make us some ravioli. Those were days when a big home-cooked meal had a magic appeal.

We had plenty of time while on the ship to pick up quite a Navy vocabulary. Such words as bulk head, companionway, galley, deck, head, port, starboard, fan tail, fore, aft, and rack; we learned to use with ease. The most common phrase used on the ship's speaker system was, "Now hear this." This phrase preceded every Navy announcement that came over the speaker.

An announcement to retard all clocks one hour came over the speaker system each time the ship crossed a time zone. Sunday, following our crossing of the 180th Meridian, the announcement was to the effect that all clocks would be advanced twenty-four hours, and that the next day would be Tuesday instead of Monday. To find the difference between our time and the time in California, we had to subtract the hours retarded from twenty-four.

The Navy tells time by the bell system. A certain number of bells ring every half-hour over the speakers, depending of course, upon the time. Thirty minutes after midnight, one bell rings. At one o'clock, two bells ring. Three bells, at one-thirty. And so on, until four o'clock when eight bells ring. Every four hours, the bells start all over; so that at four-thirty, there would be one bell again. We just had to know the approximate time of day to determine the exact time from the bells.

Before going to bed at night, I often walked around the deck enjoying the fresh air before descending into the stale air of the compartment. I wasn't the only one who liked fresh air. A few fellows sneaked their blankets out and slept on deck until someone put a stop to it. An open-air movie was shown nightly on top of a hatch in the mid-section of the ship.

Usually though, I just watched the ocean and stars. The sky and water blended into a perfect blackness, which made the stars seem brighter and more numerous than ever. I also liked to watch the bow of the ship cutting through the ink-like liquid it floated in. The foam seemed to be phosphorescent and cast an eerie light as it leaped away from the side of the ship.

Two days before the ship docked, the following announcement came over the ship's speakers:

"Now hear this! Now hear this! During the night, all clocks on this vessel will be retarded one hour. This will be the standard time in Japan and Korea. I say again! During the night, etc."

We quickly figured the time, and determined that there were seventeen hours difference between San Francisco and us.

On the morning we were to dock (after twelve days at sea), we got up somewhat before 0400 hours to make breakfast which was to be served at 0430 hours. As we waited in the chow line, we could see a few buoys blinking through the darkness.

It was misty, foggy, cold and a miserable sort of day. After breakfast it was a little lighter and we could very indistinctly see land on each side of the ship. It looked more like storm clouds on the horizon. However, the land gradually materialized to the point where we could see lighthouses and buildings on the coast.

The first person we had seen for almost two weeks, with the exception of the people on the ship, chugged across our wake in a small wooden fishing boat. He appeared to have his head and ears bandaged, but he was waving a handkerchief or scarf like a wildman in response to the shouts from the men on the Meigs. Little did I realize then that the "bandage" was just a headgear to keep his head and ears warm and dry. I had a great deal to learn about the Japanese.

Yokohama harbor was tremendous. We passed through a couple of breakwaters. At one place, a small boat about the size of a tug was struggling with a long string of huge floating balls. We supposed the balls were floats for a submarine net.

The harbor was crowded, busy, and dingy looking. There were ships from many different nations at the docks or being maneuvered about by tugs. Shuttling among the larger ships were small-motorized fishing boats starting out to get the days catch of fish (*sakana*).

We kept up a steady pace of entry until a pilot boat met us and took us to our dock. It was noon when we were alongside. Soon afterward a tanker began to replenish the Meigs oil supply.

Several Japanese men came aboard and helped tie the ship in. They were small and stout and wore Western clothes. It was interesting to watch them and to listen to their language.

There was a military band waiting to greet the ship. Everyone crowded the starboard side to see and hear it. The band stood down on the ground level of the dock. Behind the band was a two-story building. On the second floor were offices where Japanese and American women were working. They were about level with the main deck.

The men were reasonably calm until an American woman apparently became over stimulated by the music and proceeded to do a barefoot toe dance on the second floor porch. Once started she couldn't seem to stop. The men showed their appreciation with whistles and catcalls of such volume and length that all troops were soon ordered off the starboard side of the ship.

Debarkation began after lunch. The first men on were the first men to get off. They filed through our compartment all afternoon from the hold. We waited impatiently to get off.

After going through the supper chow line twice, I was still hungry, so I went up and waited with some other fellows outside the officer's galley. The cooks and waiters in there were very nice. During the trip they had often passed food through the portholes to the troops. A Filipino fellow inside grabbed a whole chocolate pie off a tray and handed it out before the waiter could say anything. It surely was good.

The last of the troops finally got off the ship between 1900 and 2000 hours. We were among them. At the gangway, a man checked off each man as he started down. At the bottom of the gangway, we were to sound off with our line number, and if we had any mail, someone would stick the letters in our mouths. Some of the men received as many as fourteen letters.

CHAPTER III

First Impressions

We hurried on down the dock and then turned to follow alongside a large warehouse. In the center of the side facing the harbor was a pair of large sliding doors. Guards directed and hurried the incoming troops inside. Once inside, we were given some cards, and were crowded into a small space at one side of the warehouse. Here we remained for better than two hours waiting for a train.

While we waited we compared cards. There were now about thirty six of us with the same APO number, which meant we would all be together, for awhile at least.

After Vincent Priola had finished reading his letters, he and I walked out a nearby rear door to see what we could see. There was a narrow gauge railroad track about ten feet from the door. A string of boxcars were on it. They looked like toys. The boxcars had spoked wheels and seemed to be about half the length of an American boxcar. On the floor of one of them were some rice grains.

Three Japanese men came by while we were outside. One of the group needed a shave. All of them were wearing worn out Western style garments, which included some of our army clothing. Two of the fellows wore wooden platform shoes called *geta.* They were held on by a strap between the big toe and the next toe. The other fellow wore a cloth and rubber boot-like affair, which to our surprise, also had the big toe separated from the others. All three men were short in stature.

They smiled and nodded as they approached us. I pulled out a <u>Pocket</u>

Guide to Japan that had been given to us before sailing, and decided to make a stab at speaking Japanese. The three little fellows lined up in a row in front of us, and I asked them which direction was north. It tickled them heartily, for their grins grew larger and they nodded their heads in vehement agreement. I had a suspicion that they didn't understand their own language; but I tried again and again to ask them which direction was north. What ever it was, the joke got better each time I told it, but they never ceased to agree with me.

Priola wanted to try his luck with the language. He had heard that we were going to Fuchu, so he asked how far it was from Yokohama. After a couple of loud repetitions, one fellow turned to the others and said, "Ah! Fuchu". Then they began to say "Fuchu" individually and in chorus each time it was mentioned.

By this time, there was a crowd of GIs trying to ask them questions from the booklet, but neither side was accomplishing anything. Suddenly, one of the Japanese said "M.P." and all three of them rushed off. We went back inside to await the train.

It must have been 2300 hours by the time we boarded the train. We packed our bags between and under the straight-backed wooden seats and had the aisle all but impassable with baggage.

Before the train started moving, an officer in charge explained that we were going to Fuchu, a distance of about thirty miles, and that it was going to take three hours to get there. He also said to throw any cigarette butts through the holes in the floor. The holes were about six inches in diameter and spaced about ten feet apart in the aisle for the passenger's convenience.

Most of the men went right to sleep, but I tried to stay awake to see the colorful paper lanterns and neon lights with strange "characters" on them, as the train crossed some of the side streets. The windows soon began to steam up and, I too, fell asleep.

At Fuchu, we lined up outside the train in a group slightly resembling a formation, and waited to be assigned to a bus. While we stood there, a young Japanese fellow (he looked about sixteen) jumped off the train with an oil can in one hand and a flashlight in the other, and busied himself with examining the springs and wheels of the train. I will admit that I ventured a look, too. From the jogging we took, I supposed that the wheels were flat on one side.

The sergeant in charge of the bus asked if we would like to eat breakfast before we turned in. Everyone said yes, so he had the Japanese driver take us to Tachikawa Air Base. We followed the sergeant into the mess hall. What a contrast it was to that on the ship! The dining area was bright, clean, spacious, quiet, and above all, steady as a rock. The cooks and "boy-sans" loaded our trays with hot cakes, fresh fried eggs, bacon, cereal, and all the milk we wanted. Then we took our trays over to the four-man tables and sat down on a chair for the first time in two weeks. Some luxury!

After breakfast, we climbed into the bus again and wound our way about six miles further along the narrow dusty road until we came to Showa Air Base. The bus turned into an area at the rear of some large hangers. A *torii*-like sign near the street read, "Home of the 474th Signal Aviation Construction Company". We were home.

The barracks situation looked bad that morning. It was difficult to walk between the beds and footlockers, let alone find room for more beds. Some of us got cleaned up before we went to bed around 0600 hours. It must have been about six o'clock, for a few men that our noise woke decided to get up and prepare for the Saturday inspection.

I hadn't been in bed five minutes, it seemed, when a nasty old first sergeant came in waking all of the new men up. Actually, it was 0800 hours and almost time for the inspection, so he wanted us to make ourselves scarce.

Following a brief orientation, we walked around the base and down to the service club. It was the nicest service club I had seen. At that time, Miss Sarah Cooper, of New York, was club director, and Miss Jeanne Langdon, of California, was program director.

Along one wall were several writing desks with paper and ink provided. Across from this were pool tables, and a ping pong table on the other side of the room. Between, was a large dance floor. There was also a free juke box, a lounge, a shuffle-board, magazines, a Japanese language class, *jujitsu* lessons, a place to wrap packages, a floor show on Wednesday, and a dance band three nights a week. Each Sunday there were tours to nearby places of interest.

Japanese girl workers, who lived in the dormitories at Tachikawa, were bussed over for dancing partners; or the men could bring in their own girl friends.

In the afternoon we had our money changed to Military Payment Certificates (MPC), or script, and were issued ration cards for soap and cigarettes.

That first evening, we all went to the service club to see what the dances were like. This particular band specialized in noise rather than music, but played American songs.

A tiny, forty-eight year old lady that everyone called, "Mama-san" made Priola and I promise to dance with one of her "nice girls". Mama-san was the girls' chaperone, and she extolled the virtues of her girls until we couldn't refuse.

As a joke, Priola pointed to Richard Scott and Kenneth Jones playing pool at one of the tables, and hinted that they wanted to dance. In a bound, Mama-san had them both collared and began pulling them toward the dance floor. They didn't know what to do except drag their heels. She introduced them to two girls and they danced, although both declared that they didn't know how.

After that experience we went over to the Airmen's Club to see the floor show. Japanese professional musicians, jugglers, magicians, dancers, etc. put on the shows. That night a powerful, little, bald-headed, seventy-five year old man was a showstopper. He came out after the usual run of magicians and dancers. He and his middle-aged son juggled some sticks between them for awhile. Then they balanced on some large balls and did some other acrobatics. At the end of his act he put his hands on the floor between his legs, raised his feet off the ground, and hopped around the room like a frog, using only his hands. For a seventy-five year old man, everyone thought his skill and strength was marvelous.

One evening, Mama-san conducted a tea ceremony (*Cha-no-yu*) for our benefit in the service club. Due to lack of time and proper atmosphere, together with many interruptions, the ceremony was in a rather abbreviated form. Nevertheless, she explained in great detail, and eventually prepared some green tea for us to drink with her tea set.

There are many articles used in the *Cha-no-yu*. There must be a water jar, a bamboo dipper, and a bamboo mixing brush about the size and shape of a shaving brush, a ceremonial tea bowl, and many other utensils. Mama-san was extremely proud of her ceremonial tea bowl. It looked like a poorly made clay bowl, as it was very plain and irregularly shaped, but she valued it highly. Such bowls often have a long history, and are definitely preferred by tea experts.

When Mama-san was ready, she called Mori Moto and Hisako Hara over to help with the demonstration. We all kneeled on the floor around her, as is the custom, while she began serving a tiny teacake. Since no sugar or cream is used in Japanese tea, a sweet is eaten first to bring out the flavor of the tea. This cake looked like cranberry sauce, but it had a dry texture and a slightly sweet taste. It had to be cut in a prescribed manner in a certain number of pieces, and then served according to ancient rules.

The guests are not supposed to talk while the hostess is preparing tea. Nothing must distract from the performance, and absolutely no error must occur. There are hundred of rules and formalities which must be observed to the letter. Every utensil has to be in a prescribed place, and used with precision. There is no part of the ceremony that is not governed by an exact rule. The whole formal ceremony lasts several hours and usually includes dinner. Of course, Mama-san had to be brief to keep our attention on her demonstration.

Tea was introduced into Japan from China as a medicine. It counteracts the acids in the fish eaten by the Japanese and supplies iron and vitamins A and C to their diet, according to Mama-san. Most factories and large places of business have a break during the morning and afternoon so that their employees can enjoy a cup of tea. Wherever there was a fire, their seemed to be a kettle on to heat water for tea.

Next morning, Sunday, most of the former Fort Riley men showed up at the service club for coffee and donuts. A short while later we were boarding a bus for a tour of Tokyo. None of us had passes, so Miss. Langdon called the company and got permission for us to go.

The road to Tokyo was narrow and very crowded. Traffic moves on the left side of the road. The houses and shops in the towns are built on the edge of the road, and the telephone poles are often in the street. Most of the Japanese-made cars were as small or smaller than the English Austin. A motorcycle-truck was also predominant as a means of transportation.

In the country, farmers had planted their crops right up to the edge of the road. Anyplace a plant would grow, one was planted. The crops indicated a good fertile and friable soil.

We hadn't gone very far when I saw something I didn't know whether to believe or not. I thought I saw an old man urinating alongside the road as he watched traffic go by. Sure enough, a little further along there was another fellow urinating. Before the trip was over, we had seen about a dozen men relieving themselves along the street. The Japanese didn't think anything about it, but I noticed that the two Japanese girls on the bus always turned their heads away.

Tokyo was the third largest city in the world. It was very modern looking. The *Ginza* (Tokyo's famous main street), was broad and lined with large department stores. Inside and out, the department stores seemed to be of the latest design. A young lady was stationed at the top and bottom of the escalators to help the customers on and off. Usually there was only one escalator and it was moving upward. The people lined up the length of the store to ride on them. I didn't see any escalators in Japan that moved downward, although there must have been some.

There were also elevators and a flight or two of stairs. The elevators were always full. The risers on the stairs were rather low by American standards and very tiring to climb; but it was undoubtedly easier climbing for people in tight *kimonos* and stilted shoes than a higher riser would have been.

Most of the larger stores had a roof garden where parents could leave their children while they shopped. One store, for example, had some play equipment such as swings and teeter-totters, a goldfish pond, and a cage containing several monkeys.

As a whole the merchandise in those stores was more colorful than the same materials in the United States. It seemed more varied, too. One could buy alcoholic beverages, meat, fish, canned goods, flowers, all kinds of toys, both Eastern and Western style clothing, all kinds of material with beautiful patterns, trees, exquisite vases, cloisonné, china-ware, silver, books, radios, television sets, blankets, straw or wooden pillows, bright quilted sleeping jackets, bamboo for every use, furniture, etc., all under the same roof. There seemed to be no limit to what the store would handle.

Near the middle of most of the stores selling television sets, would be a raised platform with a set turned on for demonstration. A magician or juggler on the screen would have an audience of a hundred or more people, blocking two or three aisles, straining to watch the performance over each other's heads.

There were other stores, not quite so large, specializing in individual items such as cars, motorcycles, jewelry, and optical equipment such as microscopes and transits. Scattered among these large modern buildings were souvenir shops and tiny stands selling novelty goods. Street peddlers were also common.

Electric streetcars, filled to capacity, followed rails up and down the center of the street. Buses, blue motorcycle-trucks, small Japanese cars, large new American cars, and hundreds of bicycles vied with each other for space on the street. Every vehicle had a horn of some kind, which the driver blew with a maniac's persistence. Never before had I heard such horn blowing.

Strange as it may seem, the Japanese people usually ignore a horn being tooted at them. To them it means that the driver has seen them and therefore will not hit them.

Next, we rode around part of the Emperial Palace grounds. It is separated from the city by a wide moat. The sloping sides of the moat were of huge gray stones apparently fitted together without the use of mortar. Far below, floating on the water was the brownish, wild looking ducks. The grounds itself appeared to be a beautiful well cared for park.

The driver stopped the bus in Ueno Park. It seemed like a holiday there were so many people around. Some of the people wore Western-style clothing, but most of the women wore Eastern-style clothes. The *kimonos* that the women and some children wore were beautiful. Even a few of the older men wore a drab robe-like outfit. There were a lot of school children there, too. The boys wore black suits with brass buttons and a black cap. The schoolgirls wore a sailor suit dress. It was an interesting mixture of East and West cultures.

After awhile, some of the fellows began to inquire among themselves as to the location of a latrine. After what we had seen, we wondered if the Japanese had such an institution. While wandering around we found what looked like it might be one, but no one dared go see. It was a stone structure approximately eight feet square. There was no door on it. About twenty feet from the opening sat two women eating their noon meal.

Finally, a Japanese man went in the opening and relieved himself in the stone urinal to the left of the entrance. Although he was in full view of the women, he didn't visibly affect their modesty.

Someone remarked, "I can't stand out here all day. Who will go in with me?" We all did. While some were inside, others blocked the view from the door. To the right of the entrance were two stool closets, only there were no stools in them—just a hole in the floor. Also, the Japanese people carry their own paper with them.

We congratulated ourselves that we got out of there before any women arrived. We simply were not used to Japanese customs yet. We had a lot to learn.

CHAPTER IV

474ᵗʰ Signal Aviation Construction Company

For what seemed like a long time, we new men were leading a great life. We couldn't be assigned to a platoon until our orders arrived and had been checked. In the meantime, there was no work for us to do. The men in the company hired Japanese boy-sans to clean the latrine and pull K.P. Since we weren't in any platoon, we didn't have to fall out for work call.

There were several Japanese factories at Showa. They worked for the American government, but were run by the Japanese. They repaired our damaged heavy equipment, trucks, and rebuilt motors, etc.

Now and then I would see these several hundred employees streaming through their check gate onto the base to work. Later, we would see them rushing off base at the close of the day. Most of the men wore Western-style business suits with a razor edge crease in the trousers, and more than half of them carried brief cases. I couldn't understand how those factories could employ so many executives.

As for the creases in their trousers, a few Japanese have been observed to remove their pants when they got on the train. They sat there in their underwear until the train approached their destination. Then they put their pants back on and step off the train as sharp as ever.

Once on the base, though, the workers went through a mass metamorphosis. They changed into old, greasy, worn-out work clothes –most frequently castoff military fatigues. I found out that they carried their lunch in the brief cases.

A few men and most women employees carried their lunch in *furoshiki* or "bathroom spread". It is a square cloth, usually silk, which is used to wrap and carry things about. It is supposed to have originated in the bathhouses of the 14th century. Clothes were folded up in the *furoshiki* while the person took a bath.

We spent a lot of time at the service club, as we had no passes and very little money to spend for *yen*. In the afternoons, we would go down there and play pool or ping-pong, then in the evenings we would go back to write letters and study the Japanese language under the tutelage of Mama-san.

The Japanese language is complicated to say the least, but it is not so difficult that the average person can't quickly learn enough words and phrases to enable him to get around with ease. There are five vowels and nineteen consonants making up the speech sounds of the Japanese. A vowel always follows a consonant or stands alone, though there is a tendency to drop some of the vowels in some cases. The language is spoken without accent, but there are slight pitch changes in certain words, which are very important. There are many words that are pronounced the same except for the pitch change. In those cases, the change of pitch, together with the way in which the word is used, determines its meaning. If the meaning still isn't clear, the character for the word may be written out.

Eleven hundred years ago, the sounds of the Japanese language were written in *kana* and made into *Gojuonzu* or "Fifty sound chart". Actually, there were 48 *Kana*, for there were two duplications. Others have been dropped until now there are 44.

There are two forms of *Kana*. The *Katakana*, taken from Chinese characters and *Hiragana* which is simplified from Chinese script. Using two dots or a small circle alongside some of the Kana has created twenty-three additional pronunciations. Besides this, there are thousands of characters. However, every school child must memorize only about 2000 of these. Few GIs have the time or the inclination to learn the *Kana*.

Getting back to the spoken language, it varies greatly in dialect in various districts in Japan. Also, there is a masculine and feminine form of the language. Needless to say, most GI's learn the feminine form from their associates. Then there is a form to use when addressing a superior, an equal, an inferior, and even for speaking to members of one's household.

Is it any wonder that the Japanese vocabulary of most GI's is limited to *sukoshi* (little or few) and *takusan* (much or many)?

The first sergeant that the men had cautioned us about, turned out to be a pretty nice guy. He was Ervin O. Easterling from Hattiesburg, Miss. Easterling got permission for the new men to go on the service club tours before we were eligible for a pass. And a short while later, he got passes for us before we had been interviewed by the C.O.

Within ten days of our arrival, the third platoon left on TDY to work in southern Japan. That same day, Priola and several others were called in for an interview with the commanding officer. He was Captain John W. Leddon, of Joplin, Mo. The men had a lot of respect for the C.O.

Priola had been a cable splicer in Chicago before he entered the service. The company needed good cable splicers, according to the Captain, so Priola came out beaming that he had been assigned to the headquarters platoon as a cable splicer – just what he wanted. Next day, some more men were interviewed. Harold Bullo was to be trained for cable splicing, so he moved over to the headquarters platoon. Eugene Bartasavage, Jack Erickson, Richard Haberkamp, and Stanley Kozenko moved to the first platoon. The first and the headquarters platoons were in the same barracks. Richard Hovorka was assigned to the second platoon, so he just had to move across the room, as the second and third platoons were in the same barracks. Hovorka had been a pole lineman as a civilian, so he was probably one of the best climbers in the company at that time. The rest of us were assigned to the third platoon. There were Gordon Gebbens, Richard Scott, Arthur Thearling, and myself. The Fort Riley gang was broken up.

One week later, the second platoon left for a TDY job on Iwo Jima. As far as anyone knew, they were going to set poles, run some open lines and string cable. Hovorka and Priola were the envy of us all, for they were going too.

After that the barracks seemed almost deserted. The new men in both the second and third platoons began falling out together for formations.

We expected to have a job to do as soon as we got overseas. Most of us had even expected to go to Korea. Now we were beginning to wonder if there hadn't been some mistake in sending us to Japan. Luckily the radical difference in culture between the United States and Japan helped ease the monotony of the days. Also the Thanksgiving, Christmas, and New Year holidays helped as well.

Every day seemed the same. At 0600 hours the bugle woke us up. Reveille was at 0630 hours, and was immediately followed by a "police call" of the area. The mess hall opened about 0700 hours. After that the barracks had to be swept and mopped.

Work call was at 0800 hours. There was very little to do in the company area, but they didn't give us any time off after we were assigned to a platoon. If it wasn't raining, someone would march us over to the motor pool to wash trucks. When a truck was washed, we drove it around the lot to get it dirty again so we would have something to do.

If the water was frozen in the hoses, the fellow in charge usually had us dust the vehicles. We often stood together talking while polishing the same spot all morning. Sometimes we got to sit in the cabs or in the back of a truck in an effort to keep warm.

The so called "weekly" and "monthlies" were taken seriously at first, but they eventually became a farce. Those were the inspections that we made once a week of the condition of the vehicles. We were to check the electrical system, lights, battery, tires, brakes, radiator, etc. Many of these things were slighted by most of the men. I don't know if I can explain it fully or not, but it seemed like the men thought they had been trained for an important job, and they couldn't understand why they were purposely placed in a motor pool to loaf.

On rainy days we either went to the line shack to kill time or worked on our personal gear in the barracks. Some fellows polished one pair of shoes off and on all day.

Dinner was served at 1145 hours, and mail call was at 1215 hours. Work call was at 1300 hours and just the same as in the morning. We would stay at the motor pool until 1600 hours. Supper chow was at 1700 hours. Then the men who had passes could go to town. "Lights out" was at 2200 hours and "bed check" at 2400 hours.

We did have a break in our routine while we were working on a couple of practice poles. Two seventy or eighty foot poles were erected a short distance from the barracks. They were spaced about six feet apart at the bottom so that we could put boards across them ladder-like to the top. The steps were three feet apart.

Donald R. "Baby Soldier" Harris, from Jacksonville, Florida, was in charge while we were putting on the crosspieces. He mentioned that the only time he got seasick on the ship was when he looked at something white like a cook's uniform. He was a young boy, but he was a good and reliable pole lineman.

We got the crosspieces spiked all the way to the top, but the last few were weak. As the poles grew smaller at the top, they were farther apart and the steps were just fastened by a toehold. Later, we took down the top twelve steps, pulled the tops together with a coffin hoist, and replaced the crosspieces securely. It was good training to get used to height.

Every Saturday morning there was an inspection. Usually it was a footlocker and wall locker inspection, and of course, a personal inspection. At other times it was an outside inspection. The men dreaded the outside inspections. They consisted of full dress, including orange scarfs and carbines. Any man getting gigged had his pass pulled for the weekend.

One Saturday afternoon following payday, Richard Scott and I rode a train to Tachikawa. On both sides, a narrow bench-like seat ran the length of each car. All but the first few people aboard rode standing up. That seemed to be the only way they could get all of their customers on the train. It wasn't hard to believe the fact that Japan is the only country in the world whose railroads haul more passengers than freight.

Tachikawa was the fourth stop from Showa Air Base. Alongside the tracks were small fields of grain and root vegetables. The grain was planted thickly in rows about a foot apart. It appeared to be rice. There weren't too many rice paddies on that level ground, but they were common on terraced hillsides and in the valleys. Each little field along the tracks had a border of shrubs around its perimeter. Later, I examined some of the shrubs and found that they were mulberry trees. The trees had been severely pruned in past years so that the trunk was only about eighteen inches high. Four to six branches from the preceding year had been allowed to remain, and were all tied together near their ends with a straw rope. This made the tree conical shaped.

By the time we arrived in Tachikawa there were so many people on the train that no one had to hold on to the safety straps. The people jammed together so tightly that they held each other up.

There was no limit to what people brought on the train with them. Many of them had lunch boxes that they carried wrapped in brightly colored material, *furoshiki*. An athletic looking fellow had a pair of skis with him. Workmen had their tools with them. Many women had a child strapped on their back. School children had their books, etc. in a backpack. Several people had huge boxes or bamboo baskets filled with what seemed like a backbreaking weight.

One grizzly, round-faced man took a large box of supposedly fresh clams off his back and set them near us on the floor. What a soggy stinking mess that was! He then began to examine his clams. Any that did not meet with his approval; he flipped on the floor and crushed them, while the nearby ladies covered the lower part of their faces with their shawls. Next, he examined the clams that he had previously removed from the shells. He proudly shuffled them around in the tray-like boxes they were in, whereupon he became the only person on the train that wasn't crowded for space.

The doors automatically slid open as soon as the train stopped in Tachikawa. There was a great surge of people and we found ourselves off the train. The momentum of the crowd carried us toward a narrow gate where a railroad employee collected our tickets.

We followed the street to the left, but before we reached the first corner we encountered a "short-time girl". As we passed her single file on the narrow sidewalk, she whispered, "Where you go GI?"

Without slowing down, Richard said, "We're just walking around". "You come to my house", she said somewhat louder, as she fell into line behind us. An emphatic,"No", from us stopped her.

Hardly one hundred yards further along, a small elderly pimp grabbed my arm, and in very bad English said that he had some nice "cherry girls" at his house. He was filthy. My first impulse was to hit him for hanging on my arm, but I answered that I wasn't interested. He was persistent, so we had to convince him that we weren't looking for "cherry girls" or any other type of girls by shoving him out of the way and into the street.

After that we had more leisure to look around the town. Only a narrow sidewalk separated the shops and markets from the main street. The other streets and alleys were either oiled or dirt and had no sidewalks. The top speed limit in Japan was thirty-five miles per hour, and in many places the limit was much lower. Nevertheless traffic moved at a dangerous pace considering the number of children playing in the streets, and even the adults on foot or on bicycles.

One of the first and most noticeable characteristics about the town was its odor. It was a sickening, suffocating reek. Today, I'm not sure what it was, for it never seemed so overpowering later as it did that first time we went to town. Perhaps we got used to it.

There are several things which blended together to perfume the air of Japan. First, there was the ditch-type sewer system which may be open, or as in the towns, covered with concrete slabs or wood planks. Second, there were the fish markets where just about any imaginable kind of sea food is left in open pans or kegs for the flies and warm air to spoil. Third, there was the "honey dipper" with his "honey bucket" wagon. A person can detect his presence a block away when the wind was right. The honey dipper is a farmer who comes to town with his oxen drawn wagon to dip human waste into his wooden honey buckets for use on his rice paddies or other cultivated land. Needless to say, this practice gives a distinctive odor to the fields on a warm day. The intensive cultivation of the soil in

Japan makes any kind of fertilizer both essential and valuable.

We ducked under the *noren* (shop curtain) of one shop after another and were fascinated by the array of colorful souvenirs that it was possible to buy. When we told the clerks who were trying high-pressure salesmanship on us, that we had no *Yen* they didn't believe us. They couldn't understand why we hadn't purchased some *Yen* on payday. We found the Japanese to be very conscious of most base activities and particularly the paydays.

From there we went down a side street for the purpose of crossing to the other side of town. There was a wide expanse of railroad tracks to cross. A railroad man had just lowered a steel cable to block pedestrian traffic as we walked up. He would crank the cable straight up or down according to the sound of a whistle in the possession of another fellow directing trains. Quite a mob gathers while the cable is down. When the man raises it, the people throw courtesy to the wind in their hurry to get across to the other side.

One side of town was very similar to the other side. It was strictly a GI town. The souvenir shops were interspersed with an occasional shoe store, fish market, fruit market, restaurant, and hardware stores where bronze pans and other Japanese house hold items were sold. Also, there were a few bookshops where brightly colored paper covered fiction stories predominated.

The Japanese are omnivorous readers. The *hon ya* (bookshops) are always crowded with students and adults reading and buying magazines and paper covered books. In the shops one can find books describing the Japanese campaigns in the Pacific during WW II, all kinds of textbooks, colorful children's books, cheap novels, etc. There are also magazines of every description, including many on photography, Communist publications, and some of the most obscenely illustrated magazines anyone can imagine. I became curious about whether there was a minimum standard of decency that had to be conformed to in publications. I was told that there was. Perhaps no publisher had reached the minimum yet.

The Japanese are very polite and considerate except when they are boarding a train. During a conversation, we watched them bow to each other as often as a dozen times, but the same people will jam a train door and none will yield an inch in their effort to gain a seat on the train, even though the train is rapidly being filled by others entering through another door. We didn't understand it. We simply followed the example of other Japanese and entered through the other door.

During the weeks we spent in the company waiting to go on TDY , we had time to become pretty well acquainted with the 3rd platoon men who arrived at the same time as we had, but from schools other than at Fort Riley, Kansas.

James O. Powers, Jr., a short blond fellow, had followed me alphabetically into every line I had been in since our arrival in California. Little did I know then that we would be in the same company overseas. His home was Wallace, N.C. James was forever entertaining the men around him with his stories.

Everett Donegan from Huntsville, Alabama was an expert at fixing a flat on the Army's complicated 6-by tires. He was quite versatile. He could shuffle his feet so that it sounded like a train engine, bark like a dog, whistle like a canary, play the saxophone, sing, and even cook.

Probably the quietest fellow in the group was George J. Sipos. His home was Cassandra Pa. He and Donegan had gone to the same wire school.

Two good friends from Illinois were Curtis R. Clendenin of Marion and Loren E Bacon from Thompsonville. Curtis told of one of their first trips to Tachikawa. A short-time girl who said in her most enticing bedroom voice, "Hello Honey", approached them. Loren replied, "Hello, Honey-bucket", and walked on. They said they could hear her cussing them in English and Japanese until they turned the corner at the end of the block.

Before the occupation of Japan, prostitution was allowed only in licensed quarters under police supervision. During the Allied occupation, the prostitutes were "freed" from police control and turned onto the streets.

In 1953 there were 300,000 prostitutes working in Japan according to the report of one Japanese commission. Japanese police were trying to regain control, and had rounded up 50,000 of these girls and placed them in licensed red light quarters. The remainder of the "short time" girls, as the GI's called them, was at large – and their numbers increasing.

The matter was beyond the control of the combined efforts of the Japanese police and the military police. Most commanders advised their men to stay away from prostitutes, but if not, to use prophylactics. Prophylactic kits could be obtained from free dispensers in most latrines and orderly rooms, but many men never used them and others became careless.

Venereal disease was very common. A man with VD had a choice of two alternatives for being cured. He could go to his base dispensary for treatment and hope that the medical record didn't reach his commander, and if it did, that he wouldn't be punished.

On the other hand he could go to a Japanese doctor for treatment. If the doctor had any drug that would cure VD, the GI could depend upon it being very expensive and very dilute—perhaps too dilute to do any good. If the doctor was disreputable, it might be only colored water. In addition to these disadvantages, there was a very great danger of infection from his unsanitary equipment and methods.

What could a commander do in a case like that? His hands were tied. If he were too severe, the GI would risk going to Japanese doctors. About all the CO could do was to advise and lightly reprimand.

What do the Japanese people think of this situation? The Japanese people have a different set of moral standards than the majority of American people. Prostitution is legal in Japan. Daughters are not always as important as a son is and the Americans are very "wealthy".

On the other hand, there are many more decent Japanese people, who through long tradition of minding their own business, stoically pretend not to see and hear what is going on in the streets around them. They are appalled at the increase of prostitution, and many are resentful. They blame the allied servicemen in general and the Americans in particular for its alarming increase.

On the day before Christmas, Richard Hovorka and Vincent Priola returned from Iwo Jima to spend the holiday in the Company. They had been gone only thirteen days, but Priola was sporting a new mustache and both he and Hovorka had a suntan. We were all anxious to hear what they had been doing and how they liked TDY. The food on Iwo Jima didn't appeal to them.

Another thing that they didn't care for was the size of the island – only eight square miles. Their equipment had been slow in arriving. Meanwhile, they had walked all around the island and had climbed Mt. Suribachi (556 feet) to take pictures. They had also been deep-sea fishing.

They went on to say that the Japanese had built a large hospital inside Mt. Suribachi. Our Navy ships had sealed the entrance with their big guns, and the Japanese that were trapped inside are preserved by lack of oxygen almost as they died. Supposedly, some officers wearing oxygen masks had been inside to vouch for this. Thus, this belief has continued and perhaps grown.

Rifle and machine gun bullet scars could still be seen on the rocks and ripped sandbags. There were thousands of destroyed or partially destroyed under-ground fortifications per square mile on the island. Mt. Suribachi was covered with pockmarks from the big shells. Priola said he found a human skull with one tooth remaining as he was wandering around taking pictures.

Some of the pillboxes were scarred up, but not too badly damaged otherwise. It appeared that our heavy guns had blown all the soil from around them until the whole box tilted forward and the gun inside was aimed into the ground.

The amount of wreckage on and around the island was tremendous. On the beach were small ships, landing craft, tanks, half-tracks, etc. still lying where they had been put out of action nine years before. Inland, there were big piles of ammunition, wrecked planes, more tanks, and other weapons. Caves all over the island contained beds and other similar equipment.

In one of the caves Hovorka found a lifeboat with an American parachute in it. Both boat and chute were covered with blood. He brought back a section of bloody parachute cord for a souvenir.

A foreign company (they didn't know from what country) had contracted to salvage the equipment and junk left on Iwo Jima. It was at that time hauling it away on ships.

During the thirteen days, both men had shot up all the film they had taken with them. The pictures of the island were just as they describe it. They had several pictures of a memorial chiseled in the rock by Waldron T. Rich. In March 1945, Rich sculptured the memorial depicting four of the five Marines raising the American flag. He had been a Seabee with the Marines.

That first Christmas overseas was rather lonely. Some of us had helped wire a speaker to the roof of the guardhouse, and the week before Christmas, it and other speakers around the base began to carry Christmas music practically all day. The music was nice, but it wouldn't let us forget that we wouldn't be home.

Around Christmas time, military units began sponsoring Christmas parties for the Japanese orphans, hospital patients, and other needy people. It was a wonderful thing the way the men overseas donate their time, money, and other gifts; and it creates much good will between the Japanese and the Americans.

Showa sponsored a party in the service club. The orphans were brought on base in Air Force buses. Men from the base went along on the bus to help carry and hold the crippled children. In the service club, other men set up chairs and arranged the toys to be given away. Preparations were made in the next door consolidated mess hall to feed the children ice cream, cake, and chocolate milk. Ambulances brought bed-ridden children on stretchers.

The children filed in, wide-eyed with wonder, and were ushered to seats where they sat in groups with an adult Japanese group leader. As they came in, a choir of children sang Christmas songs under the huge Christmas tree.

The choir was under the direction of a gruff-looking, middle aged director. He stood in front waving his hands to the music. Once in awhile he would go up to one of the children, bend his head down close, and listen to how the child was doing. There was a boy on the end of the front rank who must have been some kind of a song leader, but he must have had stage fright. He stared straight ahead, his face expressionless, and his lips moving automatically.

Several times the director bent down to listen to him, then suddenly, he cuffed the poor lad's ear and sent him to the rear rank and moved another boy into the vacancy.

The sound of the little voices in that choir was unforgettable as they sang such songs as Silent Night, Jingle Bells, and Jesus Loves Me in Japanese and English. For good measure, they even sang a Stephen Foster song in Japanese.

They sang until all the children were seated. Then Japanese jugglers, magicians, bicycle riders, etc. entertained the boys and girls. Following the program, half of the children were led next door for ice cream while the other half were given toys by Santa Claus and his GI helpers. Then they switched so that all of the children had toys and ice cream before they were taken back to the orphanage.

January 1st is practically the start of a new life in Japan. It is the greatest holiday of the year. According to ancient custom the homes must be cleaned thoroughly and all debts paid by the end of December. There is a great to do about doing things for the first time in the New Year: first guests, preparing the first meals, making the first deliveries, etc. All are taken to be a prediction of good or bad fortune for the remainder of the year. Everything possible must be renewed: new clothes, furniture, broom, kitchen utensils, etc.

The word of the day is *Shinnen omedeto gozaimasu* or Happy New Year. Actually the celebration lasts seven days, which provides plenty of time for visiting shrines and temples, attending exhibitions, and other festivities.

Across the entrance to the houses and shops is hung a straw rope called *Shimenawa*, which is hung with strips of white paper called *gohei*. It is to purify the dwelling. Before the house stands the *Kadomatsu*. It consists of three stalks of bamboo and pine branches held together by rice straw ropes. All decorations are supposed to be burned on January 7th.

Hyakunin isshu is a game of poems played by adults only at this time of the year. There are two hundred cards that must be matched up to make one hundred complete poems.

Boys fly kites, *tako*, and girls play *oibane* or a game similar to badminton, except no net is used. It is played with a brightly painted battledore and shuttlecock. The girl who misses the shuttlecock often gets a daub of charcoal on her face.

All Japanese become one year older on January 1st. This is because to them each year is complete in itself. Even if a person were born on December 31st, he would be two years old the next day because he was born last year and would then be in his second year.

Toward the last of January, Clayton C. Robison, Jr. of Corrignsville, Md. returned from Iwo Jima to attend cable-splicing school. He told us that there was a superstition among the men on the island that at 1100 hours on February 23rd, the image of the Marines raising the flag on Mt Suribachi appears in the sulfur vapors that rise from the island.

Iwo Jima lies 750 miles south of Tokyo. It was the site of the most incredible fighting of the Pacific campaign during the Second World War. Never before or since have the Marines fought a tougher battle. They lost 5372 men, killed and wounded, in 58 hours.

The bombardment of Iwo Jima began on January 24, 1945. The Navy had shelled the island with thousands of tons of giant shells but it wasn't until 0900 on February 19th that the Navy landed the first wave of Marines on the shore. It was 10:35 on February 23 when a small patrol reached the summit of Mt.Suribachi and raised the American flag.

Japanese General Kuribayashi defended this tiny island with 23,000 men. The fighting didn't cease until he was killed in a final action on the northern tip of the island in one of the innumerable caves on or about March 16th.

The reader should read an account of this terrible battle for it took place only seven years prior to the present work. After the holiday season, Hovorka and Priola returned to Iwo Jima and we went back to the daily grind of working in the motor pool.

CHAPTER V

Misawa

Near the end of January, a rumor went around that those of us left in the third platoon would be sent to Misawa to put in some cable. We were certainly hoping so.

Several days later Cpl. Thomas Klassen from Chattanooga, Tenn. confirmed the rumor. He hadn't seen the orders, but he had heard it on good authority in the orderly room. Klassen was in the second platoon, but since he was the ranking man, he was in charge during the trip.

He explained that we wouldn't be working alone. Part of the second platoon had been up there for some time. He said he didn't know much about the job except that it was cable, and probably underground. As for the base, it was pretty nice. He had been there before on some other jobs.

When the manifest came out, we were all listed on it except George Sipos. Someone in personnel had left his name off the list. However, Arthur Thearling, who was on the manifest, signed up for cable splicing school, so George went in his place. The men that went on this trip were: Sipos, Loren Bacon, Curtis Clendenin, Everett Donegan, Gordon Gebbens, Kenneth Jones, Richard Scott, Thomas Klassen, Earl L Faircloth (a second platoon man who was soon to return to the States), and myself.

We were off-duty on the day before we left so that we could pack, get our clothes from the laundry or cleaner, fill out certain required forms for air travel, and ready our equipment. It was no small job getting everything in the footlockers. In addition to our regular issue of clothing, we had extra sweaters and a pair of heavy overshoes. We stood on each other's lockers to get them closed.

Next morning, the CQ woke us at 0400 hours. We turned in our bedding and loaded the lockers on a "6-by" that the night runner had parked outside the door. This done, we all went to breakfast. Richard L Benson of Gloucester, Mass. was in the mess hall frying eggs. He seemed to be the only person that was fully awake.

After breakfast we climbed into the back of the 6-by and started for Tachikawa Air Base, which was about six miles down the narrow winding road. It was chilly and the dust from the tires was billowing up into the back of the truck. The darkness was complete except for the red glow on the ends of a few cigarettes.

By 0515 hours, we had checked our baggage at the air terminal and had gone into the snack bar to warm up and drink coffee until plane time. Word soon came over the loudspeakers that the plane was loading. We walked out on the runway to a two engine plane with "CAT" (Civil Air Transport) printed on the wings and sides. Although it was an American made C-46, it belonged to an Oriental airline.

The manifest was read in the order that the passengers were to climb aboard. The highest-ranking officers got on first and on downward in rank until us lowly privates were all that were left. As we stood there waiting to get on, I began to wish that we were going on one of the big four motored C-124's that I could see silhouetted against the early dawn light. I had never been in an airplane before, so I was a little nervous about getting airsick.

Richard Scott and I took seats in front of a window that was far enough behind the wing to give us a good view of the ground. We wanted to shoot some pictures from the air. Actually, of our group, he was the only one who had flown before.

We sat in canvas seats along the sides of the plane so that the passengers faced each other across a large mass of freight lashed to the floor down the center of the plane. Our footlockers were not in sight so we assumed that the Japanese workers had loaded them into the belly of the plane or had left them off entirely. Fortunately, the latter was not the case.

There were parachutes under each seat, but I didn't know anything about using one and no one mentioned them. I resisted the temptation to try one on when Scott explained that most accidents occur on takeoffs and landings. The parachute wouldn't do any good at that altitude.

The pilot switched on the engines while a member of the ground crew stood by with a fire extinguisher. He then released the brakes and we taxied to the end of the runway. We sat there about five minutes while the pilot revved up each engine individually and then both together.

When the pilot had satisfied himself that the passengers were sufficiently vibrated, he released the brakes. We rapidly picked up speed down the runway and were in the air without the slightest jar. As we circled the field I shot a picture of Mt. Fujiyama. The sunlight on the snow-covered cone was beautiful.

My ears popped several times as the plane climbed higher. Scott, who was a civilian pilot, had come prepared for any emergency. He passed out chewing gum to all of us first timers. The popping stopped when the plane leveled off, and many of us took a nap.

The plane hadn't been in the air long before Scott jabbed me and pointed out the window. Someone had left the cap off the fuel tank in the left wing. The backwash from the propeller was blowing the fumes and liquid back over the wing. We wondered if it wasn't parachute time.

We could see more and more snow through openings in the clouds below us as we flew northward. Approximately halfway to Misawa, the pilot landed the plane at Matsushima Air Base. The sleeping passengers were awakened so that the change in air pressure wouldn't break their eardrums. We descended so rapidly that my ears were paining terribly. I could hardly hear the plane's engines by the time the wheels touched the ground.

We walked through the drifted snow to a snack bar located on the "strip", where we warmed up for about fifteen minutes. Scott showed us how to equalize the pressure in our ears, but it was still a strange whispery sort of world.

As the plane gained altitude for the last leg of our trip, the pressure on my ears lessened and my hearing returned to normal. My ears never pained again like they did on that first landing.

At Misawa, the plane settled with a crunching sound on the snow-covered runway. Snow along the runway was about four feet deep, but near the center of the strip the snowplows had piled it as high as thirty feet. It was still snowing, just as it would be every day that we were up there.

Misawa was a large, busy base in spite of the weather there. It is located roughly about 450 miles north of Tokyo, and is near the northern tip of Honshu, the main island of Japan.

Sergeant Duley met us in the passenger terminal. We climbed into the back of the canvas covered weapons carrier he was driving, and he took us to get some bedding. From there, he took us to the barracks where we were to stay temporarily. One of the first things we noticed was that most of the vehicles were mounted with machine guns and all of the men carried personal weapons to their jobs.

We drove down the main street to about halfway between the airstrip and the main gate. There the sergeant stopped the weapons carrier in front of a small barracks that was hidden from the road by a long drab warehouse.

The barracks was already crowded with men. All of the beds were double-bunked; even those that were lined up down the center aisle. The air in there had a bad odor caused by too many men sleeping without enough ventilation.

Clothes hung on open racks. Empty bottles, fruit peels, and papers littered the floor. In the latrine were three dirty wash basins with two mirrors to shave by. Also there were three filthy stools which were just a little better than useless. They would not flush half the time because of low water pressure.

The shower room was good by comparison, but it too was dirty. It was a small; tin lined room with six foot by eight-foot floor area containing three showers.

There were three boy-sans being paid to keep the barracks clean, but that must have been their day off considering what little cleaning they did.

After we had found some bunks and brought in our footlockers, it was time for chow. We ate in a large consolidated mess hall behind the base theater. The food was good and plentiful.

Later, we had time to look around the base. The theater, service club, Airmen's club, Rocker Club, and library were grouped near the mess hall. A hobby shop was a few blocks away. The Post Exchange, snack bar, and base Chapel were a few blocks closer to the strip.

The Hobby Shop was one of the nicest ones I have seen. It had large convenient well-lighted rooms for the men to pursue almost any hobby they cared too. An instructor helped beginners with photography problems and darkroom procedures. There was a room for wood working and sculpturing. Also there were painting and model building areas.

Three hostesses ran the service club at Misawa. It was nice but too small to be adequate for such a large base. It had one ping pong table and two pool tables in the back room. There were two small rooms just off the main room. One was used for a reading room and the other as a writing room. A glassed in porch opened into the main room, which made that room large enough for dancing. Another small closed in room was used as a record room.

I spent several evenings at a desk in the writing room, until one of the ladies began hinting that she didn't see eye to eye with me about wearing fatigues in "her" service club after 1700 hours. After that I spent a good many pleasant hours in the library across the street. The library was in a small building, but it had a nice collection of books and magazines. There seemed to be plenty for the men at Misawa to do in their off-duty hours.

The next afternoon, Sunday, I walked into town to look around. I was surprised at the number of bicycle drawn *jinriksha*. They are common in Tokyo, but rarer in Tachikawa. Horses pulled large sleds filled with firewood or "honey buckets". Horses and oxen are never driven in Japan. They are always led at the end of a short length of rope.

There were many Japanese carrying skis. I was also surprised at how well the people understood my Tokyo-area dialect Japanese. There is a great difference in the dialects spoken in Japan, just as there are a great many dialects of English spoken in the United States.

Few Christians who visit Japan realize that while there they can visit the "tomb of Jesus Christ". Yes, it is true. Twenty miles or so south of Misawa is the village of Herai, where the inhabitants believe that they are the descendants of Jesus.

There is a sign in English (also one in Japanese) that tells the legend. The "descendants" agree that Christ was born in Bethlehem, but declare that He came to Japan when he was twenty-one years old. He studied Shintoism while in Japan. The emperor sent Him to Jerusalem to preach to the Jews at the age of thirty-three.

The crucifixion took place, but they believe that Jesus' legendary brother, Ishikiri (whose grave may also be seen at Herai), was the man who was crucified. Ishikiri had changed clothes with Christ at Gethsemane.

Christ then returned to Japan, adopted the name Hachinohe Taro Tengu, took a wife, and had three daughters. According to the legend, He died when 118 years old.

Monday we began work, and it was real work. We were to dig some holes five to six feet deep and large enough for two cable splicers to work inside. The soil in these places was easy to dig after we had scooped the ice and snow off the top of the ground and dug through about ten inches of frozen ground; but it was cold. It was also snowing hard.

We took turns digging. As soon as one fellow would throw out a couple of shovels full of dirt, the others would begin calling, "That's enough. Come on out. We want to get warmed up too." We dug several holes and a short trench that day.

The next day, we dug the fresh snow out of the holes and trench and laid the cable. We then covered it up. In the afternoon, largely due to the effort of a friendly Air Force major, we checked out some wool-lined parkas.

We were set for any kind of weather after that. I, for one, had taken my fatigue hat with earflaps out of my footlocker and was wearing it. Many of the men had on seven layers of clothing: summer underwear, long winter underwear, sweater, fatigues, field jacket, wool parka liner, and the parka. I even carried a pocket warmer between my sweater and fatigue shirt.

There was only one difficulty with so much clothing. It was hard to work in. Most of us left the parka liner in the barracks except on very bad days.

In a few days we had all the easy digging completed. The really hard work began when we started to dig a cable trench between two streets. About one-half of the length of the trench was along and across a much traveled road leading up to a mess hall. The easiest digging on this trench was the half from the end of the road, between some barracks, to the street. It was completed in a couple of days with both crews working on it.

But the other half, along with the mess hall road and around in front of the mess hall was slow digging. Apparently, gravel and cinders had been thrown on the road at various times and had been packed down by heavy motor vehicles.

For several days we thought we were digging through a poor grade of Japanese concrete. All of us together were making only six to ten feet of headway a day with shovels and picks. It was discouraging to swing the pick as hard as one could only to have it glance off a rock, or at most, chip off a few pebbles.

Sometimes between snowstorms the sun would come out for a few hours. When it did, the rays falling on the sides of the trench would cause them to thaw on the surface. The mud and water would then rub off on the parkas, fatigues, and boots. The men in the third platoon were more comfortable than the men in the second, however. Most of the men in the second platoon didn't have overshoes to keep their feet dry.

Finally, we got an air hammer from the A.I.O. (Air Installation Office). A forty-eight inch Japanese fellow operated the compressor, which was on a truck. We thought he was supposed to operate the air hammer, too, for it was about his size. We had to lean way over to use the toy-like tool. Nevertheless, we used it because it did the job quicker after we learned to use it to the best advantage.

After about a week there were some vacancies in the barracks where the men in the second platoon were staying. We were glad to get out of the little barracks and into a larger, cleaner building. It was located on the edge of the strip and housed about two hundred transit troops. That is, it was used as temporary housing for troops on R. & R. (Rest and Recuperation) from Korea, new troops coming from the United States, men on TDY, and other such non-permanent personnel.

Some of the men who were at Misawa at that time were: two brothers, Foy and Roy Walker of Cuthbert, Ga.; Don Mooney, of Bakersfield, Calif.; Clovis A. Owens of Mobile, Ala.; Hoover H. Neal, of Soddy, Tenn.; LeRoy Palmer, of Memphis, Tenn.; Richard McPherson, of Cleveland, Ohio; Thomas G. Carr, of Binghampton, NY; George W. Frame, of Berkeley, Mo.; Raymond O. Chryst, of Miami, Fla.; William R. Grubbs, of Flint, Mich.; Slaton E. Giles, of Atlanta, Ga.; and, WOJG John C. Price.

From the windows we had an excellent view of the airstrip. The jets were fascinating planes to watch. They were beautiful, streamlined things that didn't look capable of flight without a propeller. While at Misawa, I often watched them taxi slowly to the end of the flight line. They would turn, start forward, quickly accelerating, and be in the air and out of sight in a matter of seconds. In my more reckless moods I even wished I could fly one.

One evening I decided to visit the "21 Club". When the men from the 474th went to town at Misawa, that is where they could usually found. Several people had asked, "Why don't you stop by to see the club sometime?" They described it as, "Not fancy, but nice". I don't believe that any of them ever expected to see me there. Nevertheless, they had equipped me with detailed directions on how to reach "our club".

I was to proceed straight down the road after passing through the base gate until I came to the end of the road. At that point I was to turn left and follow that street until I saw an arrow shaped sign on a post. Then I was to follow in the direction the arrow pointed for one block and I would be standing in front of the "21 Club".

The 21 Club was a two-story building that set on a corner under the only street light for blocks around. It was conspicuous for a single medieval-looking turret built on the corner nearest the street. It served as an entrance vestibule and supported a neon sign, "21 Club".

A bicycle *jinrikisha* boy waited near the entrance. He sat inside the passenger compartment trying to keep warm and dry while waiting for a customer. He kept watch through a small round window in the canvas. When someone would leave the club, he would stick his head out just long enough to call, "*jinrikisha*". His business didn't seem too good this early in the evening.

I pushed open the swinging doors and walked into a room about thirty by thirty feet. The floor was of dirty unfinished wood. A small heating stove stood in the center of the room. Army and Air Force personnel sat at round, weak-looking tables arranged around the perimeter of the room. Smoke from their cigars and cigarettes filled the upper atmosphere of the room. Visibility from the windows was limited due to dirt and the condensation of moisture on the glass.

Directly across the room from the entrance was the bar. It appeared to be about three and one-half feet high and about six feet long. Shelves on the wall behind the bar were well stocked with Stateside as well as Japanese drinks. This wall didn't extend all the way to the floor. It extended down to the height of the bar, as if the bar were pulled back after closing hours to shut the barroom off from the rest of the house.

As it was, a person standing at the bar could see into their home when the bar was pulled out and the paper sliding door or *shoji* separating the rooms on the other side was ajar.

Mama-san was working behind the bar with her baby strapped to her back. A young girl, probably her daughter and not yet a prostitute, was behind the counter helping her. Papa-san and several other children were kneeling barefoot on the straw mats, *tatami*, within their home. Occasionally, Papa-san would step into his *geta* and bring in another case of liquor. Then he would carefully step out of his shoes before re-entering his home.

I was introduced to Mama-san. The fellow who introduced us told me what a fine lady she was. " She will do anything for you. If there is something you want and you don't see it, just ask for it. She will get it for you."

As this fellow talked, I watched Mama-san and was convinced that the boy hadn't exaggerated his last statement. I believe Mama-san would get anything for them — if the price were right.

She was beginning to show her age. Her face was cold and hard. She had no love for her customers, but she did love their money. She handled their extra cigarettes for them, and often accepted their jewelry as security that they would pay for their drinks on payday. On the second floor of her building, she had rooms that she rented to her B-girls so that they might entertain their friends.

Mama-san's girls were drinking with the men in the dimly lighted room. Most of these girls had their lipstick smeared and their dresses pretty well wrinkled from being handled. Now and then some of them would get up to jitterbug to a loud stateside record on the jukebox. The noise was tremendous. Certainly no one could think of his homesickness in that atmosphere.

One weekend, five of us went skiing on the snow-covered hills just beyond the Misawa golf course. Special Services provided the skis in a small building on the golf course. Young Japanese fellows took care of all the equipment in it.

Corporal Faircloth was an old hand at skiing. He had been skiing many times in other parts of Japan. The others: Loren Bacon, Curtis Clendenin, Don Mooney, and I had never been on skis before.

A fellow in the barracks drove us out to the golf course in one of our trucks. At that time the sun was shining and there was a cold wind. We checked out the skis at the ski shack and worked our way to the top of the first hill. From the top there was a long gradual sloping trail around a gully and over to the hills where we were to ski. The wind blew from the large ice and snow covered lake behind the hills. Clumps of snow covered pines dotted the landscape. The scenery was beautiful, which is not un-usual in Japan.

Faircloth went to the top of the hill the first thing, but the rest of us made a few short ski runs from about halfway up the hill. We were falling all over the place and laughing and shouting like school children.

Mooney had the most trouble because of a broken ski strap on one ski. Each time that he thought he had the strap fixed, he would come whizzing down the hill full of confidence. Then something would give about half-way down the slope and he would be left moving at top speed, weaving back and forth on one ski, with both arms and ski poles flapping wildly in the air. A little further and he would plop in the snow, usually on his head, rather than a more adapted part of his body. He would get up laughing every time.

The rest of us were having enough trouble keeping upright without the problem of Mooney's loose ski strap. Each time we fell, the skis got tangled in an unbelievably complex mess. Getting untangled took up most of our ski time

The daily blizzard caught us out there about an hour after we ar-rived. It gradually grew more violent and colder, so we started back to the ski shack to wait for the base bus to arrive.

Several Japanese boys and girls, who had also been skiing, rode back to the base with us. They, together with a GI, began singing Christian hymns in English as we rode along. Many of the men on the bus joined in. It was astonishing to hear how well those Japanese boys and girls sang those hymns. They had learned the songs while attending Sunday school on the base.

The work at Misawa was hard. Altogether, there were approximately two thousand feet of cable to be buried at least thirty inches deep. The top ten to twelve inches of surface soil was impenetrable without a great deal of work with a pick or air hammer. Consequently, most of the men were tired out at the end of each day. After evening chow most of them would return to the barracks to write a few letters, and then hit the sack early.

An Air Force boy who had a bunk on the other side of a row of lockers from us played his radio every evening. He tuned in the Far East Network for the transcribed musical programs and record requests. "Till I Waltz Again With You" must have been popular for some time in the States before we had a chance to hear it. That song left a funny hollow feeling in a lot of stomachs. Another song that stirred up a sad pleasant feeling was Joni James singing, "Why Don't You Believe Me".

About midnight, a few days before we were to leave Misawa and return to Showa, someone who bumped into my bunk as he ran through the darkened barracks awakened me. As he careened down the aisle, he knocked a paper cup of water off a locker and onto the floor. I heard the water hit the floor and just supposed that some drunk was hurrying to the latrine to throw up and hadn't made it.

I turned over and tried to go back to sleep, but then a light came on in the barrack sergeant's enclosure where the boy was trying to get in to use the phone. The boy was talking loud, demanding to use the phone, saying, "I'm gonna call the AP's", over and over. The friends that had brought him in from town were just as insistent that he wasn't going to call. They were trying to get him to go to bed.

A sergeant in his outfit grabbed him and ordered him to go to bed. This scared the boy and he began to call, "Don't hit me. Don't hit me. I'll call my uncle. He'll get me out of this————place."

"You're not going to call anybody", the sergeant replied. "You're going to bed". We heard the next day that the boy's uncle was a lieutenant in the Coast Guard Reserve back in the States.

The boy continued to insist he wasn't going to bed. Finally, the sergeant decided to take him outside where the cold air might sober him up. As he was pulled outside, he was pleading to the sergeant not to hit him.

"Shut up or I will", he replied.

Five minutes later, they came back in, but the cold air hadn't sobered the boy. He was still raving that he wasn't going to bed. He wanted to call the AP's to lock everyone up for kidnapping him from the tavern. It did no good for the friends to explain that the tavern was closing for the night.

The sergeant and a whole gang of men that had brought the boy in, took him to the latrine where they pleaded, ordered, conjured, promised, threatened, and begged with him to be quiet and go to bed. Instead he began to cry loudly. It was a disgusting thing to have to listen to at that time of the night. After awhile he lapsed into loud sobs. No one could be heard in the latrine but him.

It was none of my business, but my conscience kept prodding me about making it my business. No one could sleep with this going on and his friends were not getting anywhere. I pulled on my boots and went to see what was going on.

A group stood by the window talking quietly about what they should do. There were several people from the second platoon of the 474th present. One of them said, "Here's a man who might get him to go to bed. Pointing at the drunk, he asked, "Will you talk to him?"

I said I would try but from the appearance of the situation I didn't have any hope. He had his shirt and tie off and was leaning against a shelf over the wash basins. His forehead rested on his arm. Except for a sob every once in awhile he was unresponsive. Saliva and mucus ran out of his nose and mouth. From the general appearance of his features, he didn't look like the sort of fellow that was encumbered with too much intelligence.

After wasting a few sentences on him that didn't stir up any response, I jerked his right arm off the shelf, put his hand in a wash basin and turned on the cold water. Then I scooped up handfuls of the water and threw it in his face. The cold water brought him out of it, I thought. He pulled himself up to a stoop-shouldered, weak in the middle compromise of good posture. Rocking back and forth a few times, he declared once again in a loud voice that he was going to call the AP's.

When asked why, he reiterated several reasons: robbed, kidnapped, and mishandled to name a few. I tried to get him settled down on the grounds that he was keeping everyone in the barracks awake. That didn't work. Next, I tried to get him to postpone the call until morning. He insisted on calling then. I explained that he would get a DR (Disorderly Report) and spend the night in jail if he called. He wanted to go to jail. I had only one card left, the old, "What would your mother think of you now?" technique. I even tossed in his girl friend for good measure.

"Mother" and his "girlfriend" held him for a few minutes, but then I noticed his eyes were beginning to cloud as though he were losing his temper. Each time he put his hand on the door to leave I had to hit it away with the edge of my hand. He now announced that he was going to fight. He crouched over and worked himself into the awkwardest fighting position I have ever seen. Everyone in the latrine laughed except him. He was dead serious. I ridiculed him into putting his hands down.

He stood rocking back and forth from heels to toes, glowering at me for a few seconds. "Are you going to let me out of here?" he asked, slipping his hands into his pockets.

"Certainly not", I answered, "unless you promise to go to bed."

"If you don't, I'm gonna take out my knife and cut you," he threatened. I tapped both of his pockets with my fingers to be sure he didn't have a knife. He didn't.

Nevertheless, he raised his right arm high over his head and extended his left arm out behind him. It also was a silly position for a man with a knife to take, but he was all prepared to stab me – except that he had no knife. As soon as he saw that I wasn't going to move from in front of the door he stopped playing with his invisible knife.

He resumed his fighting stance once again and each time he came close enough, I placed two fingers on his chest and pushed him backward two or three steps.

It was at this stage of the entertainment that the barracks sergeant finally arrived. He was a stout looking fellow. As he walked in the door, he said, "All right you two, break it up. Shake hands and get to bed."

I explained, "This isn't a handshaking occasion. This guy is drunk and I am trying to get him to go to bed."

"Okay, Sarge," he replied, "I'll take over." The crowd in the latrine went on to bed.

We could hear the sergeant arguing with the boy for quite awhile. Finally he said, "If you don't go to bed, I'll call the AP's and you'll spend the night in jail."

"Go ahead and call them."

"All right, I will", he said pulling the boy out of the latrine and toward his office. Now you sit down there and don't move", the sergeant said, pushing him onto an empty bunk outside the office door.

"If you touch me again", the boy said, rising to his feet, "you're automatically busted." As the sergeant collared him, the boy hollered, "You're busted."

The sergeant pushed him down again, saying, "Listen you, if you don't sit down and shut up, I'm going to slap you."

The boy had an answer for that too. "Go ahead and slap me. They'll take fingerprints off my face and bust you to private E-1."

At this point the furious sergeant called the AP's. They arrived a few minutes later and took the boy to spend the night in jail.

We saw him the next morning after his release from confinement. He got a DR.

A few days later, those of us in the third platoon flew back to Tachikawa in a CAT C-46. The job at Misawa was far from completed but the company was planning to reunite the platoons. The rest of the second platoon was to join their men at Misawa, and we were to join our platoon unit in the Company before going on to another job.

CHAPTER VI

Shiroi

It was twilight when the plane landed at Tachikawa Air Base. The warm moist evening reminded me of spring in Illinois.

Someone called the company CQ and asked him to send his "runner" over after us, while the rest of us piled our footlockers on a platform at the rear of the passenger terminal.

The company runner arrived in a weapons carrier an hour or so later. He wouldn't admit it, but we believed that he got lost trying to find the terminal. When we arrived at Showa, the driver stopped the "weap" in front of our barracks door to unload the footlockers. While we were carrying the boxes in, Eugene Bartasavage came through the barracks looking for Scott and me.

Gene shook hands and generally acted as a "welcome home committee" of one. He explained that he had been expecting us, so thought he would drop by on his way to the service club to see if we had arrived yet.

We picked up our bedding at supply and got settled in. Supper chow wasn't any good according to Gene, so he insisted on buying our supper at the Snack Bar. It turned out that the Snack Bar was closed, so we had to eat warmed over food in the mess hall anyway. Gene did the next best thing for us. He acted as chef for the whole crew, and treated us like kings.

Later, we all went to the service club to listen to the Japanese band and see the floor show that entertained on Wednesday evening. A lot of things to talk about had accumulated during the three weeks we were away from the Company. Time passed fast.

We didn't work the next day. The new third platoon sergeant, Herman Kimbrell of Mount Airy, Ga., assigned each of his new men to one of his four crews within the platoon. We all felt bad about getting separated, but it couldn't be helped. None of us knew anything about antenna work. Therefore we were placed in the existing crews so that we could learn the work from experienced men while on the job. After being assigned to a crew, we had the rest of the day off to straighten up our equipment, go to the laundry, etc.

Loren Bacon and I were assigned to the third crew. Corporal Jesse Jones, Jr., whose home was Memphis, Tenn. was crew chief. The men in Jones' crew told us how lucky we were to be in their crew. They claimed that Jones was the best crew chief in the company.

His crew consisted of the following men: Robert P. Berger of Farmington, Mo.; John T. Carey of New York, NY; Bennie Davis, of Longview, Texas; Valentino C. DeVaca, of Santa Fe, New Mex.; David H. Spain, of Aliceville, Ala.; Richard Wakefield, of Mystic Iowa; and Albertus Young of New York, NY.

The order of events in the company was changed somewhat now that the third platoon was together. Of course we still fell out for reveille and "police call" at 0630 hours as usual. But when we fell out for workcall, Sergeant Kimbrell turned the platoon over to Jones.

Jones would then give the platoon physical training. Kimbrell couldn't have put a better man in charge for that sort of thing. Jones was 6 ft 4 in. tall and weighed 210 pounds. I wasn't as impressed with his strength then as I was later on the job. He was undoubtedly the strongest man that I met overseas. He was also one of the best natured.

There was something characteristic about Jones other than size and strength. It was his sense of humor. He never seemed to get mad. Sometimes he would start to tell funny stories and not seem to be able to stop. He and his audience would laugh until tears ran down their cheeks. His imagination and the consequent stories were unlimited.

After going through the standard Army exercises, Jones would take the lead and circle the company area with the whole platoon running behind him. Now and then we would do some climbing on the two practice poles as part of the exercise. There was an excellent view of snow covered Fujiyama from the top of the poles on clear mornings.

When the physical training was over Jones would march us to the motor pool where we spent the rest of the day's duty hours.

Saturday evening, shortly after we got back from Misawa, a group of us who were at the service club began discussing the Great Buddha at Kamakura. We all agreed that we would like to see it. We asked Miss. Cooper, the club director, about sending a tour to Kamakura to see the *Daibutsu*. The tour for the next day was going to Tokyo, but she said that she would have it changed to Kamakura if we wanted her to. We thanked her, and told the others the good news.

Kamakura is located about ten miles south of Yokohama. It was the capital of Japan more than 700 years ago. We left Showa about 1000 hours and arrived at Kamakura shortly after noon.

The *Daibutsu* or Great Buddha sits on the wooded grounds of an ancient monastery that Emperor Shomu caused to be built in 737 A.D. Glyptic artist, Ono Goroe, cast the Diabutsu itself in September, 1252 A.D. On each side of the walk leading up to it were old stone lanterns or *ishi-doro*. Hundreds of visitors were walking around the grounds taking pictures and buying souvenirs at the little shops.

Time had weathered the colossal image of Buddha a light green color, as it had been sitting for centuries cross-legged with its eyes half-closed. It seemed to have become a part of its surroundings. It was a beautiful monstrosity.

Although it is not the largest Daibutsu, it is considered the most beautiful by the Japanese. The largest image of Buddha is located at Nara and not nearly as serene in appearance.

We bought some cards at one souvenir shop with the dimensions printed on them. The image is forty-three feet high and ninety-seven feet in circumference. The length of the face is 7.7 feet; length of eye, 3.3 feet; length of ear, 6.6 feet; length of nose, 2.8 feet; breadth of mouth, 2.8 feet; distance from knee to knee, 30 feet; and circumference of thumb, 2.8 feet. The total weight is 210,000 pounds.

Several of us paid ten yen for the opportunity to see the inside of the image. We stooped through the doorway under the left side of the Buddha. The interior was dimly lighted from open metal windows located at about the shoulder blades of the image.

As our eyes adjusted to the darkness we could make out some of the objects on display. Towards the front of the interior was a large flat stone with Japanese writing carved on it. At the right rear was what looked like an old cupboard with glass doors. It contained various ancient religious relics on display. Nearby was a steep metal stairway leading up to a landing at shoulder height on the Buddha. From this platform, one could gaze through the window openings or look up into the hollow head where a small carved image of Buddha sat.

When we left Kamakura, we followed the road about six miles further to the pretty little island of Enoshima. Enoshima is connected to the mainland by a long causeway. The driver parked the bus and we walked across the causeway to the island. On our way we passed old ladies selling seafoods to the visitors.

The main avenue of traffic seemed to be straight ahead and up a dirt road which inclined at about forty-five degrees. On both sides of the road were small souvenir shops stairstepped into the side of the hill we were climbing. These extended upward to about midway the height of the hill.

A series of wide stone stairs continued upward from where the dirt road ended. The largest Japanese flag (*Hinomaru* or "the round of the sun") that I saw in Japan fluttered in the breeze at the top of the stairs.

At the top of the stairs I followed a trail to the left to see and photograph the many ancient shrines and caves. Some of the others went immediately to the highest point on the island. It was an observation tower rising about three hundred feet above the top of the island, according to Scott.

Although it was mid-winter, the plants on the island were emerald green. Many of them had wooden signs fastened to them with their common name lettered in Japanese script and the scientific binomial in Roman lettering. It would have been a wonderful place to spend more time.

On a Wednesday morning, about a week and a half after our arrival in the company from Misawa, the entire third platoon went to Shiroi for another cable job. Shiroi was a nice, but small and apparently new base not far from Tokyo. We rode over in one of our 6-bys and a weapons carrier.

We were assigned to an empty Quonset at the end of the road leading to their antenna site. Large pine trees grew along the sides and at the back of the buildings. Crows called to each other as they flew among the pines and provided a vacation in the woods type atmosphere for the place.

Through the trees we could see a thatched roof farmhouse in a distant field. There were no other houses nearby; and it looked like a nice place for someone to live. It was a very picturesque scene.

Most Americans are impressed with the simplicity and clean appearance of the interior of a Japanese home. There is very little furniture. The bedding (*futon* or mattress) and practically everything else is kept out of sight in built-in closets (oshiire) and drawers. The floor is covered with *tatami* or straw mats from which the room gets its size. The *tatami* is approximately 3 x 6 feet in size, so the number of mats required to cover the floor designates the room size.

The rooms are adjustable in size because of the sliding doors called *shoji*, or *karakami,* which partition off the house. The difference is the paper used over the frame. *Shoji* is made of white paper manufactured for that purpose, while *karakami* is of coarser opaque paper and may have designs on it like wallpaper. There is also a rain door for the outside of the house called *amado*. It protects the inner sliding doors. Even in winter, on sunny days, the sliding doors are pushed back to allow the sun to warm the interior of the house.

For privacy while the house is open, a hedge or high fence surrounds most houses. The *kakine* or hedge is formed from many types of trees and shrubs. It is pruned once a year to the desired height and thickness.

About the only decoration in a Japanese house is in the *tokonoma*. This is an alcove, which is the most important part of a room. Guests are asked to sit near the *tokonoma* because it is the most honored place in the house. Hanging in the alcove will be a *kakemono* or scroll bearing some writing or a picture. Below it may be a flower arrangement. A polite guest will go to the *tokonoma* immediately upon entry and admire the *kakemono* and other decorations.

The *benjo* (motion place) or toilet often consists of three closets: a men's room, a place to wash, and a closet with a hole in the floor. *Benjo* is the common name, but more polite names are: *gofujo* or "honorable impurity", *habakari* or "impoliteness", *o-te-arai* or "honorable hand washing".

Most modern houses have a tile roof, and are heated by a small portable charcoal burner called a *hibachi* . However in the old style thatched roof houses a wood fire was used and needed. The hearth or *irori* was a hole six to ten feet square in the room, and was filled with wood ashes. There was no ceiling, so the smoke from the burning logs kept the roof free of moisture and insects. For this reason a thatched roof won't last long where charcoal is burned for heat.

Before dinner, we drew bedding and got everything set up in the barracks. The food in the mess hall was good, but there were never enough spoons to go around.

At 1300 hours we began the job of digging up some old cable that had been buried in an area only a few hundred yards from the barracks. The work was easy compared to the trouble we had cutting through the frozen soil at Misawa. Here the soil was only frosted a couple of inches deep and was very friable. There was no snow on the ground and the weather was warm enough that we were comfortable. We got a lot of cable dug up that first afternoon.

It rained continuously from dawn until after dark the next day, so we spent the day inside resting, writing letters and reading.

Friday was a fine clear day. The ground seemed perfect for digging in spite of all the rain that had fallen during the previous day. It was just as loose as ever. We left Shiroi in the evening so we could be in the Company for Saturday's inspection and to get paid.

The people of Tokyo must have thought we were transporting a menagerie in the rear of our truck. Donegan amused himself by whistling like a canary and imitating a dog and cat fight every time the truck slowed down. He sounded so real that the Japanese stopped on the streets to look. We arrived in the Company after 2000 hours.

The third crew didn't return to Shiroi with the rest of the platoon when it left early Monday morning. We were to go on TDY in a few days to an air base at Ashiya.

About this time the company got a new first sergeant. Sgt. Easterling had left for the States early in December. There had been two other sergeants that had followed him.

The new first sergeant took over at reveille. Instead of the usual dry formalities that we were expecting, he introduced himself, and then read off several bulletins, made jokes about them, and said to make the police call a "short one". The men liked him immediately. Some of the men had already met him, for he had made it a point to become acquainted with as many of the men as he could as soon as he arrived in the company.

M/Sgt. John E. Hendrickson was a tall, stout, cheerful fellow who had made a career out of the military. He was from Rochester, NY.

In the few days that he was first sergeant before we left for Ashiya, we had a chance to see some of his reforms go into effect in the Company. He began by making it easier for his men to get a pass. Then he had the lockers and beds rearranged in the barracks to allow better air circulation and more light to enter.

M/Sgt. Hendrickson was the talk of the company. The men were really proud of him.

CHAPTER VII

Ashiya I

As usual on the day that we were to leave, we had the day off to pack and to take care of any personal business we had to attend to. We also packed our climbing equipment and tools in a wooden box for shipment.

On several preceding days, Corporal Jones, our crew chief, briefed us on the job we were to do at Ashiya. Sergeant Donald McArthur had been in charge of the crew that we were going to relieve. He told us what they had accomplished down there, what antennas were left to be put up, and discussed working conditions. He also warned us about a "little Air Force sergeant" who would be over us as "Tech. Rep." (technical representative).

Around 2000 hours we climbed into the back of a truck and the company runner drove us over to the air terminal at Tachikawa. We checked our footlockers and tools, before going into the adjoining snack bar for coffee and sandwiches. The night was getting chilly.

Our flight was called at about 2100 hours. We had walked out to a waiting C-119, so called a "flying boxcar". It was a huge bodied, two motored, and twin tailed plane. Flying boxcar was an appropriate name. The right side of this particular plane was decorated by a large painting of a pin up girl. It was known as the "Doanie-Dee".

All of the passengers were required to wear life jackets and parachutes. At 2115 hours we had fastened our safety belts and the pilot had taxied to the end of the strip and was revving up the engines preparatory to taking off. We were soon in the air

The weather must have been fine for flying for it was a very smooth trip. Most of us went to sleep. Everyone was awakened before the plane landed at Itazuke. When the plane stopped rolling the pilot climbed down out of the cockpit and announced a short rest stop.

We all went into the terminal to warm up. It wasn't long before someone discovered a place where we could order hot sandwiches. The Japanese cooks had finished a couple of egg sandwiches when an announcement came over the speaker that all passengers were to return to the plane. Some of the men procrastinated long enough to get what they had ordered, but the rest of us went back to the plane. The cooks were probably peeved that we didn't wait for the other sandwiches.

The next stop was at Ashiya Air Force Base. Ashiya was the "Home of the Korean Air Lift" according to numerous signs on the buildings. It was 0215 hours when we arrived. Corporal Nil J. Pla-Rodriguez, who's home was Brooklyn, NY, met us as we got off the plane. He had been left at Ashiya to take charge of the work as soon as the next crew arrived.

Missing our sandwiches over at Itazuki had only whetted our appetites, so he led us to a small building just off the strip where we could order hamburgers. From there we rode down to a large building that housed transit officers, and drew three blankets apiece from their supply room.

We spent what was left of the night in a nearby barracks, which was nearly full of sleeping men. Fortunately, we found beds and slept until 1000 hours.

Jones, however, was up early. He and Pla-Rodriguez had gone down to the transmitter site to look the job over. They woke us when they got back, and we carried our three blankets along a sandy trail that followed along beside the base fence. We had been sleeping not far from the new barracks.

This barracks, B-498, was H-shaped. We occupied the lower right wing of the H as one looked at it from the barbed wire fence that surrounded the base. The latrine joined the two barracks forming the cross in the H. Air Force personnel lived in all of the other wings of the building.

We rode down to the 483rd Communication Squadron supply room and checked out some bedding. They didn't even have enough sheets and pillowcases for all of us. However, we divided what they gave us as evenly as possible and returned to the barracks.

After noon chow, most of us took a walk around the base to see what it was like. A nice theater was located just south of the consolidated mess hall. West, and across the street from the mess hall, was the service club. The service club was large and nice, but not nearly as well equipped or staffed as one might expect from its size. A hobby shop sales room was located beneath the club. The Hobby Shop itself was located west of the service club. It was a small plain building filled with model planes hanging from the ceiling and sitting on numerous benches in various stages of completion. A large PX and laundry were located across the street from each other down near the main gate. An excellent library and a post office were within two blocks of our barracks.

Japanese men worked as KP's in the mess hall. Out on the line, Japanese girls served the food, wiped the tables, and did other less strenuous jobs. Supposedly, the girls received weekly tests for VD. Men on the base were "keeping" many of them. Some of the girls who didn't have steady boy friends keeping them, "short-timed" on the side.

In the evening I walked into *Ashiya-machi*, as the Japanese call their town. A paved road stretched from the main gate of the base through the town until the *Onga-Kawa* (Onga River) interceded. On the other side of the bridge, the road continued as a narrow oiled road extending southward.

Some of the stores along the main street seemed to be reasonably clean, but most of the merchandise was too expensive. There was a lot of silver, china, and cloisonné (*shippoyaki*) in the stores. A narrow, crooked, dirt road led off to the left of the main street. It was lined for about one third of its length with bars and shops. There were more bars in the alleys leading from it. "Business girls", as the prostitutes preferred to call themselves, were active everywhere. B-girls stood around outside their bars luring GI's in, while the noise and music from within cast its spell.

Approximately an acre of land was set aside as a park at the end of the road. A huge stone *torii* provided an entrance gate. Set back from the roadway was a large thatch-roofed temple. It was architecturally beautiful in spite of its being somewhat dilapidated.

At the rear of this building were several small scale replicas of temples sitting on stone pedestals. Some were complete even to the thatched roofs. They had pieces of straw rope and small stones inside. A few had small images of Buddha carved from stone within them. One in particular had a stone head about the size of a goose egg that was still recognizable as an image of Buddha.

By following the road to the left, I soon found another business district and more bars. That street was even narrower and dirtier than the others were. Shopkeepers were dipping water from the sewage ditches with long bamboo-handled dippers and throwing the water on the road to settle the dust.

As I walked along, the houses on my right overlooked a small bay. Presently I came to a sloping wharf-like structure constructed of large stones. Some fishermen were spreading their nets out to dry on it. I walked far enough out on the wharf to be able to see the rear of the houses overhanging the water. Invariably each house had a large sliding panel of glass on that side. They had a wonderful view.

Many of the small fishing boats were already docked beneath their owner's house, but others were chugging in on their one or two cylinder motors. What a scene this would be for an artist to paint!

Nearby, I saw how a three or four inch fish was dried. It was very common in the fish markets. The eyes of the fish were pierced by a narrow bamboo shoot and the fish were hung to dry in the sun and air. The fish were too small to be gutted. There was no protection from dust or flies as the fish were hung in racks out in the open.

When I arrived back at the barracks, a sergeant was sitting on his bunk with a bottle of whiskey in one hand and a coke in the other. He had just returned from a binge in town and had brought some refreshments back with him.

Sergeant G—— was what the men who knew him called a "real soldier", but they couldn't say much else, except that he was an alcoholic. He had been in the Army for ten years at the least. However, he knew very little about antenna work.

At that time he was waiting to be called back to the Company for processing to go to the States. If he ever had an interest in the work, it was gone. He drank almost continually until the day he left.

He would drink late into the night, often accompanied by an Air Force boy who would sit with him and listen to his half-whispered stories of woe, while sharing his bottle under the cold light of the bulb over his bunk. Sometimes, after everyone else had gone to bed he would light a cigarette, then stretch out on his bunk with his clothes on, and go to sleep with his forearm straight up in the air. Someone would have to take the cigarette out of his hand before he burned himself and turn the light off. Once in awhile he would wake and turn it off himself.

On the following morning, the whole crew went down to the site. The preceding crew had set poles for several antennas and had several antennas nearly completed. They had also set up most of the short poles of the transmission line. Their tools and equipment were in a canvas-roofed shack, so when we uncrated our gaffs and belts (which included the tools that we wore in the belt), we were ready to go to work.

Every antenna pole that was then standing was between eighty and ninety feet high, except for a little pole that had to be replaced later. It was only seventy-five feet high. None of them looked very inviting. Until the work became more organized, it was decided that we would begin by straightening some of the poles.

Each pole was held upright by two sets of three guy wires. The first sets of guys were fastened on the pole about mid-way up. The top guys were fastened about four feet from the top of the pole. The guys were made of a steel cable called "messenger strand". Each top guy and the corresponding middle guy led down to one of the three anchors spaced at 120 degrees around the pole.

The anchor itself was a section of pole five or six feet long. A short piece of messenger strand was wrapped around the log and held by a three-bolt clamp. A loop was bent into the free end of the wire and held by another three-bolt clamp. The three-bolt clamp was a small strong clamp with three bolts through it, which when tightened, held the messenger strand securely. It was a very important and necessary item in antenna work.

The anchor was buried six or eight feet deep with only the loop sticking out of the ground. The tail of the guy was stuck through the loop, and then a "coffin hoist" was attached by means of "grips" which gripped the guy on one side of the loop and the tail on the other.

By watching the hand signals given by the crew chief, the men working the hoists could tell whether to take up or let off the guy, thereby straightening the pole.

We were all prepared to straighten a pole near the line shack. The coffin hoists were fastened on all three top guys. We couldn't see the men at the other anchors because of the scrub pines growing between us, but Corporals Jones and Rodriguez were signaling from a place near the shack and visible to us all.

The pole must have been about straight when Sergeant G—— arrived on the job inebriated and took over the signaling job. He began signaling indiscriminately. In a few seconds the guys were too tight, but he was still signaling with both hands to take-up. A few more cranks on the hoist and everyone quit. We called over to him that the guys were too tight, but he insisted on a few more notches.

A few more notches was all it took. There was the sound of metal snapping and the whoosh of the pole whipping back and forth through the air. The guy nearest the shack sprang away from the top of the pole as if it were made of rubber. Only a miracle kept the top of the pole from breaking off.

Everyone ran over to look at the damage and to see what had broken. The eye of a bent eyebolt still had the cable looped through it. The strain had snapped the eye bolt in two.

The last crew had used the wrong type of bolt. However, it would have been all right under a normal amount of strain. When Sergeant G——— saw the broken eye bolt, he began to transfer the blame from himself to the type of bolt. He said that he would go see some major or colonel about it, and left, probably to get another drink.

Corporal Jones hadn't said a word. He was pacing around with a grim, angry expression on his face. He looked as if he were mad enough to tear up tree stumps. After awhile he exclaimed, "What if one of my men had been on that pole then!" Jones was one of those rare people who wouldn't speak when he was angry. Someone said that he hoped Sgt. G——— would go see the major, so that he could smell the alcohol on his breath, and maybe send him back to the Company for drinking on the job.

Rodriguez asked David "Reverend" Spain and Loren Bacon if they wanted to go up and put a new bolt through the pole and replace the guy. He knew that Spain would go up it, but since Bacon and I were both new on antenna construction, he decided to see how we reacted to high altitudes.

They both went up about halfway using their gaffs with their hands on the steps. Halfway up they changed and used the steps entirely. Spain was using gaffs that he had often worn before, so he went up easily. Bacon on the other hand, had never before worn the gaffs that he was wearing; therefore to be safe he was really hitting the pole when he gaffed in.

The rest of us watched tensely from below. The sound of their gaffs hitting the pole set up an echo from the ridge above the site. When both had reached the top and safetied in, it seemed as though we all took a deep breath.

After they had attached the guy again, they came back down. Bacon was nervous but he assured me, "It isn't so bad once you get up there".

We had been in Ashiya only a couple of days when I met the most well known GI on the base. One evening, I was standing alone in the service club looking at some maps on the wall, when someone gave me a terrific slap on the shoulder. I turned about and found myself facing a total stranger who was smiling at me as if he had just recognized a long lost relative.

He asked, "Aren't you one of the men putting up the antennas down on the beach?" I said that I was, so he inquired when we had arrived, etc. He explained that he had known the men in the other crew, and asked after several of them by name.

As we talked, it seemed as though everyone who walked through there knew and called him, "Frenchy". His actual name was Eugene J. Berube, and his home was at 79 Prince St. in Lowell, Mass. Frenchy had been awarded a Purple Heart over in Korea earlier, but was now with D-Battery of the 97 AAA. His guns were on the ridge above our antenna site.

A few nights later, Frenchy stopped by our barracks and became acquainted with the rest of the men. He seemed to be a natural comedian; for he could tell even the most serious stories in such a way as to keep those who heard him laughing. There wasn't any limit to his energy.

Frenchy seemed to be everywhere. He might be in the mess hall slapping friends on the back in his enthusiasm, walking along with a dog at his heels, in the theater, PX, service club or bowling alley. It was sometimes amazing how he got around to so many places.

The entire site had been surveyed and staked out before construction had begun. The other crew dug most of the postholes. Large metal oil drums with the ends removed were placed on top of each other in the hole, and then the sand was pushed in around them.

We still had the anchor holes to dig. Jones handled the transit. By knowing whether the particular pole was a side pole or an end pole, it was easy to locate the anchor hole by measuring a certain number of feet from the pole along the line of sight of the transit.

Later, after we had the anchor holes all staked out, we began the job of burying the "dead men". The dead men were the logs with a length of messenger strand fastened to them that we used as an anchor. The logs were five to six feet long and had to be buried six to eight feet deep.

Needless to say, we dug some gigantic holes. The sand kept caving in as we climbed in or out of the hole, and sometimes it would cave in just before we lowered the "dead man". Then we would have to start all over.

There wasn't much climbing to be done during those first few weeks. There were a great many anchor holes to be dug though. Also, all of the antenna poles that had been dragged into position near the holes that they were to be set in had to be stepped.

An accurate job of stepping a pole takes some of the hazard out of climbing. The step should be right where the man on the pole expects it to be without looking. The steps had to be in a straight line thirty-six inches apart up the center of the pole. The steps on the other side of the pole had to be lined up directly opposite but staggered eighteen inches.

A badly stepped pole was not only dangerous, but it was physically hard on a man to climb it. Irregular steps threw the climbers timing off and upset his breathing.

When we got the poles stepped that were in position to be raised, we began to make guys for them. It would have been easy to cut off a length of messenger strand long enough to reach from the top of the pole to the anchor, and to call it a guy. But, that wasn't how a guy was made.

A tail of 6-M messenger strand, six or eight feet long, was cut to attach the guy to the pole. More messenger strand was cut into specified lengths to make up the guy. Each segment of the guy was separated from the others by means of glass insulators that were held in place by three-bolt clamps. Thus the guys were insulated all the way to the ground.

Each pole required six of these guys to be made and attached to the pole before it was raised.

Gene L Smith of 213 N. Summit, Girard, Kansas, was standing in the doorway of his barracks, just across the way from where we were staying one evening as I returned from chow. I was surprised to see him at Ashiya.

We had first met on the train from Kansas City to Camp Stoneman, Calif. After we arrived, I didn't see him again until he showed up in the bunk next to mine on the following day. We came overseas on the same ship, the Meigs, but separated at Yokohama. He had been sent directly to Ashiya and had been working in a warehouse ever since.

We were eventually caught up with the work until we could set more poles. Instead of sitting around idle while waiting for the necessary crane, they had us making a pretense of being busy by straightening the poles over and over again.

One weekend I went on a tour to the city of Kurume. Kurume was about fifty miles away by road, and located inland. The scenery that we could see from the bus was very pretty. Frequently the road would round the side of a hill and we could see the tiny fields in the valleys below. Many of the higher rice paddies were flooded. Everywhere it seemed, the people, from old men to children, were out tilling or planting their plots of ground.

Some of the people were using a tool about like our hoe. The width of the blade was approximately the same width as a hoe blade, but the blade was eight to ten inches long. They would swing this instrument over their shoulder and bury it as deep as they could. Then they would raise it loaded with soil and turn it over.

Other more fortunate farmers had oxen to pull a plow and turn their soil. There was one sight that I shall always be able to recall to mind. It was the first, but not the last time, that I saw a human being pulling a plow.

The road gradually meandered down to the valley. From there we could look up at the dark green pine covered hills. Here and there in patches among the pine were small bamboo forests. The frilly yellow-green foliage of the bamboo made them look like giant prehistoric ferns.

A few fruit trees were in full bloom near some of the unpainted houses. One farmer had about ten orange trees growing on the hillside behind his house. They were loaded with ripe-looking oranges. Daffodils, pansies, and other small flowers were in bloom near some of the houses.

The main street of Kurume was wide. There were a few large department stores and theaters. It seemed to be a prosperous city. We were the only GI's on the street. The people even stared at us as though they weren't familiar with Americans and hadn't become used to our strange appearance and manners.

The bus stopped near a shrine that was hidden away in some back alley. Dozens of children appeared almost instantaneously. Those that weren't able to walk were carried on the backs of equally curious aged women.

The service club had provided sandwiches, oranges, and coffee for our lunch, so we sat on the bus and ate. That is, we ate a little. The mob of little faces was too much for most of the men. I gave away my other sandwich and my share of the oranges, and left the bus to see the shrine. Some of the others did too.

When we came back to drive away, the gang of kids was still around. Grinning adults stood at the back of the mob behaving very much as all proud parents do. Some of the GI's were entertaining their audience by trying to speak Japanese and just acting funny to make the kids laugh.

With a lot of luck, the driver got the bus turned around in the narrow street without running over any children. The kids waved as long as they could see the bus departing.

From there we were to keep an appointment to visit a rubber factory. The bus wound down more streets until we arrived at the entrance to a very modern and "American" looking factory.

The main buildings were all white. They set around a well-landscaped and manicured lawn, and presented a very striking appearance in comparison to the small, crowded, unpainted buildings nearby. In large blue letters high on the side of the most prominent building, was the name of the factory in English, "Bridgestone".

At the gate, a small Japanese guide who spoke excellent English told the driver where to park the bus. Then he asked that we not take pictures inside the factory.

He said that the factory had a movie theater, a clinic, and a cafeteria for the use of its employees. He pointed each out in its respective building. We followed the guide to the building where the tires and tubes were manufactured. It was dusty on the first floor and the stench of cooked rubber was terrific. Workers with cloth masks over the lower part of their faces dumped crude rubber into machines that seemed to chew, heat, and roll the rubber into large, flat irregular shaped masses.

After breaking down the crude rubber, the rubber went to a large machine that consisted mostly of rollers over which a coarse fabric flowed. The machine resembled a large newspaper press with all of the rollers turning.

At one stage, while the cloth rolled around through this machine, rubber was pressed onto both sides of the fabric. From this machine the rubberized fabric proceeded in an endless stream to another machine that trimmed the edges and apparently squeezed up a raised area in the center where the tread would be cut.

As it issued out, workers inspected it for weak places and other imperfections. A stream of water flowed over the hot rubber to cool it as it came out of the machine.

After cooling, the rubber passed up through an opening in the ceiling past the second floor, and on up to the third floor. Here the tires were built up by four formings. Half of the workers on this floor were women.

The built up tires were then sent down to the second floor for finishing. Here also, the "green tires" were shaped. The tires were placed in an air tight, over-sized cookie-cutter type machine. The tires were placed on a platform and then the top of the cookie cutter descended and shaped the tire under terrific heat and pressure.

When the pressure on the machine was released, the hot tire would pop out in a miniature explosion, and be rolled by hand to a corner where they were stacked until moved to the warehouse on the fifth floor for curing.

Extruded tubes were manufactured on the fourth floor. About half of the workers there were also women. The guide led us up another stairs to the roof of the building. From there he pointed out two other, smaller, dirtier-looking buildings. He said, "Maybe we no go there. *Takusan* dirty and bad smell."

Someone inquired how many *Yen* the average worker was making. After giving the question several seconds consideration, he answered, "17,000 Yen a month." Seventeen thousand Yen, at that time, was equivalent to $47.23 in American money. He also said that the employees work seven hours a day for six days a week. They have Monday off.

Within a month of our arrival, Sgt. G—— was called back to the Company – much to our relief. Cpl. Rodriguez was then promoted to sergeant.

We waited about a week for a crane to arrive so we could raise the poles that we had finished. The crane was driven to the site under its own power by a Japanese fellow everyone called, "Chiisai", which is the Japanese word for "little" or "small" when used in reference to a human. He also operated the boom.

A caterpillar was necessary to pull the crane across the sand, move the poles into position, and clear areas of the pine trees. The "Cat" had arrived before the crane. A big, friendly Air Force fellow drove it. He was A/2c Terrence Mason of 204 Willow Ave., Hoboken, NJ. He could really handle a Cat.

Sgt. Rodriguez said that the first thing we should do would be to take down the seventy-five pole, so Mason attached his Cat to the crane and pulled it out to the pole.

There wasn't any messenger strand handy, so Rodriguez grabbed a length of heavy rope and went up the pole. He wrapped the rope around the pole a few times.

By this time, Chiisai began to raise the boom of the crane. Rodriguez fastened the hook on the crane through a loop in the rope, and when Chiisai had put some tension on the rope, he came down.

Bacon, Young, and I were working on one of the top guys, while Wakefield, Berger, Davis, Spain, DeVaca, and Carey worked on the other two top guys. The belly guys hadn't been put on this pole yet. We took the three-bolt clamps off our guy, as did the others, and the crane held the pole upright.

Next, we pulled the end of the guy through the eye of the anchor rod, and stood holding the end of the guy. Chiisai was to slowly raise the pole out of the ground and lay it down easily, while we were to guide the pole by pulling on the guys.

Rodriguez signaled for Chiisai to start raising the pole. The pole began to come out of the ground slowly. We could hear the rope around the pole straining, but it looked as if it would do the job.

Then suddenly the rope broke with a loud snap and the pole thudded back down into its hole. The pole slowly began to lean in the direction of the guy to our left. Young, supposing that the pole was steady, had already turned loose of our guy.

As the pole began to fall faster, we heard Bennie Davis let out a whoop, and then the noise he and the other two men were making as they thrashed through the scrub pines to escape the pole that was falling toward them.

Chiisai had four Japanese laborers helping him set up the crane, etc. These four men were standing beside the crane completely engrossed with watching the pole fall. They didn't even see that the guy that Bacon and I were still holding was going to fall across the crane. Bacon yelled, "Look out, Papa-san", as we were being pulled along at the end of the guy. The Papa-sans got out of the way just as the guy cracked across the top of the crane. We had dug grooves in the sand with our heels as the weight of the pole pulled us along.

We all ran over to see if anyone had been injured, but our three men got away safely though scratched up and scared. Cpl. Jones said, "I just stood there with my mouth open. I tried to holler at you, but I couldn't say a word. I couldn't say a word." Chiisai was certainly lucky. If the pole had fallen toward the crane, he would have been crushed in his cab unless he had the presence of mind to fend it away with the boom.

The pine trees and soft sand broke the fall of the pole, so it wasn't broken. However, many of the steps were bent out of line, and the guys were tangled among the trees. We disconnected the guys and Mason dragged the pole out of our way with the Cat.

After that was done, we moved on to another pole that had to be set up. Mason and Chiisai maneuvered the crane into position alongside a pole lying near its hole. This time we attached the crane to the pole by means of messenger strand. Then as the pole began to rise, we guided the top of it by pulling on the guys. We had difficulty, because the wind on the beach was strong and it blew the pole about. Eventually we got the pole set, and then knocked off work for the rest of the day.

During the days that followed, we set five or six poles a day whenever the wind was favorable. Now and then a guy would get a kink in it as the pole was being raised. The pole couldn't be guyed down as long as the kink was in one of the guys, so the pole was only held upright by the crane until the kink was removed. It was at these times that Jesse Jones proved his merit. Even with the pole leaning as much as thirty degrees, he would climb up it until he was even with the kink and hook a leg over a step so that he could use both hands to twist the kink out of the guy.

We had practically all of the poles set that were ready at that time before I had a chance to climb. Bacon had been up two or three times and claimed that he was getting used to it. I began to wonder if Sgt. Rodriguez knew that I had never climbed more than a twenty-foot pole before.

I thought about it so much that one night I dreamed that I was working at the top of a ninety-foot pole. The next morning at breakfast, DeVaca said, "I hear you are going to climb today."

A little later, Bob Berger asked, "Are you all set to do some climbing today?" He explained that Rodriguez said he would have me do some climbing to see if I could.

When we arrived at the site, Sgt. Rodriguez said that we would set the ninety behind the shack.

Chiisai was late arriving, and when he did get there, it took time to pull the crane out to the pole. In the meantime, we had carried our tools, three coffin hoists, the three-bolt clamps, etc. out to the pole. As we straightened the guys out in the proper directions along the ground, I looked at the pole and thought to myself, "This will be the one." Lying on the ground, it didn't look nearly as tall as it actually was. My confidence returned.

Loren Bacon came over and examined it too. "Rodriguez will probably ask you to climb it, so if he does, try it, and if you get scared, come on down. Nobody can make a man climb a pole that high if he doesn't want to."

Chiisai finally arrived and we soon had everything set. At a signal from Rodriguez, Chiisai began raising the pole. As it arced upward to a perpendicular position, the pole looked taller and taller until it looked like a toothpick enlarged seven thousand times.

The Sergeant called my name, and as I walked over to where he was standing looking up at the pole, Bacon called after me, "Don't look at the ground, but be sure your feet are on the steps solid."

"Want me to climb up there?" I asked.

"Yeah," he replied, "Think you can do it?"

I told him that I would try, and took my lag wrench, splicing clamps, and TL's (wire cutting pliers) out of my pockets and laid them on the sand nearby.

No one had any climbers handy, so the Sergeant interlaced his fingers and said, "Put your foot in my hands, and I'll give you a boost up to the steps."

He did, and I grabbed the bottom steps and pulled myself up. The steps on that pole felt like they were unevenly spaced (of course, they weren't). By the time I was one third of the way up, I was puffing with the exertion and hugging the pole.

It seemed like I had been climbing for a long time before I reached the messenger strand that I was supposed to take off. Chiisai swung his boom a little and I could feel the pole move. Then he lowered the hook so that I could reach and disengage it from the messenger strand.

Then as I concentrated on disentangling the messenger strand, the pole vibrated from the force of something being hit against the base of it. I was curious but I wasn't ready to look down at the ground yet. Next, I could hear the sound of someone coming up the pole. The wooden poles are excellent conductors of sound. The lightest tap on the base of a pole would be conducted upward and heard clearly all the way to the top.

Rodriguez came up even with me on the opposite side of the pole just as I got the strand loose. As he climbed back down, I decided to take a look at the ground. It was a long way down. The steps down each side of the pole looked like teeth on a saw. A man would be lucky to escape with a few broken bones if he fell a few feet over the steps of a pole. However, there wasn't much chance of falling very far after one had secured his safety belt, unless his belt broke. The steps would catch the man's safety belt before he had fallen a foot and a half.

As I looked down I could see what had jarred the pole before Rodrigues started up. He had set a large oil drum against the pole so that it would be easier to reach the bottom steps without our climbers on.

I was glad to get my feet on solid ground after that, but I couldn't help but think how much worse it would have been if the pole hadn't been stepped. A slip on a pole that size could be the death of a man.

The crew at Ashiya must have been the singingest gang of men in the Far East. David Spain, Bennie Davis, Loren Bacon and Robert Berger would always start singing at the top of their voices after they were safetied in on top of a pole. Usually, they sang an old hymn or sometimes, a hillbilly song.

Chiisai and some of the other Japanese workers couldn't understand how they could be singing while apparently risking their lives. They would look up at the men on the poles, then look at each other and shake their heads.

On days when it was raining too hard to work outside, we would stay in the canvas-roofed shack waiting for the rain to stop. As we sat on coils of wire and empty wooden boxes, Spain would start singing, "Just A Closer Walk With Thee". It was a hymn with a good rhythm, and soon everyone would join in. After several choruses of that, maybe Albertus Young would lead off on, "There Will Be Peace In The Valley". One song would lead to another. They never ran out of songs to sing.

One time, Bennie Davis stood up and sang, "What A Fellowship". He took off his cap, stretched out his arms, and slowly marched around the room passing his hat as if he were taking up the collection at church. Then while the others hummed, he began his sermon, "Now Chillun, today we are goin' out there an' climb poles. They ain't ordinary sized poles neither." Someone said an "Amen", and Bennie proceeded to lecture more about what we were doing until he began laughing too hard to finish.

When he stopped, Young said, "Bennie, I see you been to some of them meetings too."

"Yes", Davis replied, "'I've been to a few. When I was little, me and the other boys followed "What A Fellowship" with "Corn bread and buttermilk". Of course, we didn't sing that very loud though.'"

Even when we were riding in the back of the K-trucks to and from the barracks and the site, the men sang and hollered at the Papa-sans and Mama-sans who grinned and waved back.

At 0350 hours on March 27, 1953, an Air Force boy came through our barracks waking up different ones in his search for Richard Wakefield. Someone wanted him on the phone.

Dick had been expecting the call, and rushed out into the hall where the phone was located. In an hour or so, at 0500 hours, the call got through. As of March 26, at 0910 hours in the States, he and his wife had become the parents of a daughter, Cynthia Lee.

After the call, Dick was too happy and excited to go back to sleep, so he paced the floor until time for everyone to get up. He did his best to look and act calm, but his pride and happiness shone all over him.

Jones nicknamed him, "Pappy", and gave him the day off. As we left for work, someone said, "I think Pappy would have rather worked today so he would have someone to talk with about his little girl."

A few days later, we had another birth to celebrate. Loren Bacon received word that his wife had given birth to a son, Mikel Keith, on April 1, 1953. Loren was another proud and happy father.

At each mail call the two fathers would compare notes on the progress of their youngsters. After awhile they began to receive pictures of their children. It made them both a little more homesick to see their families.

The Japanese cherry trees were in bloom about the first of April on Kyushu. I signed up for a service club tour that was going to one of the cherry festivals in Fukuoka.

Fukuoka was a large city. It had several beautiful parks. We only visited two of them. The first park that we stopped at surrounded a small lake near a large hospital. There were many colorfully dressed Japanese rowing about the lake in brightly painted rowboats. Others walked about admiring the scenery.

Sakura, or cherry trees, lined the street in front of the park. They were an example of the most brutally pruned trees I have ever seen used for landscaping. The branches on those trees were reduced to stubs about two feet long bearing a few blossoms.

Near the street stood a popular and modern looking public toilet. Men, women, boys, and girls clustered around the doorways waiting for an opening. The urinals lined one wall while the closets for the women were opposite.

We ate lunch of sandwiches and lemonade in the bus, and then went to a larger, nicer park overlooking the bay. This park was composed of a group of wooded hills. There were many *sakura* trees scattered here and there among the other woodland trees. Trails led to all parts of the park.

From the top of one of the hills, we could look down on the bay and see the fishing boats tied up along the shore. Also, we could see hundreds of the city's thousands of small, crowded, unpainted, wooden houses.

Walking along the trails, we passed couples and families eating their picnic lunches and drinking *sake* in grassy places a little to the side of the trail. Far below through the trees we could see the larger groups of people sitting in circles eating lunch. Some of the groups were chanting songs to weird sounding Oriental tunes while they clapped their hands in time with the singing. It was very strange and unforgettable to a Westerner.

The Japanese were all in a happy mood, partially due to the occasion and partially due to the *saki*. Now and then a group would offer us a cup of *saki*. I hadn't seen so many inebriated people since New Years Day.

The Japanese cherry festival isn't anything like Americans might suppose. This festival was more like a huge picnic to us. Japanese folk just sit around and eat, drink, and sing; but they certainly have a wonderful time.

Sergeant Rodriguez and John Carey left Ashiya on April 10 to return to the Company. They were to process for return to the States. Those of us remaining would have given almost anything to trade places with them.

Jesse Jones, our crew chief, was called back to the Company about a week later. When he returned three days later he was wearing sergeant's stripes.

We constructed four, and worked on a fifth type of antenna while at Ashiya. The hardest type of antenna that we had to raise was the rhombic. The rhombics were diamond shaped with one pole on each of the four corners. Some of these poles were two hundred feet apart.

The first things we put on the poles were the harnesses. The harness consisted of a long bolt that fastened through the pole and held one or two insulators, which in turn supported the curtains. A curtain was a single strand of wire around the rhombic. We were using three strands of three-wrap-twelve wire, so they were called three curtain rhombics.

Boring the holes for the harness was a bad job. No one wanted it. It required putting a great deal of extra pressure and strain on the borer's safety belt. The bit was so dull he more or less had to force the bit through the poles. The braces were bent out of shape due to our habit of dropping them rather than laying them down when we were through.

After the holes were bored it was easy to pull the harness up on a hand line and fasten it to the pole. One harness was installed on each end pole, and three harnesses on each side pole. The harness for the end poles consisted of two cylindrical insulators called "dog bones", while the side harness had one rectangular shaped insulator called a "hershey bar".

When all of the harnesses were up, we began to string the curtains. Starting at the end pole closest to the transmission line, someone would take the end of a roll of three-wrap-twelve wire and trudge off toward one of the side poles. Sometimes we had a trail cut through the scrub pines, but more often we would try to lay the wire over the tops of them.

Someone would climb up the side pole and run the first curtain wire through the top hershey bar. He would stay up to help guide the wire through the insulator, while someone on the ground would pull the wire on to the end pole. The same thing was done at the end pole. The wire was pulled on around to the next side pole, and then on to the starting end pole.

After the other two curtains had been laid out on the ground, and one end of each had been served in on the dog bone, the next operation was to pull in the curtains, starting with the top one.

"Pulling in" required two men working on the end poles where the curtains began and ended. One man was needed on each of the other three poles to guide the wire through the insulators as it was pulled in. The remainder of the crew worked on the ground freeing the wire from the trees and shrubs and keeping it from getting tangled with the other curtains.

The top curtain was pulled in first. One end of the wire was stuck through the "dog bone" far enough to be held securely by a "gripper". The "gripper" was a metal clamp for holding the wire, and was attached to a "come-along". The "come-along" was a rope and pulley affair used to increase the pulling power of the man.

There was a great deal of straining, together with a few choice words of profanity suitable for the occasion. A man watching from the ground would signal that the line had the right amount of tension on it.

Then a pair of splicing clamps would be put on to hold the wire from slipping when the come-along was taken off. The excess wire was then cut off and the tail "served-in". To "serve-in" the tail means that each of the three strands of the three-wrap-twelve were wrapped one at a time around the lines after they had looped through the "dog bone". The antenna would never pull loose after being served in.

Behind the shack were two eighty-five foot poles setting about twenty feet apart. They loomed like a threat to us for we knew what was supposed to become of them. As the work on the other antennas progressed, the two poles became more ominous. We were going to have to construct about two thousand pounds of platform and antenna across the top between the two poles.

The A.I.O. (Air Installation Office) had the blueprints. Japanese carpenters and metal workers were cutting the timbers and making the steel braces in the A.I.O. shops. One afternoon we went to the A.I.O. and brought all the wood and steel back to the site. We laid everything out in order on the ground below the poles.

Next morning we bolted the steel braces together as well as we could and raised them by means of a couple of ropes that were tied together and run through pulleys.

When the end braces were securely bolted to the pole, we began to raise the inside beams. There were four of these beams about four by eight inches and better than twenty feet long.

It took us three days of continuous hard work to raise, fit, and bolt down the beams and steel framework. The heavy work was over then.

Sgt. Jones decided to split his crew and send half of the men to Kashii for a cable job, while the other half finished the platform.

CHAPTER VIII

Kashii

On the last day of April, Morris M. Wingo of Empire, Ala. drove to Ashiya to get a crew to work at Kashii. Berger, Wakefield, Young, and I returned to Kashii with him in the afternoon.

We hastily loaded everything into our footlockers, put them into the back of the K-truck, and were soon on our way. On the other side of Ashiya Machi, we turned to the right across a bridge that spanned a branch of the Onga Kawa.

This bridge was a rather crude structure in spite of the fact that one lane of it was made of concrete and steel. The other lane had a wooden railing, and the roadbed was made up of layers of logs about three inches in diameter crisscrossed on top of each other until both sides were nearly level. A creosote and rock mixture laid over the logs and leveled off completed the bridge.

The road on the other side of the bridge was a narrow, rutted, oiled road. It ran along the high ground between the main branch of the river on the left and the houses and fields on the right. Many of the small fields were yellow with the blossoms of a giant radish which the Japanese call *daikon*.

In a clearing near the road, smoke was billowing from a huge outdoor oven. The oven was a humped clay affair perhaps twenty feet long. At each end was a small opening. The smoke escaped from a hole in the top of the hump. On the side facing away from the road was a high narrow opening large enough for a man to squeeze through.

Kashii wasn't far from the city of Fukuoka. We arrived just in time for supper. And, what a supper it was! It was terrible. Maybe we were just shook up from the jogging we took on the rough road, for the paratroopers seemed to be eating heartily enough. It took a couple of days to get used to the food there.

After we had eaten, we drew bedding, and moved into a Quonset hut that was empty except for two paratroopers. They were SFC. Therman E. Eubanks from Texas, and Cpl. James A. Hill. Our Quonset was in the first of three rows of the huts, and was on the end furthest from the orderly room. We had the advantage of being on the end closest to the latrine, for it, the washroom, and showers were all housed in a separate building.

Kashii had two units stationed there at that time. One of them was the Quartermaster Parachute Maintenance Detachment of the 187th Airborne Regimental Combat Team. The men in the 187th called themselves *Rakkasan* or parachute from the Japanese *rakkasan hei* meaning parachutist. The other was the 79th Engineer Field Maintenance Detachment. According to one of the men in the 79th, who often came out to watch us work, his unit only had about a dozen men in it who supervised the Japanese mechanics that worked in the shops.

The PX and day room were located next to each other at the rear of the barracks. The day room had a bar where a Japanese boy sold hard and soft drinks after duty hours. There were tables and chairs, a bookcase of books, and one pool table. There was also a movie house. Dick Wakefield walked in it and later described it as having benches upholstered with gunny sacks. There was a club, but nevertheless, entertainment facilities for the men were very poor.

Kashii was located on Hakata Bay. I was told that during World War II, it was a Japanese seaplane base. There was a large stone ramp leading down into the water. The remainder of the side of the base on the water's edge had a stone wall extending its full length. *Kani* or crabs lived in the crevices of the stones.

In the evenings some of the troopers would fish from the ramp as the tide was coming in. More often, the Japanese workers would fish for awhile before going home after work. I saw them catch fish as long as eighteen inches in length. Once a fellow pulled in a small red octopus called *tako*. He was quite proud of it and took it home to eat.

The next day was the first of May – a day for Communist demonstrations in the past. All of our bases were supposed to be restricted according to what we had been told.

Jones called from Ashiya about 1000 hours and said our paychecks had arrived. We didn't know whether or not we could get off Kashii. Rather than ask someone and be refused, we got ready and climbed into the K-truck. The Japanese Security Guards at the gate stopped us only long enough to look at our trip ticket, then waved us through.

Everything seemed abnormally quiet. About halfway to Ashiya we passed a new Japanese home that was under construction. There were about twenty young men standing and sitting around it. They were all wearing bright red headbands. They all stared as we drove by, and we stared right back.

As we returned to Kashii a couple of hours later, they were still hanging around in force, but doing nothing. We heard rumors of minor incidents in Fukuoka and Tokyo, but comparatively speaking, it was a quiet May Day.

On the third day, Wingo returned to the company at Showa before starting back to the States. Robert Z. McGlumphy, of Garrison, Pa., took his place as boss of the job.

During the day seven new men moved into our Quonset. They were planning to attend "jump school" and thus earn their paratrooper badges. Five of the men were from the Quartermaster Airborne Air Supply and Packaging Company of the 8081st Army Unit that was located at Ashiya. They were: Floyd J. Dorsey, Jr., 515 N 12th St., Manhattan, Kan.; Norvel J. Valle, Star Route, Blackwell, Mo.; Gerald L. Kuck, Lakota, ND; Early L. Graham, Rt.6, Bessemer, Ala.; Arthur L. Phillips, Polk Hill Road, Cookstown, NJ. The others were Alford F. Brueggmon, and Albert W. Simons. Simons was in H Btry., 674th Airborne Field Artillery Bn., and his home was at 3309 Wall St., South Bend, Ind.

Each of the men was determined to get his badge. That first evening they joked and laughed about jumping, but underneath it all they were really scared. They brought with them several paratrooper songs which they enjoyed roaring. One song was to the tune of Stephen Foster's 'Beautiful Dreamer". It began, "Beautiful streamer, open for me", etc. Another chorus was: "Counted three thousand, waited too long, Reached for the ripcord, The damn thing was gone." They ended the song with a loud, "splat!"

McGlumphy tried to find out from the men in charge of the base what they wanted done. The blueprint that we had was long out of date. There was no cable or any other equipment on the base that we could use, and no one seemed to know where there was any.

After a few days of doing nothing, a couple of men went back to

Ashiya and brought our climbing gear back. McGlumphy finally contacted someone who said we could get supplies over at Hakata.

We drove around the base inquiring at different places where their signal outfit was located. After exhausting the supply of out of the way places, someone gave us the right information. These signalmen had the cable and supplies ready for us, although it didn't look like there would be enough cable.

Things began to move more smoothly after that. McGlumphy said we would start work. If someone didn't like it, maybe he would come out and tell us what we were supposed to be doing.

The following afternoon, Wakefield, Young, and I began to dig a post hole at the far corner of the theater building. There was a picket fence enclosing the entire area in front of the theater. There was no way to bring the K-truck into the area without destroying much of the fence. That meant that the earth auger on the truck was valueless to us. We dug the hole with D-handle shovels. When we had finished the hole we carried a thirty-foot pole that was lying alongside the nearby drive, over the fence and set it in the hole. We tamped it in solid and left. During the time we were working on this pole, a stout middle-aged Japanese fellow was usually watching us from the window of the tool supply room. His English was exceptionally good. Sometimes he would slide the window back and talk awhile. He wanted to go to the United States some day, because his cousin lived there.

We had to set a second pole about one hundred-fifty feet straight across and in front of the KCAR building. The third pole went on a line halfway between the first two. There was a wooden walk that ran in front of the KCAR building. The walk was of heavy wood, but it wouldn't support the weight of the K-truck running over it. Therefore we had to pull up a section in order to back the truck close to the building.

Our activities aroused the interest of the Japanese working in the KCAR building and those in the nearby Security Guard barracks to quite a pitch. Some of them came over to watch as Bob Berger backed the truck in.

The K-44 was equipped with a large earth auger that was mounted on the bed of the truck. The Japanese watched with fascination when McGlumphy climbed onto the truck bed and worked the levers that raised the bit to a perpendicular position. However, he really had them "shook up" when with another movement of the levers, the big auger rushed down and took a circular bite out of the soil. They behaved like kids watching a fire truck.

McGlumphy was a master showman. He stood up on the truck working the levers as if he didn't know the audience was there. Before the soil could pile on top of the bit, he would pull it up, spin the clay off, and send the bit spinning to the bottom of the hole for another load.

At about three feet, he hit a soft blue clay that was saturated with water. The deeper he bored, the quicker the water appeared in the bottom of the hole. We set the pole anyway, packed it in, and we set an anchor rod nearby. Although we thought the pole would be all right, we were afraid the anchor rod would pull out and we would be forced to use a log "dead man" instead.

The third pole was set half way between these two poles under the surveillance of an even larger and more appreciative Japanese audience.

While we were working around the theater, I met the skinny old fellow who was the janitor there. Every time he would see me, he would bow deeply. I could never bend over as far as he, but I always made the attempt. We would exchange greetings in Japanese, as he could speak very little English.

One day as he was watching us work, he noticed that we were having a lot of trouble with the frayed "end-o's" of our hand line. He asked us to wait a minute while he hurried inside the theater for some things he had in there. He came back shortly with a heavy needle, some strong string, and a leather hand protector. In a few minutes, he had done a fine job of binding up the ends of our rope. He then showed us how to tie some knots of various kinds in the rope. When he was a young man he had been a fisherman.

After we had the poles set and anchored at both ends, we strung on them the messenger strand from which we would eventually hang the cable. We drew the messenger strand in fairly snug on the poles by using coffin hoists.

That done, we figured that we would draw the messenger strand tight by attaching the coffin hoist to the anchor guy on the pole at the corner of the theater. As we took up on the guy, we could see that the messenger strand wasn't getting any tighter. We all rushed down to the other end of the line expecting to see the anchor by the KCAR building pulled up. We were surprised to find the anchor apparently as deep as it had ever been. Someone went back and cranked on the coffin hoist while the rest of us watched to see if the anchor rod was pulling out. It wasn't. Then we noticed the pole leaning and we knew what had happened. The tension on the messenger strand had pushed the pole further into the soft clay subsoil.

We had to attach the K-truck wench to the pole and pull it out again. Then we put flat rocks in the bottom of the new hole, set the pole, and placed rocks and dry earth around it. This time everything held, and it was ready for the cable. Nevertheless, we were going to hang it later.

The blueprints called for another cable line. It was to be hung from the officers BOQ, along a line of rickety poles, and terminated on a pole on the other side of a street that ran outside of the base.

The messenger strand was soon strung from the poles. Next, we laid out the cable on the ground. McGlumphy went up the street pole and hung a "cable car" from the messenger strand. The cable car was simply a contraption with a swing-like wooden seat that was suspended from little wheels that rolled along on top of the messenger strand. It had a hand brake that kept it from rolling while the man was working.

McGlumphy got into the cable car and began to hang the cable to the messenger strand. The cable was placed in a U-shaped wire device. A twist of the wrist fastened the wire hanger to the messenger strand. While McGlumphy was working over the road, Japanese vehicles were weaving past below him with all the occupants hanging out the windows trying to see what he was doing.

Meanwhile, the jump-school boys were having a devil of a time. They had to go through a period of training before they jumped. Most of them went straight to bed after supper and tossed in agony after their first day of training.

They were given calisthenics and physical training such as running and other leg strengthening exercises. If they made an error in anything the instructor would make them give him so many "squat jumps". This wasn't punishment – just an exercise that would impress the prospective jumper and help him remember as well as build up his leg muscles.

Then the jumpers were taught how to jump by jumping from a tower and letting a chute harness stop their fall. One fellow, Floyd Dorsey, was taken to the hospital with one of the vertebra of his back dislocated according to one of the men. The training was tough, but it had to be.

The men were taught to get out of their chutes over water in a very realistic way. There was a small pool near where we were working. On the edge of the pool was about an eight-foot platform and some steps where the men went up and fastened themselves into a chute harness. When he was in the harness, he was swung out to the middle on a cable that stretched across the pool. He was timed on how many seconds it took him to get out of the harness and to drop into the water. If he didn't do it in the time allowed, he had to do it over until he did.

That night, the barracks was musty with the smell of wet fatigues draped on the steam radiators to dry. After they had returned from being dipped in the pool, they were told that word had come down from regiment saying that they couldn't be qualified as jumpers there.

Those boys were really disappointed, especially the fellows from the 8081st . They were stomping around complaining that they didn't know what would happen now. Their commanding officer, Major "Whispering" Smith, didn't want non-jumpers with his outfit, so they expected to be transferred to another organization.

The next morning everyone was happy again. They had been granted permission to finish jump school. In the afternoon we saw them all out in a field learning how to collapse their chute.

By nightfall, they had been told that the permission to finish jump school had been rescinded. They returned to their respective organizations the following day.

The 187th was a sharp looking outfit. They loved to "play soldier", as some Army men would say. I used to watch them as they fell out for reveille. Their boots were polished to perfection. Their fatigues looked new and were tailored and pressed. Most of them had fresh crew cuts and wore blocked fatigue caps. They were RA. (regular army) from head to foot.

We were such a contrast to them that we supposed they were using us as a classic example of how a paratrooper shouldn't look. Our fatigues weren't tailored to fit us, and most of us had them pretty well patched up due to the rough use they got when we were working. Usually our boots were dirty or only half-polished, and our hats were never blocked.

This doesn't mean to insinuate that we were sloppy soldiers, for the contrary is true. When it came to an inspection, parade, military discipline, or anything like that, the 474th was as sharp as the next outfit. However, our work would never let us look like paratroopers when we had a job to do. If we wore a blocked hat up a pole it would just get in the way if the wind didn't blow it off. A pair of fatigues tailored nearly skin tight would hamper our work to the place where it would be nearly impossible to reach, pull, or get into the awkward positions necessary to work on a pole. On hot days, sometimes creosote would spurt out of the pole when a gaff was dug into it and splatter up our boots and trousers. Driving steps often caused the pole to spit a stream of creosote on our jackets if the weather was warm.

When we wore a hole in our clothes or ripped them, we had to patch them, for there never seemed to be anyplace where we could buy two-piece fatigues. The paratroopers could salvage their worn fatigues and obtain in trade a new pair. We asked them if they would salvage ours, but they wouldn't do it.

One Saturday as we were unloading some equipment from our truck to a nearby shed, a young lieutenant approached. He told McGlumphy that some high-ranking officers would be on the base to hold an inspection before jumping with the troopers later in the day. The lieutenant wanted us to be sure our boots were polished and lined up under our beds and everything in order in the barracks. He also told us to put on better-looking fatigues if we had them.

When the officer left, McGlumphy said, " I don't know about you guys, but I'm not going to be around here for any inspection".

We went back to the barracks, straightened up our things a little, then piled into the truck and took off for Itazuke. We were going to try to find two men who were on TDY from our company.

We rode all around the strip at Itazuke, and were ready to drive over to the main base when we heard them hollering. They were Andrew M. Raney of Long Beach, California and James D. Bowden of Willow Run, Mich. They were working with a crew of Air Force men from the 6160th Comm. Sq.

Almost before I was off the truck, one of the Air Force fellows rushed over and began shaking my hand. I recognized him immediately as an acquaintance from high school days. He was Jack Dawson of 800 South Main, Jacksonville, Illinois. We hadn't seen each other for about five years, and neither of us knew the other was in the Far East, so it was a great surprise. We reviewed old times for awhile until his crew knocked off for the day. He had been working with cable along the strip.

One evening when Young and Wakefield were down at the club, they walked up to the bar and were refused service. They were asked to leave. They refused to leave and were quickly surrounded by paratroopers. The MP's were called and escorted them back to their barracks.

When Young and Wakefield got back to the barracks and told what had happened, McGlumphy and Berger jumped out of bed, dressed, and went back to the club with them.

The club was filled with men when they arrived, but they went in and waited for something to happen. They didn't wait long, either. Their audacity almost caused a riot. Once again the MP's were called and marched them back to the barracks. After they were in bed, they could still hear the drunks in the latrine shouting derogatory remarks. Of all the people in the 474th, both Young and Wakefield would be the last to ever offend anyone.

The next morning, one of them called the Company at Showa Mae. Captain Leddon instructed them to leave. If we weren't good enough to use their club, we weren't good enough to do their work.

Before our job was completed, the cable splicers arrived from the company. They were: George Frame, Richard Scott, Arthur Thearling, Zenon R. Mocarski of Brooklyn, NY, and Joseph K. Day of Pickens, West Virginia. They began connecting the cable that was already hung from the messenger strand.

We ran short of about one hundred feet of cable, so rather than wait for it, the cable splicers said they would hang it when it arrived since everything else was done. Young, Berger, Wakefield, and I returned to Ashiya.

CHAPTER IX

Ashiya II

We had been gone nearly three weeks on the Kashii job. We were expecting to be called back to the Company at any time, since the longest period of time that a crew stayed on TDY without being relieved was approximately three months.

Bacon, Davis, Spain, DeVaca, and Jones had the platform across the top of the twin poles finished. They had also been working on a strange looking low antenna which Spain called an "inverted V" antenna. It was located at another site on the base.

The Tech Rep showed up one day with a blueprint of a "mono" type antenna that he wanted constructed. It was to reach one hundred and twenty feet in the air, but we had no poles that long.

Jones had the Cat driver level off some of the sand dunes in a circular area where the pole was to be set. Then he had a ninety and a forty-foot pole pulled into a splicing position near the hole.

Bacon, Wakefield, and I set about driving steps into the poles. It was warm down on the beach, so we took our shirts off and soon had a sunburn. DeVaca was handy with the sledgehammer, chisel, and the drawknife, so he did most of the work of grooving the top of the long pole and bottom of the short pole for the splice.

Then we put the ends together and ran a couple of bolts through them. We then bound up the splice with wire. When it was finished we stood back and looked at the pole. It had a nasty looking bend in it, but Jones thought we could pull that out when we guyed it down. We were out of three-bolt clamps so couldn't make guys for awhile. Anyway, the wind on the beach was too strong to raise the pole if we did have the guys ready.

The weather was getting hot. Every day the temperature and the humidity seemed to leap upward. With the increase of these factors, the number of insects increased proportionally. During the day, innumerable tiny flies on the beach beset us. Then at night, squadrons of mosquitoes came roaring out of the darkness to make strafing attacks on our ears. We were getting worried about malaria.

We tried to get mosquito netting from the 483rd Comm.Sq. Supply room, but they said they couldn't let us have any except as part of a full issue of field equipment. They politely suggested we try an Army unit.

This griped the men off, but as someone said, "That's the way the ball bounces".

One Saturday, we were all in the vicinity of the line shack when we heard the air alert siren begin to wail. We had had many alerts before on other bases, so didn't think much about this one. Some time elapsed and the sirens grew into a more serious phase of an air alert.

The boys up on the hill above our site were running around getting their guns ready. Some of them were staring across the Korean Strait. We began to watch, too. It wasn't long before we could see two planes coming in low over the water.

They came straight in making a simulated strafing attack on the runway. Then they climbed upward, made a big arc before diving down in follow the leader style. We recognized them as P-51 Mustangs.

The first plane dived for another runway and the planes on the ground. As it shot upward, the second plane made a pass at the transmitter site and the gun emplacement above it. If it had been an enemy plane, none of us standing where we were would have lived through that attack. He was sighted in on us perfectly. Of course, if it had been an enemy plane, we wouldn't have been standing there watching it like a bunch of kids at a circus, either. We would have been scattered out among the scrub pine seeing how deep we could dig a foxhole.

The boys on the hill were swinging their guns here and there following the planes for target practice. Sometimes the planes were so low that they seemed barely higher than our antennas. Bacon exclaimed, "I'm glad I'm not on one of those poles!" It was over in a few minutes and the planes left as quickly as they arrived.

The holes for our poles were the cause of some of our hardest work. Fortunately for us, the crew that had been on the site before had dug most of the holes. Nevertheless, we had a share to dig. We couldn't dig very deep in the sand before the sides would cave in. By the time the hole was deep enough, it was nearly large enough to bury a jeep. We chiseled the tops and bottoms out of large oil drums, set them on top of one another in the hole, and shoveled the sand back around them.

The poles were set loosely inside the drums and held upright by the guys. While we were waiting for three-bolt clamps, we set about mixing concrete to fill the holes.

Jones got permission to use prisoners from the base Correction Center to help us mix and work with the concrete. The first day they came down to the site, most of them asked Jones as soon as they got off the truck, if they could go off among the trees to answer the call of nature. Naturally, he said it was all right, but to hurry back.

They spread out over the dunes, and after awhile began to straggle back. They all showed up but two. After about fifteen minutes we began to call for them. Jones went to the top of a high dune to look around. He found both of them laying in the shade on their backs half-asleep. Jones looked mad enough to skin them alive, but he didn't chew them out too badly. They were less than a hundred yards away, but claimed they didn't hear us hollering for them.

Rather than say the prisoners worked, it would be more accurate to say they were spectators while we worked. At the end of the day, we were worn out and dusty with cement from mixing and dumping it into the post holes, while the prisoners were returned to the stockade almost as fresh as when they had left there. Most of them asked to return the following day.

A few of the prisoners were in the stockade for major crimes, but many were just young boys who were too immature to be away from home. They were there directly or indirectly because they were going through the stage that all adolescents do, whereby they feel that they know all the answers and so rebel against authority.

Davis and DeVaca usually went after the prisoners and watched them while they were at the site. One time, while most of us were working on the transmission line behind the shack, and the prisoners were spreading cinders on the drive in front, Berger came back with a worried look on his face and asked if we had seen a certain prisoner. One of them was missing. Later, he was found reading a comic book in the truck.

Whenever I could spare the time, usually during the weekends, I always enjoyed an early evening walk through the little town of Ashiya Machi. I would start out soon after supper while it was still light and not return until after dark.

Most of the time I avoided the souvenir shops and other stores that catered to the GI trade. They were all very much the same – crowded, and filled with bright colored expensive junk.

Instead, I wandered along the narrow crooked street that followed along the bay. There was always something to see. There was the woman squatting on the ground fanning the flames in her *hibachi,* while tears ran down her face from the smoke. The hibachi was her cook stove and was about the size of a medium sized flowerpot. Smoke was already billowing out from under the eaves of some of the houses as supper was being prepared. However most of the houses now have chimneys that are about six inches of metal pipe stuck through the wall – seldom up through the roof.

There was a small court between two of the houses along my route, where I stopped many times to watch the fishing boats returning. A one or two cylinder engine powered the narrow wooden boats. The fishermen had a large rack built of bamboo logs where they spread their nets to dry.

All of the houses on my right were built so that they over hung the water. The overhang was their open side. The entire walls were of glass and rice paper panels which could be pushed back so that the occupants could enjoy the cool breeze and the beautiful and peaceful scene before them in the privacy of their own home.

A little further on was a once nice house that was badly in need of repair. Some of the thick clay walls were cracked and crumbled so that I could see the bamboo poles in the wall that the clay had been plastered around when the house was originally constructed. The Japanese use bamboo in an infinite number of ways.

Nearly always, an *ojiisan* (old man) stood in the doorway on the street side watching the people going by. He presented a unique appearance. He wore what appeared to be white long winter underwear under an open *haori* or coat. Every time I saw him standing there in the doorway I was tempted to take his picture, but I never did. I was afraid it would embarrass him away from the enjoyment he received watching people passing by.

As I walked along, the daylight grew dimmer, and after awhile the widely spaced streetlights would be turned on to cast a weak glow on the street. Women shopkeepers would come out with long bamboo handled wooden dippers to dip water from the open sewage system and throw it across the road to cut down the dust. All over Japan, the people throw water on the street to hold the dust down, while the merchandise in their shops accumulate dust until it is sold. When a prospective customer walks into the shop, the shopkeeper often follows him around with a with a few strips of cloth tied to the end of a stick with which he or she furiously dusts anything the customer shows an interest in.

In the evening there were smells that a person never seemed to notice during the day. From the ditches and ground came the famous "honey bucket" smell which mixed with the odors from the fish markets, flower shops, and the sea breeze. There was the putrid smell from carbide lamps; the sweet smell of the fruit markets the odor of pine from the furniture store, and the often delicious smell of food cooking. Then there was the odor of the people themselves: the odor of their clothes, hair oil, and the strange perfume that lingered in the air for a few seconds after they had walked on.

Sometimes I could see on the rice paper panel, the silhouette of a family sitting or kneeling on the floor around a low table eating supper. The strange sounding music from their radios easily reached the street and added to the mysterious atmosphere.

At least twice on my walks, I met a handsome young man in a spotless blue and white striped kimono. He was tall for a Japanese, had his hair neatly combed in traditional style, and wore *geta*. His height and traditional Japanese garment were quite a contrast to his countrymen around him who wore Western dress, with the exception of a few much older men who wore a much drabber kimono of narrow black and brown stripes. He was hurrying to visit his sweetheart.

I saw her once, too. They made a nice looking couple. She had on a beautiful *kimono* and had her face powdered almost white according to custom.

To while away the hours between supper and bedtime, I've often seen children sitting in a group under a light playing *Jan Ken Pon*. Sometimes their mother would join the game and play with them to break the monotony of her work if they were playing in the house. It was a simple little game. Simultaneously, the players would say "Jan Ken Pon" and thrust out their hands, sometimes with the hand open and flat which represented paper, or with the fist doubled up to indicate a stone. The third way was to have the first two fingers open like the blades of a scissors.

The winner of each round was judged in this way: If one player indicated stone, for example, and another held out two fingers for scissors, the stone would win because stones will dull the scissors. Also, if a player's hand showed paper while someone else had a stone, the paper would win because paper can be wrapped around the stone. Finally, a player holding out paper would lose to a player indicating scissors, since scissors will cut paper.

Schoolboys even use this game, sometimes, to choose up teams for games.

Adults also have a grown up version of Jan Ken Pon that is called *Tohachiken.* It is more difficult because it is played very fast and takes three successive wins to be the victor. In Tohachiken, the three subjects are a man, a fox, and a gun. Holding either both hands downward or placed on the knees indicates a man. Both arms held out with the hands raised like a fox's ears represent the fox. The arms are thrust out with the fist closed for the gun.

Surprisingly enough, the fox wins over the man because of a Japanese superstition that a fox can bewitch a man. However a fox loses to a gun which has the power to kill the fox. And lastly, man wins over the gun since man can use the gun.

On my way back to the base, I usually stopped in at a "Bingo" game. It was conducted in a room about twenty-five feet square. Across the room, opposite the entrance, was a bar. On the shelves behind the bar were bottles of liquor and various prizes.

In front of the bar was a table about the size of a billiards table. At the far end of the table was a space approximately two by three feet sectioned off into small compartments that were lettered and numbered. The rest of the surface of the table was slightly sloped towards the compartmented section.

Enough space was left around the outside of the table so that the three or four young school girls that ran the games could move around with ease. There were three tiers of benches on each side and two tiers of benches at the end of the table closest to the entrance. Each bench had a board running parallel with it at elbow height that served to hold the Bingo cards.

The girls took turns singing the letters and numbers into a microphone. They had a very definite little melody that they used. The caller stood in front of the table where she could watch the compartmented section.

The other girls moved around the table, rolling what looked like tennis balls into the compartments. Sometimes, they would let a player push a ball into one of the sections with a stick provided for that purpose. When someone called, "Bingo," the closest girl would check the card. As many as three persons could win before the cards were changed.

Rain poured down all during the first week of June. To top it off, during the middle of the week, we had a typhoon alert. The wind built up towards evening until the big pine trees just outside the barracks were creaking and moaning as if they were going to be pulled up by the roots. The power went off soon after dark.

We heard some of the planes warming up their engines, and an Air Force boy informed us that they were probably going to fly some of the larger planes to a base on Honshu out of the way of the typhoon. Later, the various organizations began falling their men out to help tie down other planes and equipment and to make sandbags. Everyone had a pretty hectic night. Next morning there was no sign of the typhoon. The wind had died down and it didn't rain hard again until noon. We heard that the storm had missed us and was heading for Tokyo.

Down at the site, we had a couple of small washouts. The wind hadn't damaged our poles or lines. There was a big washout on the hill above our site that could have taken one of the guns and washed out an antenna pole, but it had been stopped in time with sandbags.

The rain beat down for several more days then quit. It was during the rain that Herman Kimbrell, and James E. Davis of Pelzer, SC. stopped in for a visit. Kimbrell was on his way back to the Company for return to the States.

During the following week when it didn't rain, we changed insulators on our transmission lines. The work wasn't too hard compared to some that we had been doing, but the heat and humidity was terrible. It sapped our strength until it was labor just to walk across the sand. It made us tired and irritable all the time.

Overnight our boots became covered with a white mold. Our clothes, hanging along the walls, became moldy, and towels wouldn't dry out. Down at the site, we couldn't keep the rust off our tools.

Fast moving dark blue-black clouds that passed over in an unending stream obscured the sky. The clouds almost seemed in pain to drop their load of rain, like a cow long past milking time with no one to milk her.

I think it was Wakefield who originated the saying, "Come on down, Raymond". It evolved out of "come on down rain". Nevertheless, everyone took it up, and would repeat the words every morning and noon as they jumped off the K-truck to go to work and again at any time during the day. If it would only rain we could go back to the barracks.

Young had his own rain making system. He would dance around in a circle in what he called a "voodoo" or "Indian rain dance". Although he lured down a few drops once, it wasn't enough to get us back to the barracks.

A week passed, and then it really began to rain. But it didn't bring us any relief from the heat as we had expected. It rained almost continuously every night and most of the day. Kyushu Island was hardest hit by the rains. According to the newspapers, two areas got seventeen inches of rain in one twenty-four hour period.

Only a couple of days passed and then we heard that the railhead of Ongagawa was under water. Volunteers were called out to help rescue stranded Japanese. Helicopters and rubber lifeboats helped in the rescue operations.

The big bases on upper Kyushu were all on high ground so suffered comparatively little damage. Still, there were many washouts that had to be repaired, and every night there were crews of men filling and placing sandbags.

Toward the last of June, Harold Bullo and Stanley Kozenko arrived at the air terminal during a bad storm. They soldered the splices in the transmission lines during breaks in the weather.

We tried to raise our 120-foot pole, but it broke below the splice as the crane raised it. We cut out the break and respliced the poles together, and finally got it set up and guyed down. Spain was the first one to go up it.

Near the end of June, the floods were still growing worse. Japan had never had such a flood before. Several hundred thousand people were homeless, more than a thousand people were dead, and more were missing. Damage was estimated at many millions of dollars.

American servicemen were a great aid to the Japanese. Volunteers were working at all hours of the day and night in rescue operations; medical teams were supplying drugs and water purification equipment to combat the dysentery epidemic; and the Army Engineers were working to rebuild the washed out roads.

The water at Ashiya went bad as a consequence of all the rain. We had nothing to drink except the boiled water and coffee in the mess hall. Sometimes the water was too hot to drink. There was milk to drink for breakfast, but we were really hurting for water while we were working. One by one the men began to drink the tap water until all but a couple of us were drinking it. It didn't have any bad effect on any of us.

The rainy season ended about the first of July, but the heat and humidity continued. Since the base had been restricted for some time, I used to walk out to the end of one of the flight lines where there seemed to be a slight breeze.

The runways were located on built up ground high above the surrounding countryside. I sat down among the weeds at the top of the hillside. At the bottom of the slope was the high base fence. On the other side of the fence was the dirt road with a few Japanese people going home from their work on the base.

Between where I was sitting and the road were several large, heavy-barked pine trees. As far as I could see, the land was flooded with water. Near the road the water wasn't too deep. I could easily see the ridges around the fields. As the land sloped toward the river, however, the water was deeper and all I could see were a few hedges and trees. The few isolated houses that were visible had the water well up in them.

Near the road, though, was a patch of dry land a little larger than a quarter acre in area. On it was a thatched roof house enclosed by a hedge and a bamboo fence. A Papa-san was plowing the remainder of the patch with a slow moving ox.

It was a serene scene. I could hear the Papa-san giving instructions to the ox, the insects chirping, and the frogs croaking. I hadn't noticed the black and white cow behind the hedge near the house until she began to pull at the leaves of the hedge.

As I sat there watching, I began to wonder just what it was in that picture that made me think of serenity. It couldn't have been the landscape for it was flooded, and I knew the first plantings were ruined, homes destroyed, and the mosquitoes were reproducing by the billions in the water.

The big C-119's were roaring in one at a time directly over this house for a landing on the strip. They made a terrific noise. Then there were the three-wheeled motorcycle trucks that sometimes went blasting by on the road.

I began to realize that the serenity came, not from the total scene, but from the man slowly plowing with the ox. There he was plowing that little patch of ground while the floodwater chewed at the ridge that separated his field from his flooded neighbors. It was so close that his ox got its feet wet as it turned around at the end of the furrow. The man never looked at the planes or the traffic on the road. Nor did he pay any attention to the cow that was eating his hedge for want of something more palatable.

It seemed as though the plowing was the only thing of importance to him then, and he followed his oxen as serenely as if his faith was so strong he could dare the water to rise onto the land he was plowing.

A few days before we left Ashiya, the Tech Rep informed us that the "brass" had decided not to put an antenna on our platform. Inwardly, we were all relieved, but rather than show it, we griped about all the work it had taken to put that platform up there.

On July 8th, four men arrived from the Company to replace half of Jones' crew. They were: Willie B. Cathey of Fairview, Tenn.; Keith J. Conley of Wauchula, Fla.; Willie D. Edwards of Philadelphia, Pa.; and Fritz D. Huffine of Jonesboro, Tenn. Huffine had been working on this job even before our crew went to Ashiya.

Bacon, Berger, Wakefield, and Davis elected to stay behind, so Spain, DeVaca, Young, and I got on the manifest of the three o'clock plane to leave. We had wanted to travel by train, but the flood had stopped all rail transportation through the tunnel linking Kyushu and Honshu islands. We were scratched on the plane at 1400 hours, so got on the manifest for 2100 hours. That was a trip we will never forget.

The plane was a C-119. It had a tremendous load on board. The whole right side of the plane was full of huge wooden crates chained to the floor. We were expected to sit along the left side, although there was hardly room to walk down that side.

We fastened on the life jackets and then buckled a parachute on over it. The pilot came aboard about that time and helped adjust parachutes, etc. He gave us a short detailed lecture telling the passengers the altitude he intended to fly at, that there was a good tail wind, and the time of arrival. He went on to explain the use of the life jacket and how to use the parachute. He concluded in a morbid tone, "If something goes wrong, you will have to jump, because there will be no way to save the plane with this load on. Don't worry about it now, though. If it becomes necessary, one of the crew members will be at the rear door to help you".

Once in the air and leveled off, I was able to relax enough to sleep through most of the trip. It was a fairly rough trip. DeVaca felt like he was getting sick, and kept waking me up by moving in his seat every time the plane hit some turbulence

As we approached Tachikawa, the pilot lowered the landing gear, and the radioman squeezed through to the rear of the plane and turned his flashlight out a window to check that the landing gear had dropped into position.

After the wheels hit the ground a couple of times and had stopped bouncing, we were still moving like all thunder. I was unfastening my parachute harness, when I heard the pitch of the propellers change and the engines begin to race. I had a sudden fleeting notion that the pilot was overshooting the runway and was going to try to get into the air again.

Less than a month before, a C-124 had crashed at Tachikawa killing 129 men, and I expect that we all had it recalled to mind at that moment. Our fears were ill founded, but we were never so glad to get off a plane before.

Curtis Clendenin was on CQ, and had his runner, Robert N. McEldowney of Corry, Pa., meet us at the air terminal. We got to bed between 0230 and 0300 hours. It was good to be back in the Company again.

CHAPTER X

Showa I

The weather was noticeably more pleasant at Showa than at Ashiya. The humidity was high, but the central part of Japan hadn't yet felt the heat that the southern island had.

At Showa we could have all the water we wanted to drink for a change. Also, we drew mosquito netting out of supply. This did wonders for our peace of mind.

From what everyone said, most of the crews would be back in a month or two, but at that time there was lots of room. There were a few men in the company that I had never seen or met before. We had just never finished up a job at the same time.

It was on a Friday morning a few days after we got back, that Captain Leddon called me into his office. He explained that the Company wouldn't be getting any more men as replacements, and that the MOT (month of travel) date of several of his office staff was only a month or so away. He asked if I would like to take the I. & E. (Information and Education) job that Robert J Sweeney of Newark, NJ. had, or have a job in personnel.

Since per diem payments ended on July 1ˢᵗ, there was no longer any 'extra money' lure to the construction work. I had already seen a great deal of the country, so I was glad to have a job in the Company. Furthermore, it increased my opportunities of getting to climb Fujiyama.

I chose the personnel job and asked when he wanted me to begin work. The Captain asked what I was doing then, to which I replied that I was preparing for tomorrow's inspection. "The men in personnel usually work on Saturday morning, so they don't stand the inspections. You can come in this afternoon, if you want." Another advantage!

Bartasavage also started working in the personnel office the following day. Later, Arthur E. Brogley of Youngstown, Ohio, started training for the I. & E. job with Sweeney.

In the front office, Anthony T. Esposito, Jr. of New Haven, Conn., was preparing to take over "operations" when Richard L. Bollig of Hopkins, Minn., rotated to the States. William P. Borrelli of Philadelphia, Pa. was the company driver at the time.

The old timers in the personnel office were chief clerk, William C. Weissborn, of Montclair, NJ.; payroll clerk, Clement W. Riha of Elberon, Iowa; morning report clerk, Ernest L. Giordano of Newark, NJ.; mail clerk, Jack W. Hess of Verden, Okla.; and the draftsman, John W. Bruder, Jr. of Detroit, Mich.

Hess was training Neil W. Beekman of New York, NY. to take his place on the mail route. A man who had just arrived overseas a month or so earlier was learning the morning report from Giordano. He was Carl J. Scozzaro of Somerville, Mass. He was in the last shipment of replacements the company was to receive. Unknown to us, SCARWAF was ending.

Before I started working in the office I was barely acquainted with any of the officers except Captain Leddon, the commanding officer. He was a living legend to his men. From the first day I was in the company I heard stories of the things he had done and could do.

One of the stories we first heard was that if we ever got in a fight, we had better win it. "If the AP's bring one of you in for brawling", they said, " the Old Man will ask if you won it, and if you can't say you did, yo' ass has had it."

There was more *esprit de corps* in the 474th than any outfit I saw overseas, I believe. It all stemmed from the leadership and the often-dangerous work. The Captain was a strict disciplinarian, but he could be one of the boys too. He always played on the company football and baseball teams. There were also stories about how he had visited sites where his men were working, and seeing that they were short-handed for some difficult operation, would pitch in and do more work than any two men in the crew.

The Captain was a natural leader and the most astute man anyone would hope to meet. He knew every man in his company by name, together with his characteristics, and what could be expected from him as an individual and in a crew. He knew who was in what crew, where it was at, and what stage of work the crew was in at any time. At times, he seemed omnipresent in his ability to keep track of everything that happened in the crews regardless of where they were in the Far East. He had a long memory for funny incidents that happened to any of his men, and he got a big kick out of telling them.

He could be rough at times if it was necessary. He expected and got, near perfection on his Saturday morning inspections. The men who got "gigged" didn't get a pass during the weekend. No one ever accused him of being unjust.

Once the Captain glanced through the windows and saw a fellow apparently returning from the PX. He couldn't believe his eyes. "Is that man from this company?" he exclaimed. It looks like M———. Low quarters with fatigues, shirt out, and it looks like he needs a haircut! Send that man into my office."

Now and then the sound of the Captain's voice would carry through the closed door. He asked the fellow something about if he thought he was in the Air Force.

When the door finally opened, Riha commented to me, "That was pretty mild. Sometimes he really gets loud and pounds on his desk. Once he broke a wooden desk file by pounding on it, and Ishikawa had to make him a new one."

Someone said, "When the Old Man chews you out, you know you been chewed." Nevertheless, the men all loved him.

The personnel officer, or adjutant, was Captain Herbert E. Cole of Ilion, NY. He was a man who knew everything about administration from finance to the morning report. We might be on the verge of pulling our hair out over a problem that seemed to us to be of Earth-shaking consequence, but he could always supply the answer or find one in the books of Army Regulations we had just been through. Nothing could ruffle him. He was the college professor type, if there is such a thing. He had been a teacher at one time. He never raised his voice or lost his air of calmness. Fritz Huffine once commented, "Captain Cole strikes me as a pretty cool old bird. I don't think he would get excited if he woke up some night and found the BOQ on fire."

Captain Cole had a good sense of humor. Many times while reading something at his desk he would begin laughing. Then he would tell the rest of us in the office about it, and often take it in and show Captain Leddon. He could also speak a considerable amount of Japanese.

Whenever he had the time he liked to watch the 474th play other teams in football or softball.

Captain Edward A. Papp of Danbury, Conn. was assigned as the Cable Splicing Officer, but he was used in many capacities including extra duty as the Motor Officer. The Supply Officer was 1ˢᵗ/Lt. Alton J. King. He had an office in a building behind the second and third platoon's barracks. He had John L. Whitten of Dallas, Texas, as his supply sergeant. Also working in supply were: Herbert R. Wilson of Muncie, Ind.; Frank Noles, Jr. of Augusta, Ga.; John Pupplo of Long Island, NY.; Stanley L Ridlon of Portsmith, NH.; Franklin D. Taylor of Memphis, Tenn.; and Wallace J. Lefebre, Jr. of Worchester, Mass.

Lieutenant Raymond D. Self, of Amarillo, Texas, and Warrant Officer John C. Price of Marrero, La. were the Project Officers. They did most of the traveling around to the various sites to check on the progress of the work and to see that the crews had the supplies they needed, etc. They would be in the company area a few days, and then Captain Leddon would send them to another site. The Captain, himself, usually went to the sites of the "big jobs" first to look the job over and arrange administrative details.

Bartasavage and I didn't have a specified job when we arrived for work in the office. We were supposed to absorb a little bit of everything for the first couple of weeks. It was fairly confusing for awhile. When there was no filing to do or no one was doing anything important enough to watch we would sit down at a typewriter and try to teach ourselves to type. It was boring to sit in the office all day.

Eventually, it was decided that Bartasavage would be file clerk and assistant draftsman, and I would become payroll clerk under the tutelage of Riha.

There were two Japanese indigenous personnel that worked in the personnel office. They were: Hisakazu Ishikawa, the office janitor, interpreter, and man in charge of all the other indigenous people working for the 474ᵗʰ; and Reiko Ikota, a tiny girl who worked as stenographer. Both of them could speak very good English.

Ishikawa-san was somewhat taller than the average Japanese man and was of a thin build. He was twenty-eight years old, but the hair on his forehead was receding back in a manner that Japanese ladies seem to go for. At least, many of the top movie actors are in the more advanced stage of the same condition.

He would usually arrive at work a little early wearing very nice Western clothes (which is the customary thing with the Japanese who work on the bases and have to commute), but then he would change into a faded, greasy set of fatigues that were literally shot through with holes. On his feet, he wore a large pair of tennis shoes that flapped when he walked.

Ishikawa-san was a fisherman, too. So much so that he sometimes signed his name Gyojin (fish person) Ishikawa. Since he lived in Yokohama he was able to spend most of his free time fishing. Weissborn had a boating magazine checked out at the library so that Ishikawa could copy word for word the article on how to make a certain boat.

Reiko-san, on the other hand, spent a little of her salary every month to buy Western clothes, and always came to work looking nice. Captain Cole made it a point to notice her new clothes, change of combination, or a new hair-do, and ask her if it was new, etc. She would be completely flattered and make a little bow and thank him. Japanese men wouldn't notice such a thing in a woman and would never comment on it if they did.

Reiko's downfall was the high-heeled slipper. She always wore them, but when she walked, they made her so wobbly it seemed as though she would fall flat with the next step.

She had worked for the 474th for a long time and was very temperamental, although not nearly so much as she had once been. Weissborn said that he could remember when she would start crying if someone looked at her wrong. That was before she caught on to the strange ways of the Americans and knew much English. Captain Cole had always been able to patch things up for her.

She had a bad tooth in front that she was sensitive about. We had some flat cardboard fans, called *uchiwa,* as compared to the folding fans which are called, *ogi* or *sensu,* in the office. One of them was painted with the face of a pretty Japanese girl. Without thinking, one of the boys picked it up and began doodling on it. He may have drawn on a pair of glasses, I don't recall, but he did blacken one of her teeth. Reiko saw it and immediately thought someone was making fun of her. Captain Cole came to the rescue again, but she didn't come back in the office for the rest of the afternoon. A few weeks later she had a new dentist-made tooth.

There was some kind of supply distribution center in the building next to the office. American women dependents were employed there, which naturally meant that there had to be a ladies toilet in the building. It being handy, that was where Reiko went when she went on "TDY", as she used to say.

One day she asked, "Is it a custom for American women to go in *benjo* (toilet) to read newspapers and smoke cigarettes?" She went on to explain, "*Hancho* (boss) woman goes in there and goofs off, and no one else can get in. I think maybe they need Japanese style *benjo*." One doesn't sit in a Japanese toilet.

After a few unsuccessful tries over there, Reiko gave up and went on "TDY" elsewhere.

First Sergeant Hendrickson warned the men in the company to get their fatigues patched up. He didn't want to see any holes in them. Well, one Saturday when the Captain wasn't going to inspect, the Sergeant announced that he was going to conduct a fatigue inspection. Everyone was to lay his extra work uniforms out and stand by his bunk in fatigues.

It developed into a very informal occasion. He hadn't gone far before he found a pair with a hole he could get his finger into, so he gave it a jerk and ripped it. After that, everyone entered into the fun of it, and helped him find holes in their buddies' clothes to rip. It made some of the men pretty mad, but he had warned them. Later he provided a truck to take the men over to Fuchu to buy replacement fatigues.

M/Sgt. Hendrickson was an early riser. He never missed being the first person up in the morning. We were just starting to get up one miserable rainy morning, when someone happened to glance outside toward the mess hall, which was located just behind our barracks, and saw Sergeant Hendrickson. He was out in the downpour with his raincoat on, digging a drainage ditch around the east side of the mess hall. Later, he said he thought the damn mess hall was going to float away.

When the men returned from TDY this time, they didn't have much hope of going out again. Priola brought some men back from Hokkaido. Gebbens and Kenneth Jones returned with their crew from Sasebo on the southern island of Kyushu. However, small groups were being sent out now and then. Spain took a group out on one last repair job before he left for the States. They were Cabenze DeVaca; Thomas W. Kelley of Buff City, Va.; and Edward Speights of Birmingham, Ala. Richard Scott left for Chitose on Hokkaido, which put a stop to our Fujiyama climbing plans temporarily.

The rest of the men in the company were digging a trench around Showa base to lay cable in. It soon became so hot and the humidity so oppressive that the Captain was only allowing them to work on it part of the day.

Captain Leddon could speak conversational French . He had served at Normandy and Ardennes, so had a good background in the language. He told Sweeney that if he could get a class together, he would donate his records, a record player, and teach the class. There were books that went with the records in the I & E office. So in addition to his other duties, the Captain became a French language instructor.

The Saturday that the 474th received a big trophy for being the "most cooperative Construction Company" we had a big inspection. Everyone, including the men in the personnel office fell out with orange scarfs and carbines. As we stood at attention, two officers presented the Captain with the award while the base photographer shot pictures.

Sweeney stopped by the office one afternoon to show us some pictures he had taken in Tachikawa. Several of them were of a young schoolboy lying in the street with no one around him. There were Japanese walking nearby, but they would just glance at him and go on. Not one of them stopped to see if they could help.

A Japanese truck had hit the boy, Sweeney said, and if it hadn't been for Richard Haberkamp who made the driver stop, he probably would have gone on. Whether by coincidence or not, an American ambulance soon came along and picked the boy up, but he was already dead.

Many Japanese have a fatalistic view that seems to translate into little regard for life. By tradition, they memorialize their ancestors and innumerable wildlife; yet, they also have an ancient heritage of minding their own business. It reminded me of an actual case I heard of about a young Japanese wife who spent the night unaccompanied by her husband in a certain Japanese hotel. The hotel was filled to capacity. During the night a drunk staggered into her room and prepared to rape her. She woke everyone in the hotel begging for mercy and screaming for someone to help her. There were several Japanese men in nearby rooms. Any one of them could have saved her by walking through the paper and bamboo partitions that separated her room from theirs, but not one of them did.

From the American point of view, this is one of the most difficult things in understanding the Japanese – the extremes they will go to in order not to interfere in matters which don't concern them. Sometimes it made them seem cruel, as if they were incapable of being kind or courteous unless it were sanctioned by some specific rule in their tradition.

Typhoons sometimes caused a little excitement and change of routine. The change of weather that always accompanied them made us feel better for a short while anyway. They were preceded by a dead calm, and then the wind would build up until it was roaring along. It was then followed by rain, but the air the next day after it had passed was unusually clear and invigorating.

When the storm warning reached number two, the base was restricted and certain precautions were taken. The large transports on nearby bases would be flown down to Itazuke or someplace out of the path of the storm. The men in our motor pool would line all of our vehicles and equipment around the motor pool bumper to bumper. Then they would attach the winch cable of one vehicle to the bumper of the next and wind in the cable until it was taut thereby tying every thing together. Everything moveable in the company area was brought inside the barracks, and we were ready.

By the way, our mechanics and motor pool men were: Gordon Chambers of Tampa, Fla.; Donald D. Bengtson of Stockholm, Wisc; Angelo DiFrancesco of Philadelphia, Pa.; Francis C. Wittkop of Freeburg, Mo.; Richard S. Gardner of Sewickley, Pa.; Thomas L. Williams of Washington, Ind.; Ronald Griffin of Queens Village, NY. Albert J. Equils of Chocowinity, NC.; Walter P. Matulis of Worchester, Mass.; Kemper J. Bacon of Auburn, NY.; and Ronda K Clemmons of Edmonton, Ky.

A typhoon never hit our area directly, but there were close calls every year. The high winds did blow some ginkgo trees over that stood near the base fence.

The ginkgo or maidenhair tree is native to China and Japan, although it has been introduced into many parts of the United States and Europe. There is only one living species, *Ginkgo biloba*, and many botanists believe that it would have become extinct had it not been cultured as an ornamental tree.

The remarkable thing is that this species has undergone no noticeable change for more than 150 million years. The Japanese call the tree *icho*, and the nut, *ginnan*. The fleshy part that surrounds the nut has a very disagreeable odor. They roast and eat the nuts like chestnuts or add the nuts to soup or a thick broth.

Pachinko is a relatively new game that is taking Japan by storm. It fascinates most Japanese to distraction. It is a manually operated upright pinball machine. Supposedly, it originated as a children's game that paid off in little steel balls, but it has become a game for all ages.

A recent count showed that there were some eight thousand pachinko halls in Tokyo alone. Each of these places are jammed with machines. The machines sit side by side all around the room. More machines fill up the center of the room.

The cashier is stationed at a counter near the entrance. The customer lays down his *Yen* and receives the appropriate number of small steel balls. In some places the balls have the name of the pachinko hall on them. Most generally, the balls cost two *Yen* apiece, but there are more expensive and plush houses where the balls sell for ten *Yen* apiece and perhaps more.

On the right of the machine is a small hole where the ball is dropped in. Below this is the handle. The operator drops his ball into place, pushes the handle down, judging by the feel of it as to how hard he wants it to hit the ball, then releases the handle.

A pin inside the machine strikes the ball and sends it in loop the loop fashion around its track. The operator watches the antics of the ball through a glass pane as it hits spinners and various obstacles in its path. If the ball should drop into the right hole in the board, a bell will ring and a new supply of balls will drop into the tray at the bottom of the machine. These balls may be played or taken to the cashier who will give the customer his prize.

The prizes are of little actual value. They are usually candy, cigarettes, or canned goods. Nevertheless, some player addicts are determined to win by means fair or foul. Magnets specially made to guide the steel balls into winning holes are on the market and in use by unscrupulous players. However, the shop owners are aware of this and were buying anti-cheating magnets to protect themselves.

On another subject, there are four interesting ways of disposing of a dead body according to traditional Buddhism: burial, cremation, throwing into a river, or giving to vultures. The Japanese once used either of the first two named methods, but now are required to cremate the body, rather than bury it.

After the body has been burned, the ashes of the deceased are placed in an urn. One of the small throat bones which is supposed to resemble a meditating Buddha must be picked from the ashes without fail. With bamboo chopsticks, the mourners will hand the charred bone to one another using only the chopsticks. Otherwise, they will never pass anything from chopsticks to chopsticks.

The cremation may take place either before or after the funeral. Following the ceremony, the urn containing the remains is taken to the burial place. Shinto shrines have no burial grounds, so if a person wishes to be buried by Shintoism, his ashes are placed in either a Buddhist or a family graveyard.

The urn is placed in the ground and a stone containing five parts is erected over it. The five parts represent the five elements, and are from top to bottom: air or sky, wind, fire, water, and earth.

The gravestones in the cemetery are close together since not much space is required. Even in the old days when a body could be buried without cremation, it didn't take much room because the remains were put into the ground in a sitting (Japanese style) position.

One can almost judge how famous the deceased was by looking at the condition of his gravestones. Superstition dictates that one can attain some of the qualities of the deceased by breaking off a portion of his grave stone.

Autumn and vernal equinoxes are celebrated by the Japanese as national holidays. Buddhists visit ancestral graves and offer prayers for the repose of the dead. Pets such as dogs, cats, insects, birds, and fish are also not forgotten on those days. They believe all living things may attain heaven. Buddhist services have been conducted to comfort the spirits of fish that have been eaten, broken dolls, and elephants that supplied ivory for carving, for example.

Togyuboku-kuyo-to is a monument erected behind the stump of a tree to which was tied the first cow to be butchered for meat in Japan. A marble fence surrounds the stump. The year was 1858. Townsend Harris, the first United States Consul General to Japan had requested beef. At that time the Buddhist religion prohibited the use of meat for food, so it was a historic occasion.

The story is told that the nearby farmers who owned cows for draft purposes became so alarmed that they built high fences around their animals.

CHAPTER XI

Fujiyama

While on the Meigs somewhere on the Pacific I became determined to climb Fujiyama, the sacred mountain of Japan. If I wasn't going to be stationed in Japan, I hoped to climb the mountain while on R.& R. from Korea.

I had read and heard a great deal about Fujiyama. The word "*Fuji*" was supposed to have been derived from the language of the aboriginal hairy Ainus, who live on Hokkaido. It means "Goddess of Fire". The Japanese words for mountain are *san* or *yama*. Either of which is used with Fuji. Thus one English translation for Fujiyama is "Goddess of Fire Mountain".

Fujiyama is the highest , the most beautiful, and the most climbed mountain in Japan. For centuries now, thousands of Japanese have climbed Fuji during the months of July and August. To some of them it is a sacred obligation to climb to the summit before they die. The accepted height for the mountain at that time was 12,365 feet. However, the Japanese considered it to be 12,395 feet high according to the stamps they brand onto the climbing sticks.

Fuji must not only be the most beautiful mountain in Japan, but also one of the most beautiful in the world. We were in Japan about two weeks before the weather cleared enough for us to see it in the distance. It was covered with snow, and loomed far above the surrounding landscape and the range of mountains between it and Showa Air Base. It looked to be only half as far away as the seventy or eighty miles that it actually was.

The beauty of the symmetrical slopes was marvelous. I became more intrigued and more determined to climb it during the next climbing season.

Officially, the climbing season opens on July 1st and closes on August 31st. To climb Fuji during the winter months would require professional mountain climbing gear, I was told, and isn't often done.

According to the records, the last time Fujiyama erupted was in 1707, but it could do so again at any time. This possibility doesn't seem to deter the flow of pedestrian traffic on its slopes. " He who fails to climb Fujisan in his lifetime is a fool; he who climbs it twice is a bigger fool", is an old Japanese proverb.

From the first, Richard Scott and I had been planning to climb the mountain together. We made more definite plans when we met on TDY at Kashii. He was going to return to the company as soon as the cable splicing was finished at Kashii. Then as soon as I got back from the job at Ashiya, we would take a three day pass and climb it.

By the time I got back in the company, two men from our unit had already been to the top. They were Horace A. Creary of New York, NY. and Clayton Robinson, Jr. Each of them was enthusiastic about his experience. They recommended that the best way to climb Fuji was to take small steps and to keep a slow steady pace.

The weather had turned cloudy and bad, so Scott and I postponed our climb for a couple of weeks. However, John Bruder gambled on clear weather on the last weekend in July. He took an overnight pass for Saturday and Sunday, and went down to Fuji Yoshida where he hired a guide and began the climb.

William Weissborn and I were writing letters in the office Sunday evening when Bruder staggered in leaning on his climbing pole in mock exhaustion. He was tired out, but he wanted to talk about his trip more than he wanted to go to bed. He said that he hadn't reached the top because he hadn't had enough time, but he had been close enough to see people standing around the rim before turning back. The weather had been perfect. He told us how he had seen the shadow of Fuji cast by the full moon, on the countryside far below. He only regretted that he hadn't had more time.

Curtis Clendenin joined us in planning our climb and we set the dates for our three day passes on the 9th, 10th, and 11th of August. However, Scott saw an opportunity of getting into Vincent Priola's cable crew by going on TDY with them, so decided not to go with us.

We talked to Herbert Wilson and he loaned us a couple of combat packs that he had over in supply. Then we went to see the mess sergeant, Francis M. McDowell. He was a big, friendly, red-haired fellow from Rt. #1, Delton, Mich. He would have liked to have gone with us, but couldn't because he still had a cast on his foot from a fall he had taken at Easter-time. He agreed to provide us with all of the C-rations we could carry up there.

Sunday, August 9th, Curtis and I finished packing our packs. We each picked up two cans of meat and bean rations and two cans of bread units. Each bread unit contained about four crackers, a smaller can of jam, candy or a cookie, and coffee, milk, and sugar in powdered form.

Altogether, I had the following in my pack: four cans of C-rations, three oranges, twelve candy bars, raincoat, high-necked wool sweater, wool glove liners, six salt tablets, shaving kit, and film. I carried one canteen of water strapped on the outside of the pack.

We were both disappointed that none of the Post Exchanges on the air bases around Showa had any color film. They hadn't had any for over a month. There was only one man in the whole company that had an unexposed roll. He was Robert Sweeney. Fortunately, he was good enough to sell us that roll.

Right after noon chow, Curtis and I started for the train station. An AP (Air Police) held us up at the gate for a few minutes while he called to see if we were allowed to take government equipment off the base. We told him that we had our first sergeant's permission, etc. Sergeant Hendrickson and the CQ had been in the orderly room when we left, and we had mentioned to them that they might have to give the AP's an O.K. for us if they called. However, the AP on the gate got permission from his own desk sergeant to let us through.

We took the train over to Tachikawa, then caught another train at 1313 hours going all the way through to Fuji Yoshida. The train passed through eight or more mountain tunnels before we arrived. The land seemed to level out near Fuji Yoshida.

When we got off the train at Fuji Yoshida, there were a hundred or more tired-looking Japanese lined up waiting to get on. They certainly looked beat. We squeezed through them onto the main street. Then we looked around. The summit of Fujiyama was only twelve miles away, but it was hidden by clouds so we could only see the lower slopes behind the station.

Since there was no bus running to the Fuji-View Hotel at that time, Curtis decided to see if he could check his handbag at the station. They didn't have any facilities for checking luggage at the station, but a man suggested that we might deposit it at a store across the street.

As we crossed the street to the store, we had to brush off the people who wanted to be our guide, sell us climbing sticks, or pointed straw hats, etc. Curtis was about to give up before we cornered one of the busy clerks long enough to explain that we wanted to check a bag.

That done, we went back to the station to inquire where we could get the bus to the mountain. By following her directions, we headed up a street past tired climbers returning on foot and packed into buses. At the end of the street we turned left. A little further along we turned right and followed a narrow dirt road through a small forest of tall Cryptomeria trees.

Close to the opposite edge of this forest was the Fuji-Sengen shrine where for hundreds of years true pilgrims have stopped to pray before starting the climb. A few hardy orthodox Japanese still walk the entire distance from this *tori* to the summit, but most of the people seem to have gone modern and ride the bus up to the starting place. Thus they don't tire themselves out walking the four plus miles to the foot of Fuji.

We caught the bus at the edge of the woods and rode up to the starting place for 185 *Yen*. As we rode along, I noticed a small apiary of bee hives in a clearing among the trees. It was the only apiary that I saw in Japan. There were also many wild grapevines loaded with unripe fruit growing on the trees.

When the bus stopped, the passengers were besieged by hopeful guides; climbing stick sellers; men with horses to ride; and boys selling straw hats. We bought a climbing stick for 80 *Yen*, and bargained for a horse to take us to the seventh station. We finally hit upon a satisfactory sum of 1400 *Yen* ($3.89).

The horses were brought over for us to tie our packs to the saddles. We got on and started up the trail. Just then a cloud blew past the summit and for a moment we could see the top through the trees. It was a beautiful, but depressing sight, for we had no way to estimate the trouble we would have getting up there. Also , in the back of our minds, I expect we were afraid we wouldn't make it to the top.

We hadn't gone very far before we came to another shrine. The Japanese fellows had our sticks branded with a stamp for 10 *Yen* apiece. A little further and we came to the first station where we had our sticks branded again. Actually there were many sub-stations for each number, and each would brand the stick for a similar price. We quickly wised up and became more selective of the brands.

The trees along the trail were all draped with a pale green moss. There was a great variety of woodland plants growing in this moist environ-ment. Many wild flowers were in bloom.

The trail was about eight feet wide through the forest. It was practi-cally straight at the beginning, but as we climbed higher, the trail became steeper and more crooked. In places, smooth lava rock jutted out where the soil had been worn off the trail. As we approached the tree line, the soil and solid rock gave way to a red cinder composition. The many large boulders, partially buried by the cinders, stood out in relief against the sky.

Our horses were experienced mountain climbers. They couldn't be persuaded to walk straight up the trail. Instead, they would weave from one edge of the trail to the other edge. Weaving from one side to the other made it easier on them to climb but must have extended the dis-tance they covered by one-third of the way.

The sun began to set while we were climbing past the sixth station. Just above this station, we passed above the tree line and were exposed to the chilly wind sweeping down from the volcano. The trail dwindled down to a narrow cinder path that continued more and more steeply upward. The tree line wasn't an abrupt line. The trees gradually grew smaller and more gnarled and twisted above station six. Their bleak, whit-ish forms were evidence of their struggle for existence. Beyond the tree line for several yards, a few small plants clutched at the mountainside, and then there were no more.

It was a long climb from the sixth to the seventh station. The horses were breathing hard in the rarified air. The trail was too narrow for them to weave back and forth any longer, so they had a steady climb. Now and then the horses would try to stop and take a breather, but the Japanese boys were in a hurry and would slap them on the rump so that they kept plodding along.

The horses stopped at the foot of the steep stone stairs leading to station seven. We paid the boys the fourteen hundred *Yen* apiece, and after wishing us good luck in broken English, they began to lead their horses down the mountain.

Station seven, as all of the stations above the tree line, was built into the side of Fuji. The outside walls were of stones and large heavy cinders. Many more large cinders were placed on the roof to help hold it down against the terrific winds that sometimes come racing down and across the slopes.

A stone wall had been erected in front of the building and filled in so that there was space to set the house and about six feet of space left for the trail which passed in front of the building.

Although the proprietors of rest station seven were desirous of our staying all night, Curtis and I stopped in front only long enough to remove our sweaters from our packs and put them on. It was then discovered that we had both neglected to bring a very important item, a flashlight.

A middle aged couple with their lively young son were just starting out with a guide who had a flashlight. They invited us to go along with them for a way. Their son, he was probably about eight years old, was climbing the mountain twice in his excitement. The parents, somewhat past their prime for mountain climbing, were climbing slowly in the darkness, but the boy couldn't wait. He kept getting ahead of the guide and clammering over the rocks in the wrong direction. He would then be called back. Soon he would go off on a tangent again.

The climbing between station seven and eight was over rock formations rather than up a cinder path. Each step upward was uneven and precarious. In a few places there were steel rods braced between the rocks and boulders with messenger strand strung loosely between them. It served as a handrail, a guide to show the trail, and as a guardrail on some of the drop-offs.

The family only climbed about two stations above the first number seven and decided to bed down for the night. We weren't able to buy a light at this station, but we could see the lights of the next station above us and it didn't look too far away.

We climbed for awhile, then paused to catch our breath. It was slow going for the stars were providing our only light. During our pauses we could look up toward the peak and see it silhouetted against the Milky Way.

In spite of taking the wrong route a couple of times, which caused us a little trouble, we eventually arrived at the next station. We sat down on a bench in front of the station. The building provided a fair protection from the cold wind that was coming down from the mountain. Papa-san came out and tried to talk us into spending the night. We told him that we wanted to climb all night. He explained how full the houses higher up were, and that he would give us a special price of three hundred *Yen*. We thanked him and said we would talk it over.

Neither Curtis nor I were very hungry, but we thought it would be better if we ate our supper then, rather than wait. It was about 2030 hours. I opened my bread unit and gave Papa-san the coffee, cream, and sugar packets. He took the hint and went inside and left us to our meal.

It was a beautiful night. Not a cloud in the sky. The stars seemed to sparkle brighter and closer than ever before in the thin atmosphere. We could even see the lights of Tokyo, seventy or more miles away. There were many other smaller cities that we guessed at their names from their location in relation to Tokyo. Every few minutes, we would see a shooting star.

The light shining through the glass sliding panel that made up the front wall, lit up the bench where we had our C-rations spread out. Inside, we could see some of the guests sitting around the charcoal fire that was burning in a pit of ashes from previous fires. The fire pit was about three feet square and built into the floor. A large heavy pressure cooker sat over the fire. A few guests were sitting at low tables at one end of the room eating rice and drinking wine and tea. It was a cheerful scene.

As we watched, a girl phoned someone, probably her employer, and carried on a shouted conversation in very good English. She told the person she was talking to that she would not be back in time for work on Monday.

The wind seemed to grow colder as we finished our meal. We were still discussing the pros and cons of continuing our climb. We were both definitely against sleeping in one of the stations because of their reputation for lice, fleas, and just plain filth. There were two other alternatives: climb all night, or wrap up in our rain coats and sleep along the trail. Climbing in the dark would be slow and tedious, and it was too late in the season to be sleeping along the trail at that altitude; so reluctantly, we took Papa-san up on his three hundred *Yen* offer.

We slid open the glass panel, ducked inside, and quickly shut it again. We then sat down on the edge of the straw mat covered floor and removed our boots. As Curtis walked over to the fire, someone asked how old he was by way of being friendly. It was probably just one of the few phrases in English that the person knew. Everyone around the fire listened attentively as Curtis answered, and then repeated it after him. Next, I was asked how old I was. I answered in Japanese, but they weren't satisfied and wanted to hear the English words, which they enjoyed repeating.

As we sat down at the fire, Mama-san inquired if we would like some hot tea. She opened up her pressure cooker and poured in some rice. Her daughter, a round faced teenager who wore thick-lensed, black rimmed glasses, sat near the fire reading in the dim light of a carbide lamp. Occasionally, she would read an amusing paragraph out loud, which would cause a burst of laughter and comments from the guests.

We hadn't been sitting at the fire long before we began to get drowsey. We asked Papa-san where he wanted us to sleep. He took us to the opposite end of the room where he had a stack of *futon* (padded quilts) piled. He took a pair and laid them on the floor of an opening built into the wall for us to sleep on. Then he laid several more on top of these for us to cover ourselves.

The wall opening was about three feet higher than the floor, about seven feet wide and deep, and extended up to the low ceiling. It looked like a choice place to sleep. Papa-san even provided each of us with a cylindrical bag of rice husks to use as a pillow. He asked us when we wanted to be awakened. We told him before sunrise.

During the night, I woke up with a slight touch of mountain sickness, although I didn't know at the time what it was. It's symptoms seemed to be an upset stomach and hot and cold flashes. I took a couple of swallows of water from my canteen, then got up and walked over to the door, being careful not to step on the sleepers that now crowded the floor. I slid back the door, took a few breaths of the fresh cold air, and felt fine again.

Mama-san, who was sitting by the fire dozing, woke at the sound of the door sliding back. I apologized for waking her, and she asked if I would like a cup of tea. I wondered to myself if she had to sit up like this every night or if the family took turns.

We woke up at 0415 hours, just as it was beginning to get light. Mama-san provided us with a small pot of hot water and two handleless cups that she set on a low table. Curtis opened the coffee, cream, and sugar packets from his C-rations, and we had hot coffee. We still weren't hungry so we ate a candy bar apiece instead of opening the last of our C-rations. We decided to eat the C-rations on top. After paying for our lodging, we pulled on our boots, and began climbing at 0445 hours.

It was a wonderfully cold, clear, invigorating day. There weren't enough clouds to make a really unusual sunrise. There was only a single streak of red. Then the first rays of the sun touched the top of Fuji. Soon the rays had traveled down the volcano and were lighting the countryside far below us.

We could see for miles. Over to the left of us was a ridge of tiny-looking mountains that had dammed up some low flying clouds behind them. The clouds, held back by the mountain range looked like a big snow field or glacier.

The wind wasn't blowing down from the mountain as it had been the night before. It was cold, but with the exertion of climbing plus the sun on our backs, we were comfortable. Before we reached station eight, we had passed the rock formations and were on a cinder trail that was nothing but a steep inclined plane. The mountainside near the trail was littered with all kinds of rubbish. There were papers, bottles, C-ration cans, fish cans, rags, round pointed hats, and especially the *waraji* or farmer's slipper. The *waraji* are woven of straw. Consequently, it doesn't take much climbing over cinders to wear them out. The Japanese who wear them, always carry several pairs in reserve. Even the last pair of *waraji* is discarded at the foot of the mountain, so that wearer will not anger the gods who live there by inadvertently carrying away a cinder or particle in his shoe, thus reducing the height of the mountain.

Usually, we could climb upward along the winding trail far enough that if one were to take the distance from our start to where we had to stop, it would appear as an "N". Now and then on shorter distances, we could squeeze out a "W" before having to stop for air.

Strange as it seems, it only took a moment to rest. We would rest for a couple of minutes and wouldn't feel at all tired. We even commented that we felt like running. Then we would start climbing again. By the time we reached the first switch-back, we were ready to stop, but we would force ourselves to go just to the next switch-back. A few minutes rest there and we would be raring to go again.

As we climbed along, more and more people appeared on the trail ahead of us and behind us from the rest stations. The women wore anything from *kimono* and *mompei* to sweaters and slacks. A few of the men wore white robes; but most were dressed in Western clothes. Their ages ranged from old people bent almost double with age, to youngsters just able to walk. Some of the women carried a baby on their backs. There were many children of school age. Some of the people take several days to climb Fuji if they are unable to climb it without long periods of rest.

There were two climbers who were very conspicuous because of the loads they were carrying on their backs. One was a fellow with a terrific load of supplies for some station further up the mountain. His pack probably weighed more than one hundred pounds. The other fellow had a seat pack on his back and a gray-haired old lady sat in the seat. The man looked only at the ground where he placed his feet. He stopped to rest surprisingly few times. We wondered just how far he had brought her on his back.

The distance between the station eight and station nine seemed an eternity. The trail had become steeper. Many times, we looked up and counted the number of stations that we still had to pass. Then when we had climbed to the next higher station and there should have been one less to count, there was often one or two more than before. This was because of the changing curvature or the slope as we approached the summit.

When we did arrive at station nine, we knew that we were going to make it to the top. According to the Japanese, station nine is at twelve thousand feet. We could look across horizonally and see a patch of snow in the "slide".

Some more hard climbing took us through the two *torii* which are at the entrance to the summit. We were on top at 0740 hours. The first *torii* is of wood, but the second one is of white stone. It must have required a great deal of labor to bring it up, considering its size and weight.

A few steps after passing through the *torii*, we turned to the left and walked down a street with "hotels" on the right and "out houses" on the left side. In the hotels, or at little stands also on the left side of the street, one could buy brightly colored pennants and bells (*suzu)* to fasten to the climbing poles. We immediately went into one of the hotels and had a station ten brand added to the others on our poles.

Next, we walked down the street to the end of the buildings. We turned right and went to the edge of the crater which was about two hundred feet behind the buildings. The crater was a tremendous jagged hole maybe two hundred feet deep. The sides were almost verticle. By leaning over the edge, we could see snow or ice at the bottom of it.

A strong cold wind blew across the crater. We were shivering so hard that we had trouble holding our cameras steady while shooting pictures. If we had any intention of following the trail around the edge of the crater, that wind stopped us.

Back inside the hotel, we watched the climbers arrive at the top. Many of them were completely exhausted. They would flop down on the straw mats, so tired they couldn't move. One Japanese woman was unconscious. It was hard to understand why they tortured themselves so. On the other hand, most of the climbers, although tired, were in gay spirits and still full of energy.

We were surprised to see the American family, that we had climbed a short way with the night before, arrive soon after we did. They were certainly tired. Even the little boy had slowed down.

Curtis and I discussed eating the rest of our C-rations, but neither of us had an appetite. We settled on a candy bar and an orange apiece. I began to give away the remainder of my candy.

The scenery was beautiful from the top. At the foot of Fuji were the blue-green forests with dark lines interveined through them that indicated roads and trails. A little further out were small irregular patches of cultivated land. We could very clearly see Lake Kawaguchi and the town of Fuji Yoshida. The ridge of mountains still had a large expanse of clouds dammed up behind them. Far down on the slope of Fuji were climbers winding snake-like up the path. Once in awhile we could see a billow of dust rising behind a human speck running down the "slide".

Away over to the right we could see some huge clouds piling up. We watched them for awhile and saw that they were coming towards us. We had been on top about an hour, so we decided to try to get down below the cloud layer before they reached us just in case they were thunder clouds. Rather than take the slide down, we started down at 0830 hours by the way we had come up. Curtis led the way. We couldn't help but run most of the distance. Most of the time we had to follow the trail, for it was too steep to risk taking any short cuts. However, whenever Curtis saw a shortcut that was just on this side of impossible, he would take it.

On some of the short cuts, he would leap over the edge of the trail with me following close behind. There we would go in a cloud of dust, digging our heels and poles into the cinders trying to stop ourselves every step of the way until we joined the trail again and got leveled off.

Our climbing sticks were certainly handy. They saved us from falling many times. The sticks helped us keep our balance while running in the loose cinders, helped us to stop, broke several falls, and even aided us to vault over boulders when we had no other choice but to try to jump them.

We were a short distance above station seven when we met the first cloud to blow across the side of the mountain. To get the full effect of being hit by a cloud, we stopped running while it was still a few yards away and waited for it to arrive. It was a warm cloud. The outer edge of it hit us in the face like fresh cotton candy. While inside of the cloud, it appeared to be a fog, and the humidity was slightly suffocating. In a few minutes the other edge of the cloud went past us and the weather was cool and bright again until the next cloud came by.

As we came past station seven, we could see a partially completed round building with a pointed roof that we used as a landmark. We knew that when we reached that building, we would connect with the trail leading through the woods.

There was another large mass of clouds approaching slowly from the right. We estimated that they would cross Fuji just about at the tree line. Then we began to race those clouds to the round building. For all of our effort, we lost the race. We were about three-quarters of the way to it when the clouds swallowed it.

We couldn't see anything below us except the clouds blowing across the mountain. Just above the round building, we remembered that there was a steep drop off, and that we would have to follow the rim of it around to our right to reach the trail below.

Through light spots in the clouds, we saw a station at about our altitude far over to our left. It was out of our way, but we decided to go down from there rather than risk falling from the ridge. A Boy-san at the station pointed out a path that would lead into the main trail.

At the next station Curtis and I rested for awhile. Our legs were shaking from the strain of running so far over such an unsure footing as sliding cinders. The heels of our boots looked as if they had been sanded. So far our exertion hadn't caused us to be out of breath. It was probably due to the fact that we had decreased our altitude fast enough that instead of breathing faster or deeper, the increasing density of the air provided us with enough oxygen.

When our legs stopped shaking, we put our packs back on and started out again. We thought it would be easier walking when we got on solid ground, but it wasn't. There was still enough slope that we had to trot most of the way. Our heels would hit the ground first and our toes would have to slap down in such a way that it tired our feet out.

Also, as the slope of Fujiyama leveled out, we began to get out of breath more frequently. We were having to travel much further horizonally to decrease our altitude proportionally. We rested more frequently.

We arrived at the starting place at 1230 hours. There was about a half-hour wait for the bus to take us back to Fuji Yoshida. Meanwhile, a Japanese boy had us half-mad at him for his persistence in insisting that we sell our sweaters and watches to him.

It was a lucky break for us that a bus from the Fuji-View Hotel was parked in front of the train station when we arrived. Curtis went over to the shop to get his bag, while I asked the Japanese driver if he thought there were any vacancies at the hotel. He said that he thought there were, so we got on.

It took about twenty minutes to reach the hotel. The bus turned into a long paved drive that was lined on both sides by Oriental lantern type street lights that looked like large bird houses sitting on poles. They were very pretty when the electricity was turned on in the evening.

As soon as we got registered, I went into the dining room and drank three glasses of water. The air on Fujiyama had dried us out more than we thought.

Our room was with two Air Force boys whom we hardly ever saw except when they slept late in the morning. Besides the four beds in the room, there was a large closet, dresser, writing desk, lavatory, and telephone. From the large picture window, we had a wonderful view of Fujiyama.

In the room next to ours was a Japanese style bath. It was a large tiled room with a bath about the size of a bath tub built right into the floor. It was filled with steaming water. On the wall was a shower.

Japanese don't take a bath as we know it. They have to be absolutely clean before they would even think of getting into the bath water. They scrub themselves with soap once or twice. Each time they rinse the dirty soapy water off. Then when they feel that they are clean enough, they will get into the hot bath water and soak.

The hot bathing habit is unique to Japan. The people claim that the hot bath is necessary for their health. A very hot bath makes them feel better and increases their appetite particularly during the rainy season when the temperature and humidity are high and the people feel tired and depressed. Also, in the winter when the houses are cold, a hot bath warms the body.

Most of the Japanese homes have their own private wooden tubs with built-in water heaters, but for those who don't have their own baths, there are community bath houses where both sexes may soak and gossip together.

The Japanese people who worked at the hotel were very friendly and tried very hard and successfully to please their customers. Soon after we arrived, we looked at our beds and saw that they didn't have any sheets on them. I asked a house boy if he would put some sheets on our beds when he had the time. He began apologizing profusely and saying he would have it done right away, etc. I walked to the door with him and thanked him. He rushed down the hall sideways, clicking his heels together, and still apologizing and calling that he would put sheets on right away.

By the time we had cleaned up, the bed was made. We laid down to relax since we still had half an hour before supper. Both of us planned to stay awake just in case the other went to sleep. The next thing we knew it was 1900 hours. We had slept for two hours. Luck was with us though. According to the room schedule, supper was to be served from 1730 hours until 1930 hours.

The dining room was in the opposite wing from us. We were met at the doorway by a very dignified Japanese head waiter in a black tuxedo. He bowed and inquired how many. When we replied, "two", he led us over to one of the tables, pulled out the chairs and held them while we sat down. That done, he returned to his post by the door, and the waitress' took over.

One waitress came over and poured water in the glasses, while another handed us a menu. Before each item on the menu was a letter and a number corresponding to the kind of soup, meat, vegetable, etc. on down the list that they were serving. There was usually a choice between three different items of food from each category. It was surprising how well the girls remembered the letters and numbers. They seldom brought the wrong order.

The food was delicious and plentiful. The service was excellent. As soon as we set a coffee cup or water glass down empty, one of the waitress' would hurry over to fill it. If something escaped the attention of the girls, the eagle-eyed head waiter would motion to them, or if they were rushed, take care of it himself.

We paid when we left. The cost was for the service, not for the food. The Fuji-View Hotel, being a special services hotel, draws its rations from the government. Thus, it only costs a dollar a day to eat in one of those hotels. Supper was fifty cents, dinner was thirty-five, and breakfast was fifteen. The special services hotels, located in various parts of Japan, are the finest thing for the service men in the Far East. Even a private can live like a millionaire in one of those hotels.

After we had eaten, we walked around the grounds. At the front entrance there was a powerful set of binoculars mounted on a post for viewing the volcano. It was dark and the stars were shining. The black lump that was Fuji was visible against the dark blue sky. When our eyes got used to the darkness, we could see a column of lights flickering dimly along the mountain trail. Through the binoculars the lights appeared brighter and closer – almost too close for comfort. We surely felt sorry for those people up there in the cold and wind. It was hard to believe that we had been one of them just the night before.

There are five lakes around Fujiyama: Lake Motosu, Lake Shojin, Lake Saiko, Lake Kawaguchi, and Lake Yamanaka. The Fuji-View Hotel was located on the shore of Lake Kawaguchi. The next morning, Curtis and I rented a rowboat and rowed out to an island in the lake. There were two rubber life rafts anchored out there to swim from.

Many Japanese were vacationing around the lake. A boat load of them would go by every now and then. Also there were some vacationers camped on the island.

After dinner, we rode the hotel bus to the Fuji Yoshida station and caught a train back to Showa.

On the following Saturday, Captain Leddon stopped John Bruder and I to inquire about climbing Fuji. We gave him as much advice as we could about climbing at a steady pace and what to take, *e.g.* rain coat, heavy sweater, and a flashlight. Remembering my need for more water, I suggested he take two canteens.

He and some other officers were going to drive down there and climb it then. Towards evening it started to rain hard and steady. It rained all day Sunday, too. We wouldn't have traded places with the Captain for anything.

Monday morning, the Captain came in cheerful and singing, but he didn't mention his trip. He went in his office and closed the door. This increased our curiosity even more. Finally, about 1000 hours, his door opened and he came out for a cup of coffee, still humming. After he had prepared his cup of coffee, he began to tell us about the trip.

He had made it to the top, but the weather was so foggy and rainy that he couldn't see his hand in front of his face. It rained all the time. He had taken two canteens of water, but hadn't needed them because all he had to do was to hold his head up and open his mouth. The Captain said that if he could find someone to go with him, he would like to climb it again when he could see what he was doing. Someone jokingly remarked that it could take the place of organized athletics on Wednesday.

Next day, a notice came out that Captain Leddon would provide food and transportation for anyone wanting to climb Fujiyama during the weekend.

Saturday, August 22nd, the CQ woke the mountain climbers at 0500 hours. Soon after there were sixteen of us eating breakfast in the mess hall.

Two of the men were not going to climb. Edward B Lenortavage of 35 Franklin St., Shaft, Pa., was going to drive a weapons carrier down and cook for us. He had the "weap" loaded with a field stove, C-rations, water, cake, sandwiches, fruit, etc.

The other non-climber was Albert Equils. He was one of the company mechanics, and had volunteered to drive a bus down there. The climbers were: Captain John Leddon, Jr.; Eugene Bartasavage; Donald Bengtson; Richard Bollig; Arthur Brogley; John Bruder, Jr.; Horace Creary; Angelo DiFrancesco; William Grubbs; Jack Hess; Richard Scott; Walter P. Weber, of Omaka, Nebr.; Herbert Wilson; and myself.

Lenortavage and Captain Leddon led the way in the weapons carrier. It was a long trip by road. It took nearly four hours to drive to the foot of the mountain. The scenery became more interesting and picturesque as we approached the mountains further south. We had to pass through the range before we could reach Fujiyama.

As the bus struggled up the steep narrow roads, we could look far down into the valley and see the small patches of farm land and the thatch roofed farm houses. The farm land wasn't by any means confined to the valleys. There were cultivated patches on the mountainsides that didn't look larger than ten feet on a side. It was hard to believe that anyone would even climb up there. Someone suggested that they probably wore safety belts when they went up there to hoe.

Since traffic moves on the left side in Japan, we were on the outside of the road. Several times we met traffic coming from the opposite direction. Equils would slow down or stop the bus on the very edge of the road and the other vehicle would squeeze by with inches to spare. Once, just as we turned a sharp, blind corner, we met a truck loaded with gravel coming down the middle of the road. Both parties fortunately got their vehicles stopped, but the Japanese couldn't back his truck up the grade. We had to sit through the hair-raising experience while Equils backed the bus around the corner again and close enough to the edge of the drop-off so that the truck could get by. There weren't any guard rails on Japanese roads.

Another time, we came to a place where a gang of Japanese workers were repairing the road. Of course, they were working on the inside of the road, but they had piles of gravel stashed down the middle of the road, and some carts, that were the same as the ones they pull behind their bicycles, filled with gravel and some tools that were blocking our way.

The weapons carrier managed to squeeze through, but it was obvious that the bus wouldn't be able to. Equils blew the horn. The Japanese moved the carts a few inches, and then looked at him as if to say it was impossible to get a bus through there. We all got out and pushed their carts of gravel up onto the gravel piles, threw their tools out of the way, and guided Equils through. We were lucky to have such a good driver as Equils with us.

The area around Fujiyama is a national park and a forest preserve. We pulled off on a side road in the park to eat lunch before starting to climb. Lenortavage began pulling the food from the "weap". I ate a cold can of C-rations then and saved a sandwich to eat on top.

On this trip I was better prepared. I left the wool glove liners, candy, and C-rations out of the pack. Instead, I added an extra canteen of water on the inside of the pack, a flashlight, can of peanuts, oranges, and a sandwich to the sweater and raincoat that I had carried before. The other canteen of water was attached to the outside of the pack. In addition, I had some C-ration candy in my shirt pockets.

After we had finished eating, we got back on the bus and rode to the starting place. Lenortavage stayed behind to hide the weapons carrier and watch after his equipment. He was going to have a hot meal prepared for us when we got down the following day.

At the starting place, we bargained for horses. The Japanese wanted 1400 *Yen*, but we only wanted to pay one thousand. They wouldn't come down in price so we started to climb on foot. That clinched the deal. They began to call after us, " O.K. Daijobu, thousand *Yen*".

Everyone except Brogley, Creary, and Hess took horses. These three walked it all the way. They started out a short while before we did, but a few stations later we caught up with them. They were tired and wet with perspiration. Most of the rest of the time they stayed fairly close to us, which was almost too fast a pace for the most endurance. We gradually separated above the tree line.

At about the altitude of station number six, a short distance above the tree line, the horses were brought to a halt, and we were at "station seven". The guides had taken a side trail at the tree line and had taken us to a station somewhat out of the way. We could see the seventh station far up the side, but we couldn't argue them into taking us any higher. This particular station did have a seven brand that they put on some of the men's poles, however.

The Japanese wanted four hundred *Yen* more to go to the next station. Captain Leddon called for a vote, and the majority wanted to ride to the next station so we told them we would pay fourteen hundred *Yen*.

The rock formations between seven and eight tired some of the men out pretty badly. The company was spread out over a lot of trail.

Those who were in the lead stopped at one of the rest stations to warm up and have some hot tea. They hadn't been there long when Creary, one of the men climbing the entire distance, passed by. We hit on the glass and called him in. He sat down on the edge of the floor. In a few minutes he laid back and went to sleep. Now and then he would moan in his sleep.

As some more of our company came in, a few of us left. It seemed as though we were making very good time.

A few stations higher, Captain Leddon made an effort to regroup the men that were lagging behind. We could see them strung out along the trail below. Brogley had also passed some of the men who had ridden horses part way.

Scott and Grubbs hadn't waited with us, so altogether they had about an hour's lead on the rest of us. Sometimes we could catch a glimpse of them several stations above.

All but a few men were caught up when Bartasavage and I started to climb again. Captain Leddon started out soon afterward and some of the others followed, but it was a given that we wouldn't all be able to stay together. It appeared at that point that four of the men wouldn't get to the top.

Captain Leddon had out-climbed his group shortly, so Bartasavage and I waited for him to catch up with us. Bartasavage stayed to catch his breath, so the Captain and I continued climbing. We were both in good physical shape from climbing Fuji only a short time earlier. It wasn't long before we had put a lot of distance between us and the nearest man below.

The two of us reached the top at 1800 hours. As we walked down the road in front of the "hotels", we wondered which one Scott and Grubbs were in. Near the end of the street, Scott came out of the Tamaguchi-Ya Hotel where he had been watching for us. He was wrapped in a Japanese robe that he had borrowed to keep warm.

We went inside the hotel and warmed up a few minutes. Scott said that he and Grubbs got on top at about 1700 hours. He had watched our progress through someone's binoculars until he got too cold to stay outside.

The Captain and I went back to look at the crater again. A bitter cold wind was blowing across it just like before. We then went part way around the crater, and climbed around and on top of a high protuberance on the rim to look around. On the opposite side of the rim from the Fuji Yoshida trail is a weather station, but not too many people go around that far.

Before eating supper of C-rations, we waited to see if everyone would arrive on top. We supposed that some of the men might have gotten together and would spend the night at a rest station along the way. However, to everyone's credit, the last of the men stumbled in by 1930 hours.

Some of the men were really worn out, but everyone of them laughed and joked about each others troubles. One big fellow claimed that there were times when he was so tired and mad that he felt like crying. The three fellows that climbed the entire distance were really beat, but none of them was the last one on top.

While we ate and talked, Papa-san spread a row of *futon* along the back wall. Soon afterward, we removed our boots and laid down to sleep. The carbide lamps fastened to the center support posts of the room were shining in our eyes and the fumes from them were sickening.

Nevertheless, most of us went right to sleep. Several were moaning and groaning in their sleep. We had to laugh at one fellow. Every time he exhaled, he moaned loudly and terminated it with a different cuss word each time.

Most of us woke up around 2000 hours. It seemed as though it should be almost daylight rather than ten PM. Scott and several others were having the alternate chills and hot flashes that the Captain called "mountain sickness". It was supposed to be the body's mechanism of adjusting to the change in elevation.

Once again, much later, I woke up. I went to the door and looked out. I turned my flashlight on a building about ten feet away. The clouds were thick enough to tunnel through, and it was raining lightly. It was raining hard at Showa we were told when we got back.

I lay back down and didn't wake up again until sunrise or *goraiko*. The sunrise wasn't too impressive except for a wide streak of red. I woke the Captain who had wanted a picture of it. He got up, went over to the door to see it, then laid back down. About five minutes later, he and the other troops woke up. They pulled on their boots and came outside to join us on the rim of the crater.

The sunrise had lost most of its color by then, but the cloud formations far below were magnificent. Five or six thousand feet below was a great expanse of clouds that hid the earth from view.

The wind was too cold to stay outside very long, so we all went back in the hotel and began cooking our breakfast on the charcoal fires. The aroma of cooking beans soon filled the air of the room.

There was a Japanese boy next door who was in a great deal of pain. He had fallen and broken his collar bone as he started down the "slide" the day before. A stretcher crew had arrived to carry him down. About at the tree line, I met a doctor coming up the trail. He had no pack, canteen, or climbing stick. If he got up there in time, he surely did it the hard way.

It was 0620 hours when we left the top. No one, except for myself, wanted to go back down the way we came up. At station nine our paths separated. Captain Leddon led the others onto the "slide".

The route down was perfectly familiar to me on this trip. It enabled me to take more and longer shortcuts than Clendenin and I had done before. Also since I was well rested, I was able to cover more distance without resting as much.

Down in the slide, I could see billows of dust rising behind the main group of the men as they ran along. They were making much better time than I was.

I met Brogley at a station on the tree line where the trail from the slide and the route I was taking joined. He was tired out. We sat and talked awhile. Everyone else had already passed this point. I encouraged him to take a horse down, but he wouldn't hear of it.

Among the trees around the base of Fujiyama, I took a lot of short-cuts. One of them brought me back on the trail right behind Hess and Wilson. They were hiking along slowly, so another short cut put me far ahead of them.

Equils had the bus parked at the starting place. Almost everyone was in it discussing their adventures. The first men to get down arrived at 0740 hours compared to my arrival time at 0840 hours. It had only taken them an hour and twenty minutes to get down by using the cinder slide.

After awhile, we drove down the road to a place where Lenortavage had hidden the "weap" and had set up the field stove. He had made hot coffee, had the C-rations heated, and had what was left of yesterday's cake sitting out. After we had finished eating, we loaded the equipment back into the truck, and started back to Showa.

CHAPTER XII

Showa II

When Clendenin and I stopped at the Showa base gate to show the AP's our passes after we returned from the first mountain climbing trip, the guard remarked that we had returned just in time to be restricted to the base. The indigenous personnel were going on strike.

Supposedly the strike was brought about by the recent cuts in allocation of the Air Force funds. The Japanese that I talked to all had their own ideas for the cause of the strike. Some said that it was because of changes in the regulations concerning hiring and firing, etc. Others were striking because they had been laid off or had been reduced from a forty-eight hour week to a forty-hour week. It may have been all of these reasons, and more too, or none of them, but who can say.

Not all of the Japanese went on strike. Accommodations were made for any of them who wanted to stay on base to do so. Yamataki-san, janitor for the second and third platoons, always stayed and worked during the strikes. He needed the money and strikers didn't get paid for the days they were on strike. Some of the men from the mess hall and the mechanics sometimes stayed on base.

To the 474th fell the job of walking guard mount on Showa while the Japanese guards were on strike. Some of our men had a lot of fun and got even with a few of the AP's that they knew to be "chicken shit". The AP's supervised the guard mounts and therefore had to go around every so often and check on each post. If the men walking the post recognized the AP as one of those kind, he would stop him and make him lay his identification card on the ground. Then he would order the AP to retreat so many paces while he looked at the ID card. If it were in order, the guard would let him proceed to the next post where he often had to go through the same procedure.

The strikes usually lasted three days. Two weeks later, another strike was called, but it didn't go through for some reason or another.

Quite a bit of excitement was caused among the Americans and the Japanese when the first B-36 bombers landed in the Far East. One of the giant bombers landed nearby after flying non-stop across the Pacific. The roar from the ten engines, six pusher-type propeller engines and four jets, shook the buildings on the bases and rattled the frail wooden houses of the Japanese for miles around as it came in low and slow to land. We had never seen anything like it.

The men in the 474th were pretty much a cross section of men one might find anywhere in America. There were only a very few men that made serious mistakes and several that were unusual in the sense that they were eccentric or couldn't do anything right no matter how hard they tried. However, there wasn't a man in the company that didn't belong there. Each man contributed to the legend of the company.

In spite of the hard, often difficult work and often depressing temperatures and humidity, tempers seldom reached the breaking point. There were two fellows though that jumped at the chance to pound one another as hard as they could hit, but it was all in fun. They were careful to hit on the arms and shoulders. In fact, they were the best of friends and would do anything for one another.

There was one man in the outfit who was obviously trying for a bad conduct discharge. After a certain number of court martials, the government will discharge the man in the interest of the service. No one could understand this man's reasoning either. He already had ten or more years of service in. At any rate, he would hardly be in the company a couple of weeks before he would go AWOL or something, and have to be sent back to the stockade.

The Captain didn't see any reason to keep sending him back to the stockade, and tried to get him discharged. It took a long time for the recommendation to go through, but at last it did, and the fellow was sent to the ZI.

Possibly a fellow who cut up his Japanese girlfriend with a broken beer bottle committed the most serious offense by a member of the 474th. She was unconscious for a day or so, and the doctors thought she would die.

The attack occurred in the evening. He had been keeping the girl and had even hocked some of his clothes to pay her. He had probably been drinking pretty heavily that evening, too, so when he discovered she had been "short-timing" on him, he lost his head and tried to kill her with a beer bottle.

Afterward, he came back to the base. The AP's made bed check that night looking for him. He saw them, and slept outdoors all night. They caught him the next morning. He was court martialed and sent to the stockade.

On the lighter side, there was a young fellow who wasn't sure what he wanted out of life. Every second week he made a radical change in his life's ambition, which was much to the amusement of everyone in the company.

Once he came to the conclusion that he was a great singer. Of course, he was urged on by tongue-in-cheek compliments from all of his buddies. To him it wasn't the words or even the melody of the song that mattered; it was the tone of his wonderful voice. He had a loud deep voice, but it had a terrible quiver that delighted everyone who heard it. It wasn't long before he didn't have to be asked to sing. He would walk up and ask you to listen to him. When the victim couldn't listen any longer and keep a straight face, he would call someone else over and say, "Just listen to ——'s voice", and he would sneak off.

When the boy felt he had reached the pinnacle of success as a singer, he decided to combine careers with song writing. He claimed to have sold some songs in Tokyo.

Suddenly, he decided that he should give up his career as a singer and songwriter. When his buddies found him on his knees beside his bed, they asked what he was doing. He replied that he was praying, and announced that he was going to devote himself to being a "Brother".

He wasn't a "Brother" very long before he came around to tell me that the "Old Man" had made him the happiest man in the company.

"Why, how is that?" I asked.

"He's transferred me to the motor pool, and I'll get to be a mechanic."

"I'm glad to hear that ——. That will be something you can use when you get out of the army."

"Yes," he replied, "I've always wanted to fool around with motors."

When the Captain heard about him being a singer, he said, "He's about like the guy we had at the BOQ. He ordered one of these Charles Atlas kits and went around flexing his muscles. His arms weren't as big around as two of my fingers."

In spite of the fact that this boy used a whole bucket of grease to lubricate a three quarter ton weapons carrier (crammed the grease in from the top while it ran through an opening in the bottom and onto the ground), he worked and tried to do a good job. Once he got ready for a typhoon single-handed when he had CQ at the motor pool.

The Captain called him into his office one day and complimented him on the interest he had shown in his work and thanked him for the job he was doing.

When he came out of the office, bursting with pride, he had a new ambition in life – to be a thirty-year man in the army.

There was another young fellow in the company that the Captain didn't know what to do with. The boy reported in that he had "scratched the paint" on the fender of his jeep. The Captain's version was different. "This is the second time he's torn up that same fender and in the same way, too. He's like ———. I don't know what to do with him. I've already had him every place I could think of where I thought he couldn't do any harm. Maybe Special Services could use him in the Hobby Shop. At least he won't be in the company area."

Boone was a tall slender fellow from what I had been told about him. He had rotated back to the States before I arrived in the company, but his idiosyncrasies hadn't been forgotten. Wakefield used to mention Boone a lot, but it was Park A Close of Lawrenceville, Pa., that told me most of the tales I heard about him. Boone could easily be identified among any group of men. He invariably wore a raincoat and a pair of sunglasses. Go to the movie and he would be sitting in the front row with his raincoat and sunglasses on. If you asked him why he was wearing the glasses, he would reply, "So's I can see the show in technicolor".

"One night Boone came through the main gate dressed in his glasses and raincoat, but with no pants on", Close said. He marched right into Security Headquarters and said, "Some SOB done stole my pants." According to Close, when Boone went before the CO, he let him off, because if he could get through the gate without his pants on, there wasn't much he could do about it.

Out on the job somewhere, the crew would ride to work in the K-truck. Once, after everyone had been working for some time, someone asked, "Where's Boone?" During the search that followed, Boone was found sitting in the back of the K-truck. No one had told him to get out.

The Hobby Shop became an increasingly busy place as more men returned to the Company area. Some of them started large projects like furniture or boats. Stanley Kozenko and Arthur Thearling combined efforts to build a rather ingenuous boat that they called a "Catamaran". It was constructed of two auxiliary fuel tanks such as the ones carried by the Sabre Jets.

A thirty horsepower engine was mounted on the braces that joined the two halves of the twin hulled craft together. The motor was rebuilt from salvaged parts.

They cut an opening in each tank large enough to sit in. Then they installed padded seats for comfort and safety. The Catamaran also had rear fins and a steering device that was operated by a steering wheel in the right cockpit.

It took Kozenko and Thearling around 600 hours to build their boat, and they used to operate it on Lake Sagami which was at Yose.

Curtis Clendenin, Richard Scott, Kenneth Jones, Gordon Gebbens, and others had all made model airplanes at the Hobby Shop. Gebbens even designed and built a small model racer that used a miniature jet engine for power. A group of us went out to the baseball diamond where Gebbens had staked his racer to the end of a long wire for the trial run. Either we couldn't get the jet hot enough or the starter battery was too weak, for we couldn't keep the jet running. Now and then the jet would sound off with a report like a shotgun, and a streak of flame would shoot out the tailpipe, but it wouldn't do any more though we tried until after dark.

Men weren't the only persons to use the Hobby Shop. Once, I was surprised to meet Anne Thompson of Eugene, Oregon down there. She was the pretty young lady who filled Miss. Cooper's vacancy at the Area "A" Service Club. At the time she was sanding down a bass bow that she had made for her bass viol. She also had a nice voice and sometimes sang in a quartet in church.

Court martials and pre-trial investigations were a nuisance at times. The officers on the base went according to a roster. When their names appeared on the list accompanied by a time period – say two weeks – they would have to handle any case that might come up in those two weeks.

Before the Army conducts a court martial, there is a pre-trial investigation where an officer, or officers, weigh all the facts of the case to determine whether there is sufficient evidence to prosecute. When he has heard all sides of the case, he then makes a recommendation as to what should be done. A pre-trial investigation involves almost as much paper work as a court martial.

The Captain was stomping mad one afternoon. He was conducting a pre-trial investigation at the time, and he had just read an article in a magazine depreciating the army court martial because of the high rate of conviction, etc. "Of course there's a high rate of conviction", he said. "That's what the pre-trial investigation is for, to see if there is a cause for a court martial."

Robert Sweeney used to attend the investigations with the Captain and tape the proceedings. The recording was for the benefit of the clerks who had to type up the statements and recommendations later. The Captain always made it clear to the accused and witnesses that what they said would not be used for evidence. It was just an investigation and not a trial.

Later, if a court martial were recommended, we would have to go through the whole thing again. Only there would be a great many more details and additional paper work. Sometimes it kept us working in the office until late at night.

At this point, it should be emphasized that the Captain and our office staff did not work on cases involving the 474th. To my knowledge there were none anyway. We worked on cases involving other companies around the base.

There were many run of the mill cases, and Reiko could help us type the paper work on them. But then there were the sodomy cases. Although she typed too fast to comprehend the meaning of everything, we only gave her the clean parts to do. Much of her work was copying, which she did very well, rather than translating which would have involved her understanding.

A sodomy case is about the most revolting thing there is to listen to and work on. We had the misfortune to get two of these cases from the same outfit on the base. Again, another qualifier, this doesn't mean that it necessarily involves the permanent personnel of that outfit. Sometimes a man is attached to another outfit in a different locality just long enough for an investigation and trial.

At the end of one sodomy investigation, in which the accused was a sergeant and the accuser a private, the private came in and asked that his charges be dropped. He said that he could have been mistaken about what happened. There were witnesses, but they had seen nothing that could be called justifiable evidence. Also, the sergeant had a fairly solid story.

There was nothing for the Captain to do but recommend that there be no court martial. Still we had to type up all the disgusting paper work of the investigation. The trial may have been dropped, but where there is room for suspicion in such cases – well, one wonders.

Yip, was a dog that Vincent Priola had had inoculated and brought to the Company from Iwo Jima. Yip wasn't like the several other dogs that lived on the base. He could think for himself. When he wanted to go to Tachikawa, he would get in a truck from the mess hall that made a regular run over there. If he hadn't completed all of his social calls, he simply wouldn't be sitting in the truck when the driver was ready to leave. Later in the day, he would return with someone else from the Company whom he might chance to meet. Yip recognized all of our vehicles from a distance, so he never had a worry about transportation.

Yip wouldn't take sass from any dog. Once at police call, a larger black dog stepped out of line and Yip was starting to take him down a notch, when some of the men broke it up. Alvin "Old Folk" Davis of Warrenton, N.C., commented, "Them dogs gotta be court martialed next week."

There was a telephone pole outside of the mess hall with an overhead light on it. Further down the pole was a switch that appeared to be the light switch. Francis McDowell, our mess sergeant, happened to notice it one evening after supper and gave it a flip to see if it worked. He hadn't much more than turned it loose, when a fire truck came roaring down there and stopped behind the mess hall. Japanese firemen from the base were swarming helter skelter all over the place looking for the fire.

George Frame and Richard Bolig had a similar experience, Weissborn told me. Frame was on CQ when they discovered smoke billowing from cracks around the doors and windows of the distribution building next door. They turned in the fire alarm and proceeded to kick down the door. To their surprise, there was no fire. Some DDT bombs had gone off and the vapor, which filled the building, was seeping through the cracks.

Nine days before our air force replacements arrived, the 474th men began to set up bunks for them in the first platoon barracks. All of our men were going to move into our other barracks. Later, the men even put sheets and blankets on the beds for them. We were certainly crowded in our barracks, and we knew they would be too. We were getting anxious to find out what was going to happen.

The Air Force arrived about 1900 hours. It was like dropping a heated hornet's nest into their barracks. Some of them threw their bags on a bunk and ran out the door screaming that they were going to the club for beer. Others took it more calmly. The 474th veterans were amused at their behavior and lack of discipline.

Next day in the office, we loaned them our typewriters and helped them all we could, but mostly we tried to avoid their confusion and noise.

Their officers would walk into their barracks, but no one called the men to attention. They said they were in the Air Force and didn't have to call attention unless it was their CO.

Later Captain Cole and Corporal Riha paid them in the next room. Riha came back pulling his hair. A sergeant had saluted him when he came up to sign the payroll. Another fellow laid his closed wallet in front of Captain Cole until the Captain asked him to find his ID card.

To top off the day, Retreat caught three airmen on the parade ground. They stood at attention holding their caps over their hearts. One of their sergeants must have seen them for they never pulled that stunt again.

The second day brought the first of many major problems to them. Even before they knew what the living conditions would be like, they wanted to know how soon they could bring their dependents over. Then it was how soon could they make more rank. By the fifth day, it was the bowling team, and next they had their first sergeant arranging trips to the Fuji View Hotel over the weekends.

When M/Sgt. Hendrickson left for the ZI, Sgt. Frame became the new first sergeant of the 474th. Our field first was SFC Gleason E. Kent, Jr. of Seaside, California. Speculation increased as to what was going to become of the men in our company. Bartasavage said they had the, "Fuchu Fidgets".

The name of the outfit that replaced the 474th was the 16th Communications Construction Squadron. Major Erwin A. Hoag was the commanding officer. They had been stationed in Oklahoma before being sent to Japan.

The men in the 16th could tell us about 3-D movies, which most of us had never seen, but they were at a disadvantage over there because they had no one in their outfit who could show them the ropes about Japan. They had to learn about Japan by experience.

One boy learned too fast. They had hired some Japanese boy-sans to polish shoes, make their beds, and clean up the barracks. This fellow wanted to impress the boy-sans with his importance so that they would do a good job of making his bed. Now, the Japanese use the equivalent of "number one" to mean the very best, which is *ichi ban* in Japanese. So he went to great length to show them how he wanted the bed made. Every so often he would tap himself on the chest and say, "Me *dame*", which he thought meant "number one". Each time the boy-sans would have fits of laughter. *Dame* in Japanese means "no good".

Another fellow learned how the Japanese store human waste in open concrete cess pools at the edge of their fields. The "honey bucket" man goes to town leading oxen or horse which pulls a narrow, flat-bedded wagon. On the wagon are the wooden honey buckets.

He stops his wagon in front of the house he will be working at, unloads the buckets he will need plus a long handled dipper, usually ties a towel over his mouth and nose if it is warm, and is ready to go to work.

The human excrement is dipped from the cess pool and poured into the wooden buckets. Some straw is generally stuck over the rim of the bucket so that there will be a tight fit when the lid is put on. The straw serves a double purpose. It keeps the lid from slipping in and makes it easier to get the lid off again.

When the buckets are full and the cart loaded, it is hauled out to his land where it is dumped into the storage place. Later, the farmer will dip it into a bucket suspended on each side of a yoke and carry it to the field where he will dip it onto the ground around his plants.

This boy, I believe, was trying to guide the driver of a truck in turning around. At any rate, he apparently had stepped up on a storage sump to get a better look down the road and went in up to his neck. They say he rode back in the truck stark naked.

He will be leery of backing into something the rest of his life. However, he wasn't as bad as the fellow in our company. Almost every time this boy got drunk, he managed to fall into a honey bucket hole with at least one leg. He declared the Japanese people got so they would cross the street holding their noses when they saw him coming.

In spite of the fact that the 16th Communications Squadron lacked military discipline from an Army standpoint, they had some good men. Their first sergeant, Glen L Moss from Okmulgee, Okla. was friendly, cooperative, hard working, and I might add, the most overworked man in the outfit. Henri A. Gervais (mail clerk) of Pawtucket, RI was certainly one of the most reliable.

Some of the others were: Lowell D. Elkins (chief clerk) of Texarkana, Ark.; Marion W. Felmet (finance) of Bennington, Okla.; Clarence E. Foster (morning reports) of Montgomery, Ala.; Paul A. Russell (records) of Reading, Mass.; Alvin N. Carlson of Madison, Wisc; and Harold E. Weir of Kokomo, Ind., both in operations.

There were also William M. Tooke, Sr. from Tulsa, Okla.; Ernest D. Norton of LaCenter, Wash.; Olaf M. Berentson of Boone, Ia.; Ronald D. Hartzell of South Nampa, Id.; Gaylord L. Noorlun of Ada, Okla.; and Thomas W. Gehret of Johnstown, Pa.

When word came down that the 474th was to receive a Meritorious Unit Commendation, we began to drill in company formation in preparation for the event. However it looked as though we had drilled in vain, for the presentation was to be on Saturday morning, and storm warnings for typhoon "Tess" went up on Friday. All Friday afternoon and evening there were high winds and rain.

Saturday dawned calm and bright. It was a beautiful day. The atmosphere was so clear that distant Fujiyama was visible practically all day. The only signs of the typhoon were the leaves and branches on the ground and some lines down in places.

At 0700 hours, we fell out in the company area in full dress uniform complete with our orange scarves. We got into buses and rode over to FEAMCOM Air Station. It turned out that we were the only Army unit to be present.

Captain Leddon marched us to the far left of the reviewing stand that was built on a runway behind some hangers. Air Force units began to arrive and continued to do so until there were about twenty outfits lined up down the runway to the left of us. Then the band marched out and took up a position on our right.

After going through the customary formalities for the benefit of the General, the band began to play as Captain Leddon and Arthur Brogley, the Guidon carrier, marched down to the reviewing stand.

The Citation was read as follows:

The 474th Signal Aviation Construction Company, Far East Logistical Force, distinguished itself by exceptionally meritorious conduct in the performance of outstanding service to the United Nations, from 1 August 1952 to 31 May 1953. During that period, the personnel of this company made an outstanding contribution to the successful accomplishment of the Far East Air Forces mission through their construction, repair, rehabilitation and maintenance of communications systems throughout the theater. Demonstrating keen technical proficiency and close attention to duty, the Company accomplished prodigious construction feats despite operational obstacles, extreme weather conditions and the necessity of operating at many different locations. In addition to the major projects accomplished in Misawa, Iwo Jima and at locations in Korea, the Company performed various duties for Communications Squadrons at widely scattered locations in the theater, consistently demonstrating cooperative spirit and productive team effort. Through their collective diligence and determination in discharging urgent responsibilities imposed by combat operations, and through their outstanding resourcefulness and devotion to the best interests of the military service, the personnel of the 474th Signal Aviation Construction Company greatly enhanced the effectiveness and capability of communications systems in the Far East Air Forces, and the United States Air Force.

Following the reading, Major General Paul E. Ruestow, Commander of the Far East Air Logistic Force, "in the name of the President of the United States as public evidence of deserved honor and distinction", tied a red streamer inscribed "KOREA" signifying the award of a Meritorious Unit Citation on our guidon. This streamer is still in the hands of our reunion committee and is displayed at the annual reunions. All members of the 474th during that period are entitled to wear a small wreath embroidered on a cloth patch on the lower right sleeve of their uniform.

After the presentation, the Captain and Brogley returned and took their places in front of the company. The band led off, followed by the 474th and the other outfits, and marched in review past the General. It was very impressive.

One afternoon, I took a long walk down the road leading to Tachikawa to take a few pictures. As I was returning, I passed a new elementary school house. Many times I had noticed the progress the workers were making as they constructed the building. Now the school was completed even to the point of being painted two toned, which is a rarity. This made the building a nice contrast to the drab unpainted homes and shops nearby.

It was a long, narrow, single storied building. Length wise it ran north and south. A narrow hallway ran the length of the building on the west side and along the south side making the hall L-shaped. There was a hinged door at each end of the L.

However, the main entrance was centered on the east side of the building. It opened into a vestibule about the size of one of the classrooms. There was a stair at the back, for this part of the school was two storied. The principal's office may have been up there. On each side of the vestibule were shelves where the students could leave their *geta* while in class.

The main source of light came from the windows on the east side, but there were windows on the on the west side as well, that enabled light to pass across the hallway and into the room.

There were three rooms on each side of the entrance. The grades seemed to go progressively higher in each room as they went from north to south. There was even a small laboratory located just north of the entrance.

Each room was equipped with many small tables hardly a foot and a half high. There were two small straight-backed chairs at each table. An eighteen-inch high blackboard ran the length of the room and was placed surprisingly close to the floor. A few characters were written on some of the boards.

One or two of the rooms had crayon drawings made by the children, tacked around the room. Also, there was a colorful paper chain crisscrossing a room from its corners to the electric light in the center. It reminded me of an elementary classroom in America.

Since April of 1947, boys and girls have been able to attend classes together in all grades from primary through high school. Before that, girls went to separate schools and even had different textbooks. Also, women could not attend the universities. Women are encouraged to attend college now, but as of the time of this writing, most universities had neither the facilities nor the curriculum to accommodate them. Male students had a tendency to ignore the female students or to treat them indifferently.

Most students lived in the city around the university because there were very few dormitories. They generally ate the food they brought from home rather than buy it on the campus.

Social life was practically nonexistent except for departmental clubs. There were no professional coaches or athletic directors although most schools had athletic competitions.

As usual in almost every case, the Japanese people knew that Showamae was going "off limits" several weeks before we received official word of it. The narcotics peddling and prostitution must have been getting out of hand. Even at that it should have been off limits months before.

It was interesting, but pitiful, at times to read in some American newspapers how the morals situation in Japan was exaggerated. I have never seen an American "morals report", but cannot imagine how it could have been exaggerated.

Several months ago we read an article about what someone called a "sex circus" at Chitose. The high official that was sent to investigate this and other reports didn't even go to Chitose, but he declared that it was all "exaggerated". Some of our men who have been to Chitose say otherwise.

Tachikawa also had a "sex circus", I'm told. There was a place the men called the "Turkey Farm" where every obscene and abnormal sexual activity imaginable was performed before an audience. It was placed off limits several times, but only for periods of short duration.

Though these places are widely known to the GI's, they are too obscene to be popular with the majority of the men except on a one-time basis. The men seem to shy away from the girls who take part in these demonstrations. Nevertheless, I'm told that the "Turkey Farm" is always full to capacity.

What was the matter with the investigators that the authorities sent to Japan? Were they being duped on carefully guided tours and false information, or were they deliberately misrepresenting the obvious facts when they returned to the States?

CHAPTER XIII

Nikko

Richard Scott and I picked a wonderful time of the year to visit Nikko. It was the middle of October.

It took us about an hour to get from Tachikawa to Kanda, a suburb of Tokyo. From there we had to go to Ueno station, another suburb. From Ueno, it took three and three-quarter hours to reach Nikko, which is a small city approximately one hundred miles north of Tokyo.

I was a little surprised at the Japanese on this train. They are usually ultra conservative and rarely eat in public, but as lunchtime rolled around, they began to behave like kids at a picnic. At each station stop, some of them would lean out the open windows and call, "*Bentoya-san*", which I didn't understand for some time. Finally I realized that they wanted *kisha bento* or train lunch.

The person, usually a woman, selling *kisha bento* would hurry up with a basket or cart loaded with small wooden boxes, oranges, tangerines, soft drinks, and small pottery containers full of tea and covered by a small cup of the same ceramic material.

Two of the wooden boxes usually made up the lunch. One box would contain *osushi* or boiled rice flavored with vinegar. The other box might contain a piece of fish and several types of vegetable. Another delicacy might be a rice roll covered with fish or a vegetable and wrapped in nut-flavored seaweed.

Nikko is a shrine city that contains the most beautiful and famous shrines in Japan. Mere words cannot describe the magnificence of some of those ancient gates and temples.

After leaving the train station, Scott and I walked some distance through the town to the temple area that was located somewhat behind the town.

For twenty-four miles along the main road into Nikko there are giant Japanese cedars or Cryptomeria trees on each side of the highway. Some have been destroyed due to various natural causes, but nevertheless there are more than 15,000 trees still living of the original 18,404 trees.

Some three hundred years ago, Masatsuna Matsudaira, *daimyo* or lord of Kawagoe, made an offering of *sugi* (cedar) sprouts to the Toshogu shrine. In addition, he and his followers planted and cared for the trees. Other local *daimyo* made offerings of *torii*, or *ishi-doro* (stone lanterns), or money. Matsudaira-san, however, was too poor to make such an expensive gift, and so humbly donated the trees and labor to care for them.

On the other side of the road that runs in front of the temple area is a bright red bridge that spans the Daiya River. There is a locked gate to keep people from walking on it, for it can only be crossed on April 17, June 2, and October 17, and then only by the Imperial Messenger's procession.

This "Sacred Bridge" is ninety-three feet long, and is often called the "Snake Bridge". According to the legend, a priest named Shodo Shonin saw Mt. Nantai and wanted to climb up and see if a god lived on the mountain. He started out, but soon came to this river which he couldn't cross, so he recited the Buddhist Sutras. Suddenly, an old man appeared on the other side of the river and hurled a red and green snake across. The snakes joined with others and grew large enough to make a bridge.

The priest was now afraid to cross the river on the snakes, so he stopped a farmer, Jimbei Yamasuge, and had him lay sedges over the snakes before he would cross. This supposedly happened twelve hundred years ago. The original bridge was washed away in 1902, but was rebuilt two years later.

From here, Richard and I followed a walk leading back into the temple area. All the temples were constructed without the use of nails. The first temple we came to was the *Sanbutsudo* Temple (Three Buddha's Temple), which is the largest building at Nikko. It is 112 feet long and 84 feet high.

The first Sanbutsudo Temple was built in 848, but it was removed, and when Shintoism separated from Buddhism in 1877, it was torn down.

The present temple was completed in 1887. Inside the temple are three wooden statues painted with gold lacquer. Each one sits on the petals of the lotus, and is about twenty-seven feet high. On the right, as one faces the statues, is *Senji-Kannon* or one thousand-handed Buddha. Actually, there are only forty hands, but each one is supposed to hold twenty-five "good lucks". He will give people anything they want.

The middle Buddha is *Amida Nyorai*. He is the main Buddha. To the left of this is *Bato-Kannon* or horse-headed Buddha. This Buddha protects all animals, but especially the horse.

To the right of the broad steps leading up to this temple is an ancient Japanese cherry tree. Some say that it is four hundred years old.

Behind the *Sanbutsudo* Temple stands a bronze pillar called a *Sorinto*. It was made by a priest, Tenkai Sojo, in 1643 to keep evil spirits away from the temple grounds.

Nearby are two bronze lanterns donated by silk merchants in Osaka, Sakai, and Nagasaki. They sit where they are because in feudal times merchants were in such a low social class, they could not put their gifts on the Toshogu shrine grounds.

After leaving the *Sanbutsudo* Temple grounds, Scott and I turned onto a wide shady street leading to the Toshogu Shrine grounds. This shrine and the tomb of Iyeyasu Tokugawa, the founder of the Tokugawa shogunate, are the main attractions of all the many famous things there are to see at Nikko.

Iyeyasu Tokugawa lived from 1542 until 1616. The Emperor Gomizuno gave him the name Toshogu. Iyeyasu's son Hidetada, the second shogun, had his subjects build a mausoleum at Nikko that was completed in March, 1617 and his ashes were brought there in April.

Yemitsu, grandson of Iyeyasu and the third shogun, thought it was too small and ordered his subjects to rebuild the shrine to its present day size in the year 1624. His scheme was to take so much in the way of contributions to the shrine from the *daimyo* that they could not revolt against him. He must have been successful for the Tokugawa Shogunate maintained peace in Japan for almost three hundred years.

A large stone torii indicated that we were approaching a Shinto shrine. The columns were about three feet in diameter and rose to about thirty feet high. The stones were brought from the southern island of Kyushu by ship in 1618.

Beneath the torii were ten wide stone steps that are called, "one thousand people's steps". This is because one hundred people are supposed to be able to stand on each step and look at the shrine. In feudal days, farmers and merchants could not go beyond the torii so stood on the steps to see.

Nearby stood several beggars or *kojiki* in white kimonos bowing deeply to the people passing by. They all had at least one artificial limb.

Further along on our left stood a five storied pagoda or *gojunoto*. It is a Buddhist symbol, but the Japanese government allowed it to remain as part of the Shinto shrine even after the two were separated. Tadakatsu Sakai contributed the original pagoda in 1650, but it was destroyed by fire in 1815 and rebuilt in 1818. Like Buddhist gravestones, each of the stories represents one of the five elements: sky, wind, fire, water, and earth.

The front gate of the Toshogu Shrine sets at the top of a flight of stairs. It is called "Nio-mon". We had to buy a ticket at a booth at the base of the steps in order to pass through. The ticket also enabled us to see the *Futaarasan* Shrine, *Rinnoji* Temple, and the Treasure Museum.

There is a Korean dog in each of the two rear niches, male and female. The female dog may be recognized because of the horn on her head. Empress Jingu supposedly brought the dogs back from Korea.

Inside the Nio-mon are many lanterns. Most are of stone, some of bronze, and two are of iron.

There is a sacred stable where a white horse used by the emperor was kept. Since the monkey is considered a mascot of the horse, there are many carvings of monkeys on the building. This is where the original of the three monkeys, "See no evil; Hear no evil; and Speak no evil" are carved. The Japanese names are: "*Mi-zaru; Kika-zaru;* and *Iaw-zaru* respectively.

I was surprised to find that these monkeys were just one of eight panels of monkey carvings, and that each lintel represented a period in the life of man.

Lintel number one shows a mother monkey speaking to her baby. The second lintel is the see no evil, hear no evil, and speak no evil carving. They are practicing what their mother taught them. On the third lintel a young monkey is gazing at something in the distance which depicts the ambition of youth. Lintel four is of one monkey looking up and another one looking down. This indicated how social position is nearly limitless. Three monkeys are carved on the fifth lintel. One is weeping over his failure while another tries to console. Another still looks ahead with ambition. The sixth lintel has one monkey hanging from a tree branch and another sitting idle. It means that they have become lazy in mid-life. People recognize in middle life that they can't achieve all of their hopes and wishes and give up trying for them. The seventh lintel shows a monkey approaching water while another attempts to stop him. Although he can't swim, he is going to try. This means that in later life people are likely to take gambling chances. The eighth lintel is a carving of a pregnant monkey which takes one back to the first lintel.

The most beautiful edifice at Nikko is the *Yomeimon* Gate of the Toshogu shrine. It is also called *Higurashi-mon* or "Day spending gate", because one could look at it all day and not grow tired of it. The carvings on all the buildings in the temple area are incredible, but the work done on the *Yomeimon* Gate is even more wonderful.

There are many carvings of dragons and Korean dogs to keep out evil spirits. Also, there are carvings of Chinese saints and others of children. Each group of carvings has its own story.

A statue of an old minister in the imperial court sits in each of the two front niches. They watch the evil-minded people as they walk through. A gilded dog sits in each of the rear niches for the same purpose. The one on the left has a blue mane and tail and the other one has a green mane and tail.

Each compartment of the ceiling is painted with a dragon that won't take its eyes off you. The famous painters, Morinobu and Yasunobu did them.

Except for one thing this gate is recognized to be perfect. The designs on the pillar furthest to the left are upside down. It is said that the builders made this mistake on purpose so as not to incur the wrath of the gods on the shrine.

Connected to each side of the *Yomeimon* Gate are long corridors where *daimyo* once sat for certain ceremonies. Each panel is exquisitely carved from one piece of wood. Pine trees, peacocks, bamboo, flowers, etc. stand out in high relief and are beautifully painted in red, green, gold, and blue.

Nearby is the *Yakushido* temple (Buddha of Medicine). Scott and I left our shoes on the front steps among the dozens of *geta* and walked into the temple. A priest stood across the room. He waited until the room was full; then he had the people kneel down while he praised the virtues of an amulet the temple was selling at the exit.

When he was finished, he asked the people to file through the hallway to his left. A gate was pushed open and the Japanese stampeded. It was dark in the hallway and in the back room, but our eyes soon became adjusted so that we could see a large dragon painted on the ceiling. It must have been forty feet long.

The people were held back just inside the doorway by a rope enclosure. Another priest explained what they were to do, then one at a time he allowed them to stand under the dragon's head and clap their hands together. If they were standing in the right place they would hear the dragon cry. Children and adults alike grew so excited they could hardly wait their turn. Only the priest seemed to be taking the matter seriously.

Scott brought his hands together almost hard enough to shake the building. The roar he got from the dragon caused the Japanese to laugh in appreciation. Some of the children who couldn't clap loud enough to make the dragon cry were still clapping outside of the temple. Yasunobu Kano painted the crying dragon on the ceiling about 1650.

On the lintel of the Sakashita-mon gate, which is the entrance leading up to the tomb of Iyeyasu Tokugawa, is a carving which is known to every school child in Japan. It is a small carving of a sleeping cat that was done by a sculptor named Jingoro Hidari. His last name means "left hand".

He was the most skillful sculptor that ever lived in Japan. So skillful, in fact, that jealous rivals cut off his right hand according to the story. While many great craftsmen made many carvings, Jingoro Hidari made only this one carving at Nikko.

The cat sleeps among peony blossoms, for the sleepiest time of the year is when the peony blooms. The cat reportedly keeps all rats and mice out of the buildings.

The spirit of Mt. Nantai is enshrined in the Futaarasan Shrine. There were bits of paper tied to some of the trees in the area. Each paper had a fortune written on it. If the person who takes one doesn't get one that he or she likes, that person will tie it on a branch and give it back to the god.

A "ghost lantern" stands in the southwest corner of this shrine ground. The story is that a courageous *samurai* was passing the shrine one night when he met a ghost. Instead of fleeing, the *samurai* drew his sword and struck at the ghost until it disappeared. The next morning, the people of Nikko discovered that this lantern had several notches cut in it with a sword. They confined the lantern under a wire cage so that it couldn't molest anyone else.

There just wasn't enough time to see everything. The giant trees began to shade the area too much to get good pictures, and we still had to confirm our reservations at the Nikko-Kanko Hotel. We started back down to the street again.

For 125 *yen* we purchased tickets which would allow us transportation to the small village of Utagahama on Lake Chuzenji. We boarded a bus that took us to *Umagaishi* (horse return), which was a cable car station. People who used to ride horses this far had to send them back when they reached this place because the trail was too steep and narrow for the horse to go further.

Our cable car was almost halfway up the 1200-meter track when another cable car suddenly emerged from a tunnel coming straight at us. At the last moment, both cars swerved out on a bow in the tracks and passed alongside each other.

The angle of the tracks at the steepest point near the top is approximately thirty-seven degrees. The floor of the cable car is stair-stepped in order to compensate for this and have the seats level.

Akechidaira is the name of the upper station. The sun was shining brightly on the mountaintops and the trees were beautiful in their fall colors. We were not able to see any of the monkeys that have been observed among the trees.

There was a long line of people waiting to ride a suspension cable car to *Tenbodai* (Sightseeing Place) on a hill above Akechidaira, so we decided to go up there when we came back.

From Akechidaira, we took a bus the final mile or so to Utagahama, passing through two tunnels on the way.

A hotel bus came after us and took us to the Nikko-Kanko Hotel. It was a long, white, two-story mountain resort situated above Lake Chuzenji. A short walk through the timber led to a boathouse on the edge of the lake. The two-bed rooms all had private baths and rented for three dollars per day at the hotel. Meals in the dining room averaged one dollar per day.

In season, the Nikko-Kanko featured swimming, sailing, hiking, fishing, skiing, and ice-skating. Lake Chuzenji is said to have been stocked with various fish imported from Colorado. There were also areas nearby where hunting was permitted.

The next morning, we were up early to go see Kegon water fall. After breakfast we asked the headwaiter to prepare us box lunches so that we wouldn't have to return for dinner. A Japanese boy said that if we would wait a little while, a hotel bus would take us to the falls. Eventually, we got there. The place was packed with Japanese tourists. Busloads of people were arriving and leaving all the time. Whole classes of school children in their black uniforms and "sailor dresses" were waiting their turn to see.

We worked our way up to a ticket stand where we paid forty yen for an elevator ticket. Then we got in the line of people waiting for the ride down. When the elevator stopped at the bottom, we got out and followed a long, damp, dripping, concrete tunnel that suddenly emerged onto a concrete and steel observation platform near the bottom of the falls.

It was a wonderful place from which to view the falls. The blue sky, the red, greens, and gold of the trees, the water plunging past the lava formations, and the rainbows on the mist were indescribably beautiful.

The dimensions of Kegon waterfall are 330 feet high and 25 feet wide. From about halfway down, twelve small waterfalls spring from the cliff. The name of the waterfall was taken from one of the Sutras of Buddhism.

In May of 1893, a young high school student committed suicide there. Before he jumped, he peeled the bark from a nearby tree and wrote a message on the trunk. His last words must have made a big impression on the Japanese, for it is said that more than a hundred people go there annually intending to take their own lives.

We spent some time down on the platform taking pictures and admiring the scenery. Japanese photographers, professional and amateur, were doing a great business taking pictures of the many groups and individuals with the falls in the background.

Up on top again, curiosity prompted us to follow a wagon trail along the rim of the river gorge and through the woods. We stopped to look at a cable that was fastened to some timbers at the top of the cliff and led to somewhere far below. It was obviously unsafe, but while we were jokingly arguing about who was going to ride it down first, we discovered a crevice in the cliff nearby.

I jumped down into the crevice and climbed down to where a maple tree was growing out of the face of the rock. I had just told Scott that I didn't think we could get down to the river bed from there when he squeezed past where I was gripping the tree trunk and began pussy footing across a narrow projection under the overhanging ledge.

It was easier going after we got past the overhang, but our rubber soled boots would have provided us with a more secure footing than our slick soled low quarters. We emerged from the undergrowth under a concrete bridge that spanned a swift flowing stream from *Shirakumo* Falls (White Clouds Fall). Here, we followed a walk with steps the rest of the way down.

By leaping from boulder to boulder, we crossed the stream and followed the opposite bank around a bend so that we could take full-length pictures of Kegon Falls. We ate our box lunch sitting on a huge boulder in mid-stream. The falls seemed more beautiful every time we looked at it from a new location. Climatic conditions in those mountains, together with the greater variety of plants, had brought out the fall colors much more than around Tachikawa.

Further downstream, an old woman, all alone, wearing drab *mompei* and a scarf over her head, was sifting sand and gravel through a screen. We speculated on what it would be used for, but we would never know for sure.

After lunch we followed the trail back up the way we had come until we reached the bridge. Crossing the bridge, we wound around hillsides on a well-defined trail until we arrived at a point slightly above the observation platform.

Rather than go back, we decided to ride up in the elevator again. The ticket taker at the top was surprised that we didn't have tickets. Scott explained to him in English with elaborate gestures that we didn't have tickets because we climbed down. He didn't understand, and the discussion was holding up the line so he motioned for us to go on.

The hotel telephone operator phoned us at 0630 hours the next morning according to our plan. We ate breakfast, checked out, and the hotel bus took us as far as *Akechidaira* to catch the cable car to *Tenbodai*, the sightseeing place higher up the mountain. We decided to walk up. We left our bags at the station house and started up the steep incline.

From up above, the station house looked like a small airplane hanger. Looking in the opposite direction, we had a magnificent view of Lake Chuenji, Kegon Falls, Shirakumo Falls, and Mt. Nantai. The whole area was surrounded with multi-colored tree covered hills. Autumn is the perfect time of the year to visit Nikko and vicinity.

An interesting incident occurred on the train between Nikko and Tokyo. The train didn't have seats facing to the front and rear as the train had that we came up on. Instead it had the more common bench type seat that extended along each side the full length of the car. The seats could be raised in order to gain access to a small compartment under them.

As the train came to a halt at one station, a group of Japanese police boarded it for a raid. With one or two men to each car, they made a methodical search, mostly under the seats. The people sitting in each section of a seat didn't make any move to rise until the officer asked them to. The policeman in our car examined all of the compartments except the section where Scott, several Japanese, and myself were seated. He then went into the next car. While he was gone, I asked the fellow next to me what they were looking for. He replied the equivalent of "black market rice".

Shortly, he came back with the officer from the next car. I understood them to say they had found nothing. However Richard and I stood up and motioned for them to look in our compartment. They were full of apologies, but they were glad not to have had to ask us to stand up in order to examine it.

There was a big demand for black market rice in Tokyo and other large cities. Rice was the only food item still rationed in Japan. Reiko told me that two hundred yen would buy enough rice to last one person for three days on the legitimate market.

CHAPTER XIV

Showa III

Loren Bacon was the first man from the Company that we met when we reached Showa. He had just returned from Korea. He, Fritz Huffine, Dale E. Wendlandt, of Hillsdale, Wisc. and Andrew Raney had gone to Korea on August 22nd. They had split into pairs over there. Bacon and Huffine were together, and Wendlandt and Raney were together in another crew. Their plane had stopped in Pusan, and they had seen Seoul and much of the little bit there was to see in that part of Korea. They didn't like it at all.

Wendlandt and Raney returned to Showa several weeks before Bacon and Huffine. Raney had shown me some of the snapshots he had taken of some of the buildings in Seoul. There were many bullet holes visible in the larger buildings. The Koreans dressed differently from the Japanese. They wore a shallow slipper rather than a *geta*. The women often wore long skirts that practically came up to their armpits. A short jacket or blouse covered the rest of their body. The children were often filthy and caked with dirt. The youngest ones were naked or simply wore a shirt. They saw bearded old men in top hats and white robes.

A week or two after his return, Bacon had CQ duty. We sat in the office for some time discussing what he had seen and done while in Korea. He also mentioned how dirty and uncared for the children were that he had seen. They would steal anything. Once he saw a small boy lift the pen and pencil from the shoulder pocket of a sergeant as he bent over to get in his jeep. They approached the GI's on the street to ask for candy and cigarettes, or if he wanted a woman.

Pickpockets were numerous and the black-market was an enormous business. Koreans walked around the fenced tent compounds wanting to get anything for the GI's in exchange for American clothes, food, or equipment. Many of them were just waiting to cut the fence so that they could sneak in and steal anything they could lay their hands on in the tents.

There was a whole street or alley in Seoul that was lined on both sides with booths handling black-market items. They had all kinds of military clothing, blankets, boots, field equipment, and even jeep tires, Bacon said. When a blackmarketeer was asked the price of a particular item, he or she always asked, "In *hwon* or script?" They preferred to be paid in MPC. Bacon said that he saw one woman with a roll of American money that must have amounted to three hundred dollars. One hundred eighty *hwon* was the exchange rate for the dollar at that time.

Some of the Koreans were living in houses constructed of sticks, mud, and C-ration boxes. The main means of transportation was the A-frame. A cooley could carry a prodigious load on his back. He saw men along the road with their A-frames piled eight to ten feet high with hay, so that they looked like a walking hay stack. Women carried everything balanced on their heads.

Bacon got to see a buddy, William Blue from Indiana, who was in a tank corps. Blue told him that the North Koreans had beat on their tanks with sticks trying to find a hole in which to drop in a grenade.

The Koreans had an interesting way of using our empty beer cans. They would flatten the cans and fasten them together some way. Then they would run them through a machine that looked like a wringer. This corrugated the cans into sheets about four by eight feet in size. One could still read the labels on the cans.

By the end of October everyone was back in the company. It was very crowded with everyone packed into one barracks, but food was plentiful and good, and many of the men had their hopes high that the whole company might go to the States as an intact unit. Actually we were living in a rather cheerful and optimistic atmosphere.

On the last day of October we had an extra large payroll. Captain Cole and I went over to the finance office at Tachikawa early in the morning to pick it up. Usually, on payday there wouldn't be very many men in the company. Checks would be made out for the men on TDY and we would just have to mail them or have an officer hand carry them to the crews. This time we were going to pay everyone in the company in cash. Fortunately, the company had been losing strength due to men rotating back to the States, but there were still a lot of men left.

The cashier counted out the packages of MPC for our payroll plus four hundred dollars worth of *yen* (Y 144,000). He tossed it into a bag which Captain Cole and I took into a nearby room to count. We opened each package and counted each bill. There was nearly $17,000 worth of MPC.

When we got back to the company, we had to count out the MPC for each man and put it into his envelope that was previously marked with how much he was to receive. We kept the envelopes from one pay-day to the next. By reusing them we could find any mistakes before the men lined up. Also, the men didn't have to stand in line so long.

All of the *yen* had to be counted out in ten-dollar piles and be stapled together. If we came out short on the last pile, we had to go through all the piles to find which one had too much. We always went to great lengths to come out right the first time.

The men signed the payroll as they came in the door. Then they walked over and reported to Captain Cole, who removed the money from their envelope, counted it, and handed it to each man to count for himself. The man then went to the next table where he could buy *yen* if he desired to. Finally, either Bruder or Bartasavage collected a certain amount to pay the indigenous personnel such as the janitors and KP's. As a formality, either Wendtlandt or James W. Trapp of Peak, S.C. sat by with a carbine as guard.

We had money in our company fund, which we had to start using up, so in the afternoon we had a big company party. Our men had built a large fireplace and a long wide barbecue pit of stones less than five months before. Both were located in a shady area across the road from the athletic field.

The food was certainly delicious. There were large barbecued steaks, fried chicken, baked beans, potato salad, cake, lemonade, etc. Also, there were a few cases of hard and soft Japanese drinks.

Northwest of the company area and across the road was a place called the Showa Country Club. Actually, it was just a miniature golf course and a golf driving range. M/Sgt. David O. Wilson of the 474th designed the course in 1952. Volunteers helped construct it from available surplus materials at no direct cost to the government. The balls and golf clubs were provided free on the miniature golf course, while there was a fee of fifteen cents per bucket of balls for the driving range. This fee paid the wages of a Japanese boy-san that took care of the course and gathered the balls from the driving range.

1ˢᵗ/Sgt. George Frame had known for a long time that I had an abiding interest in plants. Whether we met at Misawa, Kashii, or in the company, the conversation usually came around to plants. One day our talk drifted around to growing plants in nutrient solutions, and I commented that I would like to see the hydroponics farm at Chofu if I had some way to get over there.

Frame asked if I thought anyone else in the company would want to see it too. If so, he might be able to arrange transportation if I would make the arrangements for a tour of the farm at Chofu.

I arranged to have forty men tour the place the following week and Frame borrowed 6-by's from the 16ᵗʰ Comm. Sq. to take us over. Chofu is near Tokyo.

The Tokyo Quartermaster Depot, 8080th Army Unit, managed the Hydroponics Farming Center. Hydroponics is derived from the Greek word *hydro* meaning water and *ponic* meaning work. Thus the name given to the system of growing plants in a nutrient solution without soil.

Soon after the Japanese occupation started, the Army discovered that it needed a nearby source from which it could obtain fresh, but perishable vegetables. It was practically impossible to get clean salad vegetables from the Japanese because of their practice of fertilizing their field with human excrement. The danger, of course, was from the eggs of intestinal parasites carried in the uncooked salad fruits and vegetables.

During WW II the Army had set up successful hydroponics farms on Ascension Island, Iwo Jima, and British Guinea. So the farms were soon started at Chofu and at Otsu. Chofu is the larger farm. The first vegetables were harvested from the gravel beds in 1947. It wasn't until the Korean War started that they began operating on a large scale.

Not all of the vegetables produced at Chofu are raised in the gravel beds, however. As we drove through the guarded gate, it seemed that all of the fields within the enclosed area were planted in crops. The guide later explained that the vegetables growing in the fields were planted in "purified soil", *i.e.* soil that had been specially treated to kill any organisms which might be harmful to humans.

The guide told us that the hydroponics section consisted of ten open plots and one greenhouse plot. A plot was an area of five acres. One five-acre plot contained 87 beds that were 300 feet long. Each bed was further divided into three separate sections that were set at successively lower levels. The upper section was 120 feet long, the middle section was 100 feet long, and the lower section was 80 feet long. The beds were all filled with fine gravel.

At the lower end of the plots were large sump tanks. It was here that the chemicals for the nutrient solution are mixed. The six main elements in the nutrient solution are nitrogen, phosphorus, potassium, sulfur, calcium, and magnesium. In addition, small amounts of the trace elements were added. They are copper, zinc, iron, boron, and manganese. Great caution must be exercised in adding these trace elements to the solution because they are necessary to the plants in very small amounts. If their concentration in the solution is too much in excess of the plant's requirements, they can be extremely toxic to the plants.

After the chemicals are mixed in the sump tank, the solution is then pumped to a header tank at the upper end of the plot. This is about the only mechanical operation. Once the solution is pumped to the header tank, the beds are irrigated by gravity.

The solution may be turned into the upper bed section until it is filled to about one inch below the surface of the gravel. When this level is reached, a hose may be dropped and the solution will flow by gravity into the next section. After the third and lowest section has been filled, the connecting hoses are dropped and the solution drains into a collector ditch which in turn flows into the sump tank. Normally the beds are irrigated three times a day.

The greenhouse plots were very similar to the open plots except the entire five acres were covered with glass. It was one of the largest greenhouses in the world at that time. Most of the plants grown in the open plots and soil fields were propagated in the greenhouse and later planted outside. The vegetables grown on the farm were: lettuce, radishes, cabbage, cucumbers, onions, parsley, chard, peppers, eggplant, leeks, green beans, cauliflower, and tomatoes. A few of these are only grown to maturity on the soil plots.

Acre for acre, hydroponics farms can produce a greater yield with a somewhat shorter growing season than a soil farm. At Chofu it is possible to get three crops a year. Most of the vegetables are sent to troops in Korea while the excess is eaten in mess halls in Japan.

How is the farm operated? Japanese employees, mostly women, do the seeding and transplanting. The chemical laboratory, staffed with Japanese technicians, constantly checked the nutrient balance of the plot solutions and made recommendations depending on their analysis. A team of horticulturists, entomologists, and plant pathologists daily tour the entire farm in search of disease and insects. A spray team acts on the advice of these men as to where and when to apply an insecticide or fungicide.

The farm has its own packing shed, vegetable chill room, and ice plant. The farm has harvested as much as 150,000 pounds of vegetables, washed them, packed them, and shipped them out in one day.

When we got back to the Company later in the afternoon, we heard where the majority of the men in the Company were going to be sent when the 474th broke up. It was to be the 802nd Engineer Aviation Battalion stationed at Itazuke on Kyushu Island.

The office personnel would have to remain behind until the Company officially ended sometime in January. About twenty men would stay for normal rotation since their MOT date was near at hand. All the other men would start south in about a week.

The *Shichi-go-san* festival occurred on November 15th of that last week. A tour left the service club to visit a shrine in Tokyo. *Shichi-go-san* literally means "Seven-five-three". Parents with children of these ages go to a shrine to give thanks to the child's tutelary deity that the child has reached one of these ages. This festival is believed to be over four hundred years old.

A boy is usually allowed to wear a *hakama* or pleated skirt for the first time when he attends this festival during his fifth year of age. When seven years old, a girl usually receives her first *obi* or sash to wear to the festival.

A Shinto priest at the shrine read an address followed by a prayer for continued patronage for the children. Then the children filed through the shrine and were given gifts or charms. The boys were receiving a twig with leaves on it and a small arrow. Open stands all around the shrine area were selling *ame*, a confection that chews like taffy and comes in round sticks less than half an inch in diameter and a foot or more in length. The candy is put into elongated paper bags on which various lucky symbols are painted. The symbols were: a crane, tortoise, pine, bamboo, plum, and an old man and woman called *Takasago-no-jijibaba*. The man carried a rake and the woman a broom for the purpose of raking in good luck and sweeping out evil respectively.

The crane is believed to live 1000 years and the tortoise 10,000 years. They symbolize long life and youthfulness. The plum indicates vigor because it will bloom even with snow on the ground.

It is interesting to see the small boys wearing *hakama* because in modern times they are seldom seen except when worn by old men.

The little girls are truly lovely in their gorgeous kimonos. They usually have their faces powdered ghostly white and wear red coloring only on their lower lip according to the old custom.

We all ran out of film shooting pictures of the children. The parents were justifiably proud of their youngsters and eager to have them pose, but the kids didn't know what to think about it.

There was still $396.03 in the company fund, so a committee made arrangements for one last party at the Golden Dragon restaurant in Tachikawa. At 1730 hours, we got into 6-by's and rode over. Edward Speights of Birmingham, Ala. started calling Jody cadence at the top of his voice as the truck pulled out, and when he ran out of wind, someone else took it up. The noise and gayety even made the Japanese turn and stare. Bennie Davis was laughing so hard the tears ran down his cheeks.

For dinner we had a banquet of steak, French fried potatoes, corn and peas, shrimp cocktail, apple pie, and a martini.

Japanese steaks are famous for their tenderness and flavor. Each head of cattle is shown every consideration before it is slaughtered. It is closely penned and fed all of the nutritious food it will eat for two weeks before it is killed. It is not allowed to exercise, but every day the animal is given a massage with special attention paid to the regions of choice cuts. Besides all of this tenderizing care, the beef has an unexcelled opportunity to age to perfection in the inadequately refrigerated Japanese markets. Japanese beef was good and safe.

Captain Leddon was called upon for a speech. In closing, he advised the men, "Remember that you have done a fine job, but when you get down there, don't make yourselves obnoxious by always mentioning how you used to do something in the 474th. Most of the men down there have been in Korea and have done a fine job too." He thanked everyone, and concluded, "Delinquency has been surprisingly low – believe it or not. This has been a good company."

The last few days were pretty hectic. There were all kinds of work to be done that couldn't be finished until the last minute. Transportation had to be arranged, orders cut, shipping orders worked out, partial pay given to the men shipping, etc. In the barracks the men were trying to squeeze all of their belongings into their duffel bags; and packing boxes of extra clothes and souvenirs that had accumulated to be sent home.

Everyone was restricted to the base the last night because they had had a physical and "short arm" that day. However, there was hardly anyone in the barracks later in the evening. Almost everyone was down at the service club or at the Airman's Club. Later, practically everyone was at the service club – even Captain Leddon.

There were several "fifths" from the Airman's Club "floating" around in paper sacks at the service club. The contents were added to cokes on the sly. There was ice cream and cake to eat also.

Unfortunately I left soon after the ice cream and cake was served, thereby missing out on some of the excitement. A couple of AP's came into the service club and tried to take one of the largest men in the 474th outside. He wasn't intoxicated or causing any trouble and he didn't want to leave. One of the AP's caught him by the coat and backed him against the wall. Another fellow tried to break the AP's grip, so the second AP hit him across the mouth with his nightstick and knocked him down. The people that saw all of this, sober and otherwise, didn't approve. They began to crowd around threateningly. One of the AP's pulled his automatic and slipped a cartridge into the chamber for additional support. They then handcuffed the big boy and took him and his friend, whom they had bloodied up, to the station.

Meanwhile, Captain Leddon was called back to the service club by Jeanne Langdon who warned him that trouble was brewing. He ordered Alpheus O. Kearney of Norlina, N.C. to fall the rest of the 474th out and march them back to the Company. The Captain left them and went down to the guardhouse. He said that when he got back he had better find everyone in bed. Such a scurrying as there was then! It was almost comical to see the sober and near sober men trying to get the drunk ones in bed and keep them quiet. Everyone was so excited they couldn't keep quiet or sit still long enough to unlace their boots. One fellow kept saying that he had never seen the "Old Man" so mad. Two or three fellows were "heaving their guts out".

From what we heard later, the "Old Man" really chewed AP's that night. He brought the two men back to the Company, and then he walked around the barracks until nearly everyone was asleep.

Someone told me that some men from the 97th AAA who witnessed the trouble, ran back to their outfit and began organizing a mob to try to free the two men held by the AP's. They also had to be quieted.

Meanwhile at the Airman's Club, a boy from the 16th Comm. Sq. was on duty as "sergeant at arms" when a boy from the 474th began breaking glasses and throwing them across the room. He said he was almost afraid to do anything, but another fellow from the 474th, Daniel H. McDowell of Pepperell, Mass., picked him up like a bag of feathers, and carried him outside at arm length in front of him.

The next day dawned early. Reveille was at 0500 hours, and we were at work in the office an hour later. The Captain came in with his usual enthusiasm. When discussing the previous night, he said rather proudly, "Boy, what a rifle company they would make".

Half of the men were to ship at 0830 hours. They loaded their bags on the buses that would take them to the train station. They didn't seem so excited then. Maybe they were feeling the after effects of the night before, but more likely, they hated to leave.

Captains' Cole and Leddon and everyone else saw them off. Afterward, Captain Leddon came in the office and paced the floor with his hands clasped behind his back as if he didn't know what to do. Captain Cole suggested that they go for coffee.

The second half of the troop movement left at 1645 hours. We all saw them off again. Captain Leddon commented to Cole, "There goes the 474th – and a chapter in history. It was one of a kind." There weren't many of us left. We began eating in the 6412th Area "A" Consolidated Dining Hall at noon.

Fritz Huffine and I went to a show in the evening, and later stopped by the service club for "Dagwood sandwiches", but it seemed almost too lonely. We went back to a practically empty barracks. It also was lonely, but nice and quiet for once. From out of the darkness at the other end of the room, I heard Huffine comment, "Fifteen months I've been waiting for this night."

CHAPTER XV

The Official End

There was considerably less work to do now that there were only about thirty men left in the Company. Within a week, George Frame, Ronald M. Bartley of Salem, Ill., James Davis, John Pupplo, and Douglas Taylor of Blue River, Kentucky, went to Fuchu for return to the ZI. Also, Captain Papp and Major Edward A. Sweeney of Alexandria, Va., returned to the States. We seldom saw anything of Major Sweeney except around payday. He was on permanent TDY (temporary duty) at Yokohama. Clement Riha became first sergeant when Frame left.

In the afternoons and evenings we often had time for some interesting discussions. Once the talk came around to a strange pagan ceremony that one of the men in the office had witnessed at a shrine on the road between Nagoya and Komaki Air Base. He called it the "Fertility Shrine".

Many of the men in the company had seen the shrine and festival during the time they were on TDY at Komaki. Some had shot pictures of the affair (some of the pictures had purposely been blurred by the Japanese who printed them, they said), and one fellow had even brought back a large carved souvenir of what he had seen.

On the occasion of the fertility festival, people flock to the shrine grounds as participants and spectators. From a small building, fifty or more carved human penises of all sizes are removed and carried on the shoulders of the persons who want their infertility cured. The largest penis, approximately five feet long, is carried on the shoulders of four men to the "Fertility Shrine". Here the people throw money into a box, clap their hands, and pray for fertility.

I could understand GI's going to watch something like that, but I was curious if many foreign women attended. He replied that everyone goes, but only the American women turn away and blushed.

On the day before Thanksgiving the Captain got another pre-trial investigation. It was another sodomy case. We made recordings of the investigation all that day, but we didn't have time to take it all off the tape, which meant that Scozzaro and I had to spend Thanksgiving morning taking it down on paper.

Early Thanksgiving morning we had the worst earthquake that I had noticed while in Japan. The tremors and noise woke me from a sound sleep. Suddenly, I felt the bed shaking as if someone were trying to wake me. At the same time I heard a loud noise that sounded like hail on a tin roof.

I sat up to see who was shaking the bed, but then it occurred to me that it was an earthquake. Across the aisle I could see a whole row of white T-shirts sitting up in bed. I asked what time it was and Robert Berger replied that it was 0250 hours. The barracks seemed to shake for a full two minutes.

As I went back to sleep I thought what a strange noise for an earthquake to make, for I had noticed the stars were shining. It never occurred to me until morning that our barracks didn't have a tin roof and anyway the attic would deaden any sounds from above.

Then I realized what had caused the noise. All the empty metal wall lockers had been "walking" around on the concrete floor of the barracks. We hadn't heard the noise during any previous light earthquake because the lockers had been full and heavy enough to sit solidly on the floor.

Bennie Davis said that during the quake he had watched the street lights out on the road. If they went out, he was going to move on out of there fast.

Bennie Davis, Robert Berger, Ezekiel Gilmore, Jr. of Calvert, Texas, Howard D. Coil of Jefferson, Iowa, and Stanley Ridlon left for Fuchu early Thanksgiving morning, and Tommy H. Spaulding of Middletown, Pa. was sent to Itazuke.

We had a wonderful Thanksgiving dinner. It lasted from noon until after supper. One could come in at any time, or several times, and eat. The menu read: turkey and noodle soup, soda crackers, sautéed wafers, shrimp cocktail, roast young tom turkey, Virginia baked ham, poultry dressing, cranberry sauce, cream giblet gravy, snow flake potatoes, candied sweet potatoes, fresh whole grain corn, fresh green beans, celery hearts, lettuce wedges, assorted salad dressings, assorted pickles and olives, assorted candies and minced nuts, fresh apples and oranges, fruit cake, mince meat pie, pumpkin pie, Parker House rolls, bread, butter, fruit punch, and coffee and cream.

One Sunday afternoon, Scozzaro, Close, Riha, and I went for a jeep ride in the mountains toward Mitake. It was rather cool in the open jeep, but the scenery was still beautiful even though it was almost December. The small-leafed Japanese maples were a bright crimson.

Not all of the people around there had to pump their water from wells. Many of the houses obviously had running water. Bamboo poles, two inches or more in diameter, were used to convey water from nearby springs to the house.

In order for water to pass through the stem, the nodes or joints had to be hollowed out. This was done by cutting a thin section down the length of the bamboo. Through this opening a sharp knife or chisel could be used to open up each node. Then the thin section was wired back in place to complete the homemade water pipe.

We stopped along the road to watch some Japanese foresters bring pine logs down from a mountain to the road. There was a deep gorge with a river between the mountain where they were cutting and the road. The logs were brought down one at a time on a suspension cable and piled on a platform next to the road to be hauled away by truck.

When the Japanese harvest the pine growing on a mountainside, they leave great patches where it looks like a giant razor had swiped it off clean. There were no visible stumps, and from a distance, one can't see any vegetation at all on the denuded slopes. However, timber is too valuable a product to the Japanese for them to leave the slope bare for very long or even to wait for nature to reforest it. They replant the patch with seedling trees, row on row, close together, as soon as possible.

As we drove back, we saw a couple threshing rice beside their house with an electric threshing machine. I had wanted to get a picture of one for some time, so Scozzaro stopped and we all went in.

They were just finishing up, but they were very proud of their thresher and were glad to let us take pictures of it. The man and his wife (she looked fifteen years older than he) gave us a demonstration on how the teeth on the rotating drum pulled the grain from the straw. They were very friendly. As we drove away, I thought how lucky they were to have a machine like that. Some of the Japanese were still threshing their grain by beating it with a strap attached to the end of a stick.

Largely due to the efforts of Captain Cole to get the final twenty-one men, nearly due for return to the States, home in time for Christmas, they left the company on December 11th. They were: Park Close; Joseph Day; Merwin R. Flagg, of Santa Rosa, Calif.; Clement Riha; H. L. Stone, Jr., of Decatur, Texas; Herbert Wilson; Donald Bengtson; William Borrelli; Horace Creary; Angelo DiFrancesco; Richard Gardner; Fritz Huffine; Thomas Kelly; Zenon Mocarski; Don Mooney; Marvin L. Morrow, of Scotia, Nebr.; Jack Shewsbury, of Arista, W. Va.; Dale Wendlandt; Louis Dixon, of Lackawana, NY; Pete Herrera, Jr., of San Antonio, Texas; and Elias B. Swire, of Hackberry, La.

Four or five of them brought in a case or two of canned beer and they sat on their beds drinking it until late at night. They got pretty drunk and kept the others awake for a long time.

The alcohol hadn't worn off by morning and they didn't want to get up. They weren't thinking clearly enough to finish packing their duffel bags and they had left the barracks a mess. One of them had knocked a fire extinguisher off a post and onto an empty bed. The fluid had run out and soaked through the bed. There were beer cans and other junk all over the room and one of them had urinated in a wall locker rather than walk to the latrine. The officers never heard of their escapade on that last night.

Yamataki-san and some boy-sans from the airforce barracks came over to clean up the mess. Later, the 16th Comm. Sq. began to move into their new barracks. The entire remaining 474th Signal Co. (Bartasavage, Noles, Scozzaro, and I) moved into a small room at the northwest corner of the building.

We received some bad news a few days before Christmas. Mrs. John E. Hendrickson wrote that her husband had passed away only six days after he got home. He had had a heart attack while on a hunting trip. The sad news was relayed on to the men who had gone to Itazuke.

A few days before Christmas I was walking down a street in Tachikawa when a gang of little schoolgirls turned into the street ahead of me and proceeded toward me. As they approached they suddenly began to talk excitedly and then became quiet as mice. I thought something was up, for as we passed each other, they were all looking into my face, just as all kids will when they want to say something but are a little afraid. I smiled at them and walked on.

I hadn't gone but a few steps, when one of the little girls bravely came running back. She held out her hand and placed a damp, sticky, piece of Christmas candy in my hand. She then started to run back to where the other little girls were clustered, watching. I called her back and placed two ten *yen* coins in her hand.

It didn't seem possible that Christmas was only a few days off, but suddenly I knew that it was. That sweet little girl left me walking on air the rest of the day.

About this time, the two remaining officers received their assignments. Captain Cole was assigned to the 66th Signal Battalion, Fort Bragg, North Carolina, and Captain Leddon was assigned to the 314th Signal Construction Battalion, Fort Leonard Wood, Mo. Captain Leddon seemed disappointed. It would make his fifth time as a company commander.

Also, I happened to see an order on 1st/Lt. Werner Meyer of Petersburg, Illinois, that came through the office just a few days after I received a card from him. He had requested an extension of his tour and was being reassigned from the 39th Fighter Interceptor Squadron in Korea to the 6408th M.&E. Squadron in Japan. We had roomed together on Green Street in Champaign, Ill., while we were attending the university. Lt. Meyer had graduated as an aeronautical engineer and was commissioned into the Air Force. He had been flying a Sabre jet on missions in Korea.

Many times in the afternoon when all the work was caught up and the office was empty, Reiko, Ishikawa, and I would get into discussions about Japan. Only once in a while would they ever mention World War II, and then it was just to date an event or something like that, but they, like other Japanese, didn't seem to mind answering all kinds of questions about it.

Reiko was a young schoolgirl at the time. She had no idea what the Emperor looked like. His picture was kept in a building near the school, where the children would go to pray to him. Once a year, she said, the picture was removed, but she never saw it because she was bowed to the ground. It wasn't until Hirohito denounced his divinity that she, and millions like her, realized he wasn't a god.

The Japanese newspapers never mentioned their war loses. Not until the day the first American bombers dropped their loads on Tokyo, Yokohama, Osaka, Kobe, and Nagoya, did the people know they weren't winning.

When the occupation troops began to land, Reiko's family fled to the country from Tokyo. Thousands of city people moved to the country in fear. The people were surprised, though, that there were none of the atrocities committed that their leaders had told them would be.

Still, the children and women stayed off the streets, and men peeked from partially open doors at the strange looking American giants passing by. Within a year some of the people began moving back to the cities. Some worked for the terribly high wages the Americans were paying.

Reiko said that many Japanese didn't like their Prime Minister Yoshida, or Britain's Winston Churchill. When I asked if she liked Eisenhower, she replied, "Japanese people liked MacArthur". She wasn't sure whether or not she liked Eisenhower.

She liked the way Americans give women equal rights and the new status of women in Japan as a result of our occupation, but she wasn't sure that it would last after we leave. I wondered myself. I could see many evidences of the Japanese going back to their ancestor's ways. Sometimes it seemed as though the Japanese hadn't grasped the ideas of their human rights and civil liberties. Control seemed to be slipping from them into the hands of the government.

While many small farmers obtained land during the agrarian reform of the occupation, much of it is of such limited area that they can't make a living on it. Consequently, it has changed hands. The rich are growing richer. Maybe the *zaibatsu* are coming back.

The American military occupation of Japan was the most successful in history. We have made impressions on the Japanese and their way of life, both good and bad, which will last from generation to generation.

When I first arrived in Japan I had several opportunities to talk with a number of highly educated Japanese men and women. I was astonished at the way they talked of a Japanese "collapse" when the Americans pulled out. On the surface Japan appeared very prosperous, but it was prosperity based on the Korean War and the foreigners living in or visiting the country. The main effort seemed to be to accumulate American dollars at home by filling war orders, providing mechanics and houseboys, and from sales of consumer goods in their department stores and shops.

At the time this chapter was written (1954), Japan was one of the most densely populated countries in the world, and the population was increasing by more than a million people a year. Following the war, Japan was left with little more territory than its homeland. The natural resources of the main island are limited and insufficient. Consequently Japan must import vast quantities of raw materials in order to maintain an export trade.

We can laugh about it now, but at that time Japan's products were usually more expensive and often inferior in quality to similar Western products. This was due to the high cost of raw materials, to inefficiency, to obsolete machines, and the need for more trained workers to turn out a given product. None of this applies today. Japan has undergone a re-markable recovery thanks to the United States of America.

It didn't seem possible that it could happen so often, but on the day before Christmas the Captain got another pre-trial investigation. This time it was a narcotics charge and the O.S.I. (Office of Special Investigation) presented definite proof in the form of a urinalysis that the boy was guilty. A court martial was recommended.

We had the same wonderful menu for Christmas dinner that we had at Thanksgiving. We filed into the mess hall and the KP's, in paper party hats, piled food on our trays. We took a seat at one of the tables that were lined up end to end. A choir of older Japanese boys and girls sang Christmas songs under the gaily-decorated tree between the tables and near the entrance.

Inside it was Christmas, but outside it was barely cool and there was no snow. I was a little sad. We were separated from our unit. Mail was slow. So far I had only received one Christmas card. I consoled myself that next Christmas I would be home and had even started counting the weeks that I had left in the army.

On January 3rd, I went with the service club tour to Ueno Park in Tokyo. We went through the Art Museum that had a display of modern paintings by Japanese artists. I like Oriental art of some kinds, but those paintings weren't impressive at all. They looked more like Western artists had done them.

The wide gravel plaza leading up to the *Niju-bashi* Bridge which spans the moat to the Emperial Palace grounds was roped off near the street. Japanese police were on guard to keep people from going under the straw rope. Only the day before, the Emperial grounds had been open to the public on one of its annual occasions. Thousands of people were jammed into the areaway waiting to cross the bridge. When the gate was opened the mass surged forward. Sixteen people were trampled to death and hundreds were injured. They must have thought they were getting on a train.

In different parts of Tokyo we saw various groups of firemen parading down the street. They wore their blue *happi* coats (sign coats) with a large white character printed on the back. Occasionally, they would stop and set up a tall bamboo ladder in the street. They would then gather around and hold the ladder erect by hand and with "fire poles", while one of their members climbed to the top. The fellow on top would perform acrobatic feats such as hanging downward by one foot, sitting, standing, or even lying down on top of the ladder, and many other balancing stunts. These "reviews" by the fire brigades are called *dezome*, because they take place on the sixth day of January. Those that we saw must have been practicing for the main exhibition.

Several times we received telephone calls from the men at Itazuke to tell us about something that had happened down there, or to complain, or a few times just to talk. One must certainly talk loud on Japanese phones. They have a very weak current. What they had to say usually boiled down to the same thing – they weren't happy.

The 16th Comm. Sq. still seemed to be operating in a quandary. There was no formality about their orderly room. The boys would come wandering in out of uniform to the point of wearing shower shoes, shorts, and a blue dress cap until Sgt. Moss put a stop to it. Reiko was embarrassed several times.

Reiko held up better than I expected though. Several times we warned them that she had a very sensitive temperament, but they persisted in teasing and joking with her in a manner she didn't understand. There was one fellow who liked to tease her by putting his arm around her and pretending he was going to kiss her. She would get up and run over behind our desks. I was sure he was going to precipitate trouble, but she took it all right.

Then it happened unexpectedly. One of them jokingly said to her, "All you do is drink coffee and go on TDY". The tears came thick and fast. An officer stated that there was to be no more teasing or joking of any kind, but a day or two later, the boys were back at it again. I often wondered if she continued to work for them after we were gone.

Instead of using a front room for the CQ at night, the 16th Comm. used their office. That meant that there was a continuous stream of men through there in the early evening. Some would come in and sprawl over the desks, go through any papers that might be lying around, and some even took typewriter paper to write letters on. We could no longer work in the office at night for all the noise and confusion.

Though it seems that at times I have written rather harshly about the 16th Comm. Sq., I recognize that it was potentially a good outfit. They had some good men, and they had heavier and better equipment to work with than we ever had. When an entire outfit suddenly moves to a new location as strange and foreign as Japan, and finds itself with an unfamiliar job like antenna work, it is no wonder that it becomes disorganized.

When the 16th becomes adjusted to the environment and the work, and order is restored, it has possibilities of becoming one of the best outfits in the Far East.

Ishikawa-san taught me the fundamentals of the national indoor game of Japan. It is called *Go* or *Igo*. In its simplest form it is similar to checkers, but it is much more complicated in its higher forms. It is said to be more difficult than chess.

Go is a Chinese game which was introduced into Japan about the eighth century, but it has been developed to such a degree in Japan that the Chinese go to Japan to learn the finer points of the game.

The *Go* board, called *Goban*, is square and has nineteen lines crossing it each way making 361 crossings, or *me*. The board is often made of gingko wood and is three or four inches thick. It is further heightened by short stubby legs that make it a convenient height for the players kneeling on the floor.

The game is played with 180 white and 181 black stones called *ishi*, representing day and night respectively. The weaker player takes the black *ishi*, and is offered the opportunity to place *ishi* on any or all of the nine "advantage points" on the board before the game begins. The Japanese also recognize nine degrees of proficiency in the game. The ninth degree is the best.

The object of the game, as Ishikawa explained it, is to take possession of as much of the board as possible. The *me* surrounding the opponent must be occupied to obtain possession. When the *ishi* is placed on the *me*, it may not be lifted again unless captured by the opponent.

On the Saturday morning before we left, Bartasavage and Scozzaro set up an incinerator that the men in the 16th motor vehicle shop had made for us from an old oil drum.

When Captain Cole arrived, we began burning all the old company records. Captain Leddon also came down and helped.

On Monday, Captain Cole finished signing the morning reports, and said goodbye. We began clearing the base. That afternoon, Captain Leddon was awarded the Bronze Star. In the evening, Scozzaro took our baggage to Tachikawa station for shipment.

I was finally able to get a call through to my friend Lt. Meyer at Kisarazu. It was good to talk to him again. He was going to fly down to Itazuke the next day, but wasn't going to stay long.

On January 19, 1954 we three went to the office a little before 0800 hours. Captain Leddon came in humming and singing. We sat and talked, while we impatiently waited for the weapons carrier to arrive to take us to the station. The Captain discussed everything from heating a jeep at Misawa to the places where his men had worked.

We weren't keeping up our share of the conversation, but the Captain didn't notice, and reminiscenced about some of the humorous incidents that had happened in various places the 474th had worked. He told about the time a fellow named Butler, who had been in the company, was working by himself way up the line from everyone else. He happened to be watching, when all of a sudden Butler seemed to go crazy. He was stamping the ground, running in little circles, and fighting himself something furious. He and the crew ran up to see what had happened. Butler had jerked up some underground cable and had thrown dozens of cockroaches all over himself.

Another time, on Iwo Jima, Clayton Robinson was riding a cable car out in the middle of a span when two men let the cable slip. Robinson was left bouncing and swinging like wild in the middle. Robinson got a good scare, but he wouldn't come down until he finished. The Captain said he was pretty mad at the two for letting the cable slip, but Robinson did look funny up there bouncing around.

The "weap" arrived, but it was hard to say goodbye. We really hated to leave, but the 474th was gone.

CHAPTER XVI

Itazuke

We didn't have to wait long at Tachikawa for the train. Actually, it was fortunate that we shipped our footlockers to Tokyo the night before, because we didn't have time to take care of them that morning. The day before, when we presented our TR's (travel requests) at the Tachikawa station to pick up our tickets, the ticket agent said that we had better ship our baggage that evening. We would catch up with it at Tokyo, and it would travel the rest of the way to Kyushu on our train.

The train from Tachikawa to Tokyo was just as we expected – only more so. We had never seen it so crowded. We squirmed inside the door just far enough to get hold of one of the steel pipes that were spaced every so often down the center of the cars. It was pretty uncomfortable for we couldn't straighten up or change position to relax at all. The engineer was having difficulty closing the automatic doors for the people pressing in.

About halfway to Tokyo, a middle-aged woman began to work her way toward the door nearest to where we were standing. As the train came to a halt at a small station, she made an effort to get off, but was still about six feet from the door when the train pulled out.

At the next station she asked the people standing in front of the door to let her out. A few people moved a little, but still she couldn't get out. Carl Scozzaro noticed her plight and was getting mad because the people standing in front of the door wouldn't let her out. He told us that he was going to push them all out of the car if they didn't let her out at the next station.

She was only about two and a half feet from the door by the time the train reached the next station, and she was getting desperate. She began to ask to get off as soon as the train began to slow down. It was a losing fight, for there was a crowd waiting to get on.

Scozzaro braced himself on our pole and began to push on the woman. It looked like he was going to mash her against the wall of people standing in the doorway, so I applied a little pressure to the man in front of her. This caused him to push two or three people in front of him off the train and made an opening large enough for the woman to squeeze through. I'll bet those fellows thought that she was the strongest woman they ever saw.

We had approximately half an hour to wait in Tokyo station before our train was to load, so we walked into one of the beautifully modern Western-style waiting rooms. Nearby were many other shops such as restaurants, bars, clothing stores, bookstores, florists, etc. The central section of the large sprawling station was the Western-style Tokyo Station Hotel.

Tokyo terminus is one of the worlds greatest. Each day, some 400,000 passengers pass through the station, and around 1650 trains come and go in that period. During the war part of the station was destroyed. Now it has been rebuilt and is being expanded on adjacent railroad property.

The government owns the railroads in Japan. It is approximately a 12,500-mile system for all four main islands. About 1040 miles of it is electrified. The whole railroad system has a surprisingly accurate schedule. It used to be, and perhaps still is, that the engineers had their salaries docked if they failed to arrive and depart on time.

At 1000 hours our train began to load. We were ushered into a first class car that was equipped with large windows and comfortable reclining seats. All these seats were reserved. Exactly on time, 1030 hours, the train pulled out of the station.

Soon after the train started, a boy-san came through and announced that the club car was open, then handed out a paper printed with the price of beer and *sake*, etc. At noon we went into the dining car and were met in the doorway by an army man who probably supervised the meals served to any troops that might be on the train. We gave him a meal ticket and signed his roster. We had ham for dinner and roast beef for supper.

The scenery along the route was truly beautiful. During much of the afternoon, we could look out to the left and see the dark blue Pacific, the rocky coast, and the weather beaten pine trees. On the right we could see the ever present mountains, the thatched roofed farm houses and small fields, the circular straw stacks built up around a pole or young living tree, and as we traveled further south, scattered orange trees loaded with fruit. It hardly seemed real.

Not far out of Yokohama, the train passed close to beautiful Fujiyama. Snow reached far down its symmetrical slopes and was lost to view in places due to an intervening ridge of small mountains. As the train curved on around Fuji, it afforded innumerable opportunities to get some magnificent pictures of the mountain.

I was amazed when a Japanese fellow showed me what it was going to cost the American government to send the three of us to Itazuke by train. The figure was Y 26,820, which amounted to $ 74.53 at that time. This included the cost to ship four footlockers, three meals apiece worth Y 128 each, and first class accommodations from Tokyo to Hakata station, a distance of 1,173 kilometers or 733.5 miles.

We passed through all of the large cities near the eastern coast from Tokyo and Yokohama southward. Some of them were: Nagoya, Kyoto, and Osaka. In the evening we were asked to get off the train at Osaka just long enough for a compartmented car to be added to the train.

There was a narrow aisle down one side of the compartmented car from front to rear. The other side was enclosed in numerous compartments containing two uppers and two lower bunks that converted into seats facing each other in the daytime. The bunks were at right angles to the length of the car, which made them extremely short for most Americans. In the wall of the car was a foldout wash basin. There was hardly room to turn around, but at least it was private.

During the night we passed through Kobe and Hiroshima. One would never guess that Hiroshima had been atom bombed in the last war. The small-unpainted houses and shops already looked like they had been standing there for years and years.

The train was approaching the southern tip of Honshu by daylight. While we were eating a breakfast of hotcakes, a boy-san converted our beds into seats. After we had finished breakfast, we returned to our compartment to enjoy the last few hours of our trip. We had passed through many railroad tunnels on this trip, but the one we were looking forward to was the tunnel under the ocean between Honshu and Kyushu islands.

I began to note the length of time the train was in each tunnel as we approached closer. In this way I hoped to estimate the length of each one. We were in the last tunnel approximately five minutes. When we emerged on the other side, I recognized a small mountain and knew we were at

Moji on Kyushu. I was disappointed, for the tunnel connecting the two islands was apparently five miles or less in length.

The train was scheduled to be in Hakata station at 0958 hours, and it was.

We located our footlockers in a nearby building, made a call to the 802nd E.A.B., and then stood around in the baggage building waiting for transportation. It was misting, and although the main street running past the station was of concrete, there were so many puddles in its depressions that passing vehicles were splashing the pedestrians.

In an outside corner of the station, an old man and a boy were crouched under the eaves. They were both filthy and ragged. After awhile the man came over to us and held his palm out, silently begging. He was so filthy and diseased that we didn't want him near us. The boy didn't get up to beg then. He seemed to be in the dream world of a narcotics addict.

William Grubbs came after us in a weapons carrier, and we arrived at Headquarters Company half an hour before noon chow. Headquarters Company was situated on the main base while the line companies were down on the strip. Captain Harold F. Burandt was the commanding officer of the company. The first sergeant told us that we would be interviewed at the personnel section at 1300 hours, so we waited until chow time in one of the tents.

Frank M. Gantz of Aspers, Pa., came in to visit while we were waiting. He said that he was the mail clerk, and began to answer our questions concerning the 802nd. He painted a pretty dismal picture of the situation, but said that it was good now compared with what it was when they first arrived. The 474th had straightened it up a lot, he said.

We ate in the consolidated mess which was located about two blocks up the street toward the main gate. I had eaten there once before while working at Kashii. The top three grades didn't have to wait in line. They went into their dining room and sat down. A Japanese girl brought them a plate of food. The lower three grades had to file past a serving line and carry their own food into another dining room. There were young waitresses in their dining room, too, but they just set the four main tables, poured the liquids, and ran for "seconds" if there were any. It was a good mess hall.

At one o'clock we walked into the battalion personnel office. The officer was busy at the far end of the room, so we waited a few minutes behind an enclosure just inside the door. The reception we received while penned up there rather put us on the defensive in our surprise. Several of the boys working in the office began to criticize the way we had kept our records in the 474th. In addition, an army Tech./Sgt. announced that we shouldn't count on making any more rank, and that he was personally going to investigate every man from the 474th; everyone that he found who had made rank before being eligible for it, he was going to have them demoted. I thought to myself, "Not if there's any way I can prevent it, you won't."

The personnel officer was (Army) Lt. Roger M. Crosby II from Palo Alto, Calif. He was an intelligent, young-looking fellow with a crew hair-cut. Lt. Crosby assigned Scozzaro to Headquarters Company to do the morning reports. The morning reports were far behind date so they were glad to see him arrive. He didn't have any regular job for Bartasavage and myself, though. He said that Bartasavage could work in the personnel office and help straighten up the records and filing system. He would find out if the base finance could use me.

I would have liked to work at base finance during my stay with the 802nd. The 802nd had already supplied them with two 474th men. They were Dennis G. Cernik and Harold A. Coleman. I met them later, and they were both good men to be working with. They worked in a light, airy office, and were quartered in a barracks away from the 802nd. They didn't have to stand formations or pull guard duty or CQ, and rarely had to stand inspections. That's what I wanted – to have as little to do with the 802nd as possible those last few weeks.

After the interview, the first sergeant (Air Force) of Headquarters Company explained various things about his company and assigned us to tents. I moved into tent fourteen. There was a vacancy there because the boys had caught a fellow stealing and had had him moved out.

The tents had wooden floors and walls, and the canvass was stretched over a framework of 2 X 4's overhead. The eight men per tent had plenty of floor space. Uniforms were hung on open racks along the sides, and field equipment was piled on a shelf over them. There was a wooden door at both ends of the tent that gave us no end of trouble keeping them closed against the slightest breeze. There were two stoves which were sup-plied with oil from individual drums at the side of the tent, but they were either too hot or not working at all – usually the latter. We never lacked fresh air in that tent.

The men in tent fourteen at that time were: Marvin F. Picha of Beemer, Nebr.; Ralph J. Dagnall of Pittsburgh, Pa.; Robert Dettinger of Eagle Bend, Minn.; Albert Hill of Roseville, Mich.; Nazzarino Fiorvanti of Conshohocken, Pa.; James E. Conley of Monticello, Iowa; and Anthony Sicurella of Niagara Falls, NY.

Next morning, I went to personnel to see if Lt. Crosby had found a job for me at the base finance office. He hadn't. They couldn't use any more help. I was going to have to spend the rest of my time in that dingy, dark, two-thirds of a Quonset hut they used for a personnel office. I inquired why they didn't use stronger light bulbs, and they explained that they were conserving electricity. I noticed, however, that most of the B.O.Q.'s across the street often had lights burning in them all night, and our tents had a couple of lights on during the day when one or none would have been sufficient. It was a rather foolish economy.

I started through the service records and Form 20's to see if I could get the longevity payments up to date. Bartasavage had a beautiful style of printing, so he was helping me recopy the Form 20's in ink.

We were soon acquainted with everyone in the office. Besides Lt. Crosby, there were: Sgt. 1st Class Caywood, a good natured Air Force fellow who was personnel sergeant; Richard W. Whitworth of Mundy, Tex., an expert on Form 20's; Raymond E. Shearer of Toronto, Kan., pay clerk; Arthur L. Bowman of Los Angeles, Calif., file clerk; Roger F. Honold of Latimer, Iowa, Form 66's; Barksdale H. Macbeth of Mystic, Conn., Form 20's; Bobbie P. Dycus of Ina, Ill., service records; Chalmous E. LaShea of Chicago, Ill., morning reports; Robert D Black of Champaign, Ill., service records; and John B. Apel of Pittsburgh, Pa., pay clerk.

I used to enjoy talking to Bowman. He had a good sense of humor. Once, after returning from the firing range, he said, "I don't need no rifle up on the front line. Just give me a light pack and some tennis shoes." He liked to tell about the "meanest chaplain on earth" that he met in Korea. "If a boy came bursting into his office – tears in his eyes – waving a request for an emergency leave – his mother dying, you know – the chaplain would turn him around and push him back out the door saying, "Dammit! Don't you know better than that?' or ' What the hell do you want?" It was comical to watch Bowman act it out. Every Sunday he preached about venereal disease, Bowman claimed.

He told how many of the GI's avoided paying for cigarettes in Korea. The boy would go to "Black-market Joe" and tell him that he wanted to borrow some money to buy cigarettes. "Joe" would loan him $2.00 MPC and the boy would buy two cartons of cigarettes at the PX. He would then give a carton to "Joe" and use the other carton at no expense to himself.

Most of the GI's who were in Korea didn't believe there were any honest Koreans. Adults and bigger boys would beat up smaller boys and send them through holes cut in our fences to steal. If the boys came back empty handed they would beat them again. Another time, some Koreans broke into an enclosure and were stealing the CARE packages we were going to give them. A couple of times, according to one fellow, Koreans burned to death when they tapped a jet fuel pipe line running across an open field.

Toward the last of January, we began to get snow flurries. The ground would be white for a few hours, but the snow soon melted. Soon after we arrived at Itazuke the Tokyo area had a heavy snow of a foot or more.

The heaviest snowfall at Itazuke occurred on the afternoon Headquarters Company went to the firing range. I had guard duty from 0300 to 0600 hours that morning. Then at 0630 hours there was a formation to go to the firing range. We climbed into a 6-by and I dozed until we reached the range. It was some distance away in the hills near the strip, I think.

The men who fired first were lucky. The sun came over the hills bright and reasonably warm. It didn't start getting cloudy until forenoon.

Those of us who weren't firing, worked in the pits pushing the targets up and down, marking the targets, and waving "Maggie's drawers" (a red flag) to indicate the misses. The targets were cloth covered 2 X 4 frames that slid up and down on guide pipes. Paper targets were pasted over the cloth, and each time the target pulled down, we would paste a small piece of paper over any bullet holes, mark the score, then raise the target and show the shooter where he was hitting by holding a small metal disk over each hit.

After lunch of C-rations, it came our turn to fire while the other group worked our targets. While we were firing it began to snow in blizzard proportions. The large flakes soon had the ground white, and when we moved back to the 100-yard range, there were times when it was difficult to see the target. We were soaked and caked in slush in no time at all.

The flakes were so large that a couple of them landing on the wooden stock between the front and rear sights obscured the front sight from view. We had to wipe them off with a finger and squeeze the trigger before more landed, all of which didn't improve our accuracy. It was fun until we began to get so cold we couldn't stop shaking.

Probably the warmest man out there was Albert Hill. He was wearing a pair of rain fatigues over his regular work clothes. He was such a comical sight that he appeared to have just stepped out of a Bill Mauldin cartoon. It didn't look like he had shaved that morning, and his steel helmet fitted so low over his ears that he could hardly see from under it.

His oversized rain suit was so baggy with all the clothes he was wearing underneath that it was a wonder he could move around. With his carbine slung over his shoulder, muzzle downward, he was a perfect picture of the disgruntled combat trooper.

They had a strange promotional system in the 802nd. In addition to the sergeant that set me off when I first arrived because he was looking to demote several of the new 474th people. None of which lost rank subsequently to my present knowledge. It seemed as though it wasn't what you knew but whom you knew in that outfit. Ralph Dagnall, a Pfc in my tent, was a crane operator. He had done the same type of work as a civilian, and probably knew as much about heavy equipment as any of the sergeants. It was a rarity to meet such a hard working, reliable person and he was next to the lowest in rank. He would have made a better officer.

Another fellow who deserved a promotion was Chalmous LaShea. He worked in personnel, and his job was to check the morning reports from all the companies before they were sent out. The knowledge required to do this efficiently was deserving of the rank of sergeant in my opinion.

I did my best to get them promoted before I left, but I'm afraid without success. I had no authority, and their crew chiefs were supposed to put them in, not me.

Loren Bacon noticed the same trouble with promotions down on the strip. He told me later that he had put a fellow in for a promotion from his crew. He said he didn't know if he was supposed to or not, but he deserved it, so he put him in. The 802nd simply wasn't the cohesive type of unit that the 474th had been.

One evening as I was sitting in the Battalion Headquarters on CQ duty, the CQ from Headquarters Company called and said that "Fritzmeyer" would be over to visit me that evening. Although he had the name wrong, I was quite pleased because it could be none other than 1st/Lt Werner "Fritz" Meyer. He had flown down from Kisarazu that afternoon to pick up some parts that they needed, and wasn't going back until the next day.

Fritz had been flying "wing man" during his missions in Korea. He was flying "wing man" for the famous Captain McConnel when he shot down his twelfth MIG. However, he said, the "wing man" seldom gets to fire his guns over there.

He described his closest call as being the time a cannon shell came up the tail pipe of his F-86 and exploded just before it reached the engine. It made a circle of holes around the fuselage, but fortunately didn't cut any hydraulic lines; therefore he was able to bring his plane back. Excitement was rare on the whole, he said. It was mostly the boring job of waiting for an "alert" or a "mission".

War hadn't changed him much. He still had the same sense of humor, and the ability to form logical and definite opinions on nearly any subject. It was really good to see and talk to him again.

With the exception of the last group of men to arrive in the old 474th most of the men that were sent to Itazuke weren't there long enough to break them of their old loyalty. It was almost impossible not to make comparisons between the outfits, regardless of Captain Leddon's parting advice not to.

Someone, I never found out who, used to have the request program on the local Far East Network station play songs for "the men of the 474th Signal Company who are <u>attached</u> to the 802nd E.A.B. This irked certain officers who correctly maintained that we were assigned, not attached, to the 802nd and that the 474th no longer existed.

Caywood had a good idea for improving the lighting in the personnel office. He decided to paint the ceiling of the Quonset white. Somewhere, he managed to finagle some white paint, but he slipped up on the painters. Everyone except Lt. Crosby had to paint the section over his own desk, but it did improve the working conditions in there.

I went to see the prize winning Japanese movie, "Rashomon", before I left Japan. It was a little weird, but the sets and acting were very good and I enjoyed it. The only actress in the movie, Machiko Kyo, was rather plain featured judging by American standards, but she was one of Japan's most well known actresses. Her gross income in 1952 was roughly three and a half million *Yen* or approximately $9,730.

An interesting thing was occurring on Kyushu in March. The American government was planning to move the R & R (Rest and Recuperation) center from Kokura to Fukuoka. Even before the plans were officially announced, the Japanese people in Fukuoka knew of them and began to oppose the move. Of course, the brothel keepers and shop owners in Fukuoka wanted the change, and were about the only ones who would benefit by it.

Influential Japanese men and women started writing articles in the newspapers against the move, and organizations petitioned the American authorities. They claimed that at least a thousand prostitutes moved to Fukuoka soon after word of the proposed move leaked out, and that as soon as it took effect, most of the remainder would move.

To move the R & R center to Fukuoka would cause a general increase in the cost of living for everyone, and many students at the local university would be squeezed out of their rooms because they wouldn't be able to pay the rent that the "short-time" girls could.

The latter is an important factor in itself. It is hard enough for the Japanese student to meet the expenses of a higher education without competing with American wealth. To lose their rooms would mean the end of education for many students, and they would be bitter at the United States for the rest of their lives. It is the students of today who will be the leaders and influential persons in Japan in the near future.

Prostitution is legal in Japan, but still the Japanese don't like Western morals, usually because they find us as hard to understand as we do them. In truth, I believe they find it harder because of the general lack of information about the West, and partially due to the outlandish propaganda about us during WW II.

While many Japanese may think nothing of prostitution, or of a man urinating on the street in companionship with his wife or girlfriend, it is a major moral issue if a man walks down the street with his arm around a woman or holding hands with her. The same is true of chewing gum or eating an apple in public – little things that Westerners never give a second thought to.

Several women wrote in about their young daughters. They claimed that the so–called "pompom" girls were becoming the ideals of mere children, and they were shocked to hear them imitating their obscene language.

I admit that many of the charges and arguments brought against us are of a relatively superficial nature and could be vindicated with a little common understanding, but when we as representatives of a predominately Christian nation, are accused of undermining the morals of a Buddhist nation by its decent intelligent people, then that calls for some thoughtful, penetrating, reflection on our part, and then some action.

When I first arrived overseas, I noticed something peculiar about the men about due to rotate home. Practically all of them were affected by a type of insanity the last couple of weeks before they left. Time seemed to hang endlessly on their hands, and although they spoke continuously of going home, the topic was always new to them. They became nervous, and worried about getting their port call. The symptoms varied with each man, but were usually present to some degree. Many times I had wondered if I would be affected when my MOT arrived.

Judging by the way the port calls were coming in at Itazuke, I figured that I would leave there about a week early. I had purchased a few gifts to mail home during that last week, but didn't have a box to send them in yet.

I was so sure that I would leave a week early that I began to notice some of the symptoms of the "insanity" creeping up on me early in respect to the date I had estimated I would leave. I didn't talk about home much, but it was on my mind most of the time, and I was getting apprehensive about why my port call didn't come.

Fortunately, I was spared all but the beginning stages of the malady, for not only did the port call come down for me a week early, but I was appointed courier and had to carry the orders to Fuchu about a week in advance of that date. That left me with only Saturday morning and Monday in which to clear the base, ship my gifts, and pack my duffel bag. Another port call came in with mine, and Curtis Clendenin was to be courier for it, so we cleared the base together.

We rushed here and there all Saturday morning, but couldn't clear the medics, etc. until Monday. Sunday, I did some more gift buying and packing, then shipped the packages on Monday and finished clearing the base.

When I went to bed Monday night, I still couldn't believe that at last I was going to Fuchu for processing to return to the ZI. It was hard to fall asleep.

CHAPTER XVII

"Figmo" at Fuchu

At 0730 hours, Clendenin and I left the company to ride down to the strip. We crossed over to a flight line on the opposite side of the field. A large black, Navy amphibian plane was warming up in front of the passenger terminal. That was the plane we wanted to go on.

We walked inside and presented our orders to get on the flight manifest, but something was wrong. Although the orders definitely stated that we were couriers, there was an error in the authority for them, etc. He had us all shook up, for if he had insisted that they are corrected, we would be delayed at least a day. We argued awhile, and made sure that he noticed the stripes on our sleeves. Finally he said he would overlook the error if our duffel bags weighed less than sixty-five pounds. We sweated it out while he put the bags on the scales. They were O.K.

The waiting room was full of men waiting to catch a flight out of there, so we didn't stand a chance of getting on the Navy plane. We wanted to go on it, because it made fewer stops and would arrive several hours earlier than any other scheduled plane going to Tachikawa.

Richard Scott, Kenneth Jones, and Richard Hovorka drove over in a jeep to see us off. Scott and Hovorka were listed on our orders, so we would see them in about a week, but Jones' port call hadn't come down yet. We would probably be gone before he got to Fuchu.

Our C-46 left the flight line at Itazuke at 0915 hours. It stopped at Ashiya, Iwakuni, Miho, Itami, and Komaki before reaching its destination. At one place the radio went dead and we killed an hour while the crew tried to locate another one.

The pilot flew that plane like the Japanese drive automobiles. At noon, I bought a sandwich at a snack bar during a layover, but my stomach was still flopping around so much I couldn't finish it.

We ate a late supper in the Tachikawa terminal snack bar and missed the first bus going to Fuchu, thanks to a conspiracy between the fellow at the desk and the boy-san driving the bus. The loudspeaker carried the announcement that a bus was loading to go to Fuchu. All the prospective passengers rushed outside just in time to see boy-san roaring away in an empty bus.

We were waiting in the lounge when a young Air Force 2nd/Lt. came up to me and shook hands. It was Merle D. Swain of Rt. 1, Alexander, Ill. My brother and I had known him for a long time. Swain had been stationed in Korea, but was just then returning from the States where he had attended funeral services for his mother. In a day or so he would be flying back to Korea.

It was late when we got to Fuchu. The boy-san let a busload of us off at one end of a large administration building. The reporting window was in the front entrance of the place. We filled out a card, received a tent number, and some verbal directions on how to reach the building where we could draw bedding.

Directions for reaching a certain location on the other side of a strange base in darkness tend to be somewhat complicated, and these were. We came away with what we believed to be an idea of the general direction we should go.

After we drew bedding and found our way back again, our next problem was to find our tents. We picked a starting place at random and eventually located the tents not far from the mess hall. By trading numbers with another fellow, we managed to get into the same tent.

We were lucky, for a large shipment had gone out that day and the area wasn't very crowded. The chow lines were comparatively short so we could eat all we wanted.

Nothing happened the next day. We weren't called for processing and didn't get any detail work. We saw Gilman A. DeMars of E. St. Louis, Ill., and Ralph S. Payne of Oxford, Pa. while watching a formation. They gave us some advice on how to avoid details, etc. In the evening, DeMars, Clendenin, and I went to a movie.

The next morning, Clendenin and I joined a large group that was just starting to process. We were herded in a long column out to a large warehouse where we had our clothing forms checked over. Army men had to have an overcoat of the old "horse blanket" type. All of our nice-looking new style coats had to be exchanged for them, and if the man didn't have an overcoat listed on his forms, he still had to take a "horse blanket" back to the States.

With that done, we stopped processing for several days and watched formations from the sidelines, just in case. We weren't going to miss a shipment if we could help it.

On the day we were supposed to report in, had we not been couriers, we joined a formation and turned in our records that we had been hand carrying. There would be no more processing for us until they gave us line numbers.

We met Jack Erickson and Frank Gantz in the mess hall that noon. Gantz brought Clendenin and me some mail that had arrived after we left Itazuke. It was surely welcome. Later in the afternoon, Loren Bacon, Richard Scott, Thomas Clark, and Richard Hovorka stopped by our tent. They were all living in a tent on the other side of the base.

Fuchu was becoming very crowded. There were waiting lines two or three blocks long everywhere; especially for the movies and to get into the mess hall.

A couple of days later it seemed as though Fuchu was going to burst at the seams there were so many men. About then a formation was called for 1230 hours to give out line numbers. We all stood or sat around in a group within the formation. Many of us had come overseas together.

There were: Curtis Clendenin, Jack Erickson, Loren Bacon, Anthony Esposito, Thomas A. Clark of Somers, Conn., Arthur Brogley, Arthur Thearling, James Powers, Richard Hovorka, Frank Gantz, Everett Donegan, Donald R. Francois of Branford, Conn., Richard Scott, and Thomas Williams.

Clendenin commented that we were just about the last of the old 474th. Another shipment or two would take care of everyone except the newest men and a few RA's. Jack Dawson was nearby with some men from his outfit. They had come up from Itazuke on the same train as the men from the 802nd.

That was a happy day for Clendenin and me. I was given a line number on the USNS General H. B. Freeman. Following that, Clendenin got a line number on another ship, the USNS Menifee. No one else in our group got numbers then, so we would temporarily be traveling among strangers.

The only other person that I knew going on the Freeman was a fellow from our tent, Roger A. Delisle. He had been in the 934th Engineering Aviation Group in Korea, and his home was Bronx, NY. He once told me that the reason Korean trains don't have headlights is because the Koreans feel they aren't responsible for the death of anyone they hit if they don't see the person on the tracks.

The next morning we had a formation for converting our MPC back into real American money. It felt strange to have the various familiar coins in our pockets again. After dinner, while the others were at a formation to get line numbers, we had a physical check for any visible signs of venereal disease.

Afterward, I went back and stood with our group in the formation. Powers was up in front of the administration building where they were reading off line numbers. He had gone up to break up a dogfight, and had stayed to look over the shoulder of the fellow reading the roster. We saw him point at something on the list, and shortly he was back to say that more of our men were on the roster. Several of them had been assigned to a third ship.

Next day, we took our duffel bags through customs. We had to empty the contents out on a table for inspection. An officer signed the customs declaration, and we repacked the bag. One foolish boy had tried to smuggle a live hand grenade home in his duffel bag. This inspection was mostly routine. The duffel bags were left in a storehouse until the following morning when we would leave for Yokohama.

When I got back from customs, everyone in our group had line numbers and were scheduled to leave during the weekend.

I was awakened Saturday morning at 0230 hours. We fell out for a formation in front of the administration building at 0300 hours and were marched over to turn in our bedding. We stood outside until the building opened, then filed through in line number order. From there we returned to the mess hall for breakfast. The chow line stretched far down the street. The mess hall looked warm and inviting as we waited outside in the chilly darkness.

At 0530 hours we started through handbag customs. Following that inspection, we removed our duffel bags from storage and were ready to go. A man at the depot gave us a car number on the basis of our line number. Scott and Bacon came walking along the platform on their way to breakfast and said goodbye again.

That train didn't make any time at all. It must have been the same train we came over on, for it must have stopped at every crossing to let another train go by. People riding bicycles on the road passed us as if we were standing still. Dinner was served on the train.

At Yokohama we debarked from the train just around a corner from where the Freeman was docked. One at a time, as the line numbers were called off, the men began to file around the corner and form into formations alongside the ship.

We could see a gang of Army men hanging over the top railing. They were the "advance party" who readied the ship for the troops, and who worked as kitchen police or on other details. On the next lower deck and near where the steps went up, was a large group of dependents. The majority of people on board were civilians and officers.

The ship that Clendenin would be going on, the Menifee, was docked nearby. It seemed much larger than the Freeman did. I wished that the Freeman was larger and thus steadier in the water, but I could only hope for calm seas. The Gen. Hugh J. Gaffey was also docked nearby.

As it happened, the remaining 474th fellows were assigned to separate ships, but all of them were destined for San Francisco. Loren Bacon said he could see the Menifee in the distance all the way across. The ships were involved in maneuvers at one point in the exercise; a man was transferred from one ship to another. As the ships passed Alcatraz Island, Richard Scott said they could see men on the walls of the penitentiary waving at the troops.

CHAPTER XVIII

The Final End

There was a steady line of men from the formation, up the gangplank, across the deck, and down into the hold of the ship. The hold compartments were a mass of confusion. There had to be a man for every rack, and a pillow and life jacket for every man.

The narrow aisles were jammed with hand and duffel bags, men trying to change into fatigues, or men trying to find an empty rack, a life jacket, or a pillow. As quickly as I could, I threw my bags on a rack, changed clothes, and went up on the top deck.

I was quite alone. The men I had been courier for were apparently returning home on the larger ship that Clendenin had been assigned to which was docked next to the Freeman. As far as I could determine, I was the only one from the old 474th on the ship.

I walked around the deck. From the other side, I could see a large sleek luxury liner loading at another dock. I wished that I were going home on it. The USNS Freeman couldn't have been much longer than 500 feet or wider than 70 feet. It was designed to accommodate 1500 passengers. According to what we heard there was a relatively small percent of troops on board. Most of the passengers were "cabin class". The ship's captain was Alex J. Zugehoer.

As the time for the ship's departure approached, the loud speaker began to warn visitors to go ashore. The announcement was also made in Japanese for the benefit of the Japanese families who were on the ship seeing their daughters off to America. There were many Japanese women sailing either with their husbands or to meet their husbands in the States.

I took a position by the railing on the port side near the bow before the deck became too crowded with men. It was a bright clear day, but it was too hazy inland to see Fujiyama. It didn't seem to matter, either. I thought to myself that this would be one time when <u>goodbye</u> would be appropriate. I didn't anticipate ever returning to Japan again – at least, not by ship.

At 1415 hours, the boy-sans on the dock loosened our ropes, and the ship began to push away from the dock, slowly, almost imperceptibly. It was a strange feeling. There was no physical sense of movement at all. It seemed as though the dock and the land were moving away rather than the ship.

The 289th Army Band marched across the dock and played to us. It seemed as though they should have played "Farewell to Yokohama". The boys on the ship shouted for them to play it until we were far out in the bay, but they never did.

The ship was moving along under its own power when a powerful American patrol boat pulled alongside on the starboard side. An MP was holding a gentleman in civilian clothes upright on the deck of the boat while he waved his arms and shouted to get the attention of the bridge.

The man the MP was supporting was visibly embarrassed and downcast, and he should have been. All troops had to report to their compartments about that time, so we didn't get to see them bring him aboard.

The compartment commanders explained various regulations, assigned men to details, etc. This was going to be a luxury cruise. We had a blanket, sheet, and even a pillowcase for our pillow. There were the several fire and boat drills too.

There were three compartment clean up details: morning, noon, and night. The morning clean up detail was the largest and biggest job. They had to clean the compartment thoroughly for an inspection by the commanding officer.

Fortunately, I got on the night clean up detail. There were six men on it, but only two or three of us ever showed up. This detail didn't take long. We just went around the compartment and policed it up.

I was hungry for supper, but didn't feel like eating much when I got into the galley. It was nice in there, too. There was none of the sickening odors of rancid or burnt grease, etc. that often drifted from the galley of the USNS Meigs. On the Freeman we could sit down on benches while we ate. It only took an hour to feed all the troops, so we didn't have to stand in line long. Best of all, we were never served green boiled eggs for breakfast.

On the second day at sea I succumbed to seasickness. I continued to respond to chow call optimistically, however, and by the time we crossed the 180th meridian, I was beginning to feel fine again.

Actually, there was very little seasickness on board and it was usually of short duration. There were a couple of hospital cases, but few of the troops felt bad more than a couple of days.

The Freeman was following one of the northern routes. I should think that it took advantage of the Japan current which arcs upward past Japan, across the Pacific and downward along our West Coast, but I don't know whether or not that was the plan. The Japanese current is known as the *Kuroshio* (Black) current to the Japanese because of the dark blue of its water.

We crossed the 180th Meridian on Thursday, so the next day was also Thursday. We gained back the day we had lost going over. On the return trip we had been advancing our watches one hour each time we crossed a time zone. We did this seven times.

After a day out from Yokohama several albatrosses replaced our entourage of gulls. The big brownish birds never seemed to tire of skimming along above our wake.

We had fine bright weather for sailing, but it got chilly as we curved northward. I was glad that I had the "horse blanket" overcoat to wear. Many of the Army men swore they wouldn't wear them, but after a few days, some of them were reconsidering their rashness.

As usual, there was a lot of card playing on the ship, but there didn't seem to be as much gambling as there was on the troopship going over. Most of the men were holding on to their money to blow it on a good time in the States.

The men were undergoing a change on the way back. They didn't talk as much about the war as they did of home and what they hoped to do. They were even content to sit silently and think or dream. When a Japanese or Korean word or phrase was used, or a "war story" told, or a comparison made, it sounded as if that person was rehearsing something he planned to say when he got home.

When the ship's paper came out in the afternoon, there was a rush to see the "Noon Report". This report was a little item listing the distance we were from the port of Yokohama, miles traveled in the past twenty-four hours and the average speed during that time. As long as the speed was close to seventeen knots, we were happy. That is approximately 19$^{1}/_{8}$ MPH.

There were a few tours conducted to various parts of the ship for persons wanting to know more about its operations. The Freeman was so well equipped with modern devises that it could almost run itself. In the bridge were compasses, radios, clocks, depth sounding devises, surface radar, and a machine like the automatic pilot in a plane which would hold the ship to any designated course.

In another part of the ship, the guide explained the water supply for the ship. An emergency supply of water was carried in storage tanks, but the main volume of water used was taken from the ocean. He said that approximately 40,000 gallons of distilled water could be manufactured from seawater every day.

On the morning of the twelfth day at sea, I had barely stretched out on the hatch cover over the forward hold when a commotion on the starboard side caused me to sit up. A plane was rapidly approaching us low over the water. As it roared over the ship we could see the Canadian wing markings. It circled the ship a couple of times before whizzing past alongside. We could see the crew in the plane waving to the men who were waving and cheering on deck. With one last pass over the ship, the sleek, two-motored plane went on about its patrol.

During the day we had a disembarkation drill. Every man was as-signed a place in a certain formation on the deck. He was to bring his duffel bag up as soon as possible the next morning and put it at the place he was then standing. When it was time to disembark, he was to take a position next to his bag and wait for his line number turn.

The Captain's dinner was served that evening. It was a banquet of turkey with all the trimmings. According to custom, it was given on the last evening of an ocean voyage.

We came in sight of land at 1400 hours that afternoon. There wasn't much to see, but it was <u>Land.</u> After supper I went up on deck to watch. By then we were very close. There was land visible on either side of the ship. Practically all the troops were up there. A few were quiet, but most were walking around shooting pictures and talking excitedly.

One's homeland never appears more beautiful or wonderful than it does to the men returning home from war on a troopship.

We watched the vast areas of evergreen covered hills and the great, rugged, snow covered mountains behind them. Here and there was a cluster of houses, and as we moved on, the clusters became larger until they were cities.

Dusk settled and we could see the bright colored lights from the cities. It was really beautiful. Later that night I walked around the deck as we glided into Seattle. The water reflected the glow from the huge neon signs along the waterfront. I could see the car lights moving up and down the steep streets and listened to the American sounds. It was overwhelmingly great to be home.

Much later, someone came down to the compartment and whispered that the ship had stopped moving. It was 0100 hours. Many men stayed out on deck all night in spite of the chill and dampness. It was a hard night to sleep.

At 0300 hours, half an hour early, some men in our compartment began to stir about. Immediately, everyone was wide awake and getting dressed. We rushed about putting our blankets, sheets, and pillowcases into piles to be turned in. The life jackets and pillows had to be carried to another compartment and be counted.

By that time our compartment was called to breakfast. The stairs were crowded with men hauling their duffel bags up to put them in position on the deck. When we returned, the racks all had to be stripped of their canvas and the ropes tied around the frames. The frames were then tilted up to make more room, and the compartment was thoroughly cleaned for the last inspection. No one would disembark until the ship had passed the final inspection.

The day broke cloudy. Men who didn't have a detail walked the deck, impatiently waiting. We were still some distance from the dock and seemed to be drifting. At 0815 hours, a newly painted tug came out and began to maneuver the Freeman back and then towards a dock.

Some of the compartments weren't passing inspection, and the men were being called back to clean them again. Eventually all the compartments passed and the men formed into formations next to their duffel bags.

As the ship came up to the dock and was being tied in, a band marched out and began to play. A mob of civilians, confined behind ropes, searched for friends and relatives on the ship and shouts were exchanged. Gangplanks were raised to the deck. A couple of hospital cases were brought off and taken away in a waiting ambulance. Then the records were removed and trucked away. We expected to get off after the dependents, but for once the troops got a break.

We hurried off the ship by line number carrying our bags with us. The duffel bags were thrown onto waiting trucks, and we got into buses. It was nice to sit in a seat again. Red Cross workers handed in coffee and cookies through the windows.

The buses took us to a large Navy base where we were to process. I didn't know then whether I would be sent on to Fort Sheridan for release, or if I would get a delay in route to go home for Easter.

They had a wonderful processing system at that Navy base. We had an orientation at 1100 hours. Following that we ate chow in the Navy mess hall. At 1300 hours, we filed through a building and received our back pay and the travel pay to our next station. At the rear of the same building were people selling transportation tickets.

My orders indicated a ten-day delay in route, so I bought a ticket for Jacksonville, Ill. I had time to clean up and eat supper before taking a bus to the King Street Station. The people of Seattle all seemed very considerate of service men. It seemed strange that so many cars could be moving about so quietly. In Japan it would have been a bedlam of horn blowing.

The train pulled out of Seattle at 2100 hours. I purposely left the service ribbons off my jacket, then laid the jacket on the seat next to me to discourage anyone from sitting there. I didn't want to have to talk to anyone.

There couldn't have been anyone happier or more thankful for being an American and to be home again.

Please see Appendix I for a list of men serving in the 474th Signal Aviation Construction Company in 1954, but not mentioned in the text.

CHAPTER XIX

The Aftermath

The Korean War   June 25,1950-July 27,1953

At the end of World War II the country of Korea had been temporarily divided along the 38th parallel with the Russians occupying the North and the United States controlling the South. The two sides had not been able to agree on a plan for reunification thereby acerbating the two rival governments. Suddenly the North Korean Communists acted to bring unity to the country on their terms.

On June 25, 1950 the North Korean army crossed he 38th parallel to invade South Korea. The following day President Harry S. Truman authorized the U.S. Navy and Air Force to aid the South Korean troops. The United Nations Security Council adopted a resolution calling for armed intervention on June 27th.

President Truman sent the first of the United States ground troops to South Korea on June 30th. General Douglas MacArthur commanded these troops and by July 8th he was named to command all United Nations troops in South Korea.

The Chinese entered the war on November 26, 1950 by crossing the Yalu River, separating China and Korea, with 200,000 men. The UN troops were forced out of North Korea. President Truman refused to let MacArthur bomb the supply depots in China. MacArthur went public with his dispute and Truman fired him. General Matthew Ridgway took his place on April 11,1951. A year later, on May 12, 1952, General Mark Clark was appointed to command the UN troops in the Far East.

Interestingly enough, the Japanese Peace Treaty passed the United

States Senate on a vote of 66 to 10 on March 20, 1952. It was on April 28,1952 that President Truman formally announced the end of a state of war between the United States and Japan.

The Korean War ended on July 27, 1953. United Nations and North Korean officials signed the armistice agreement at Panmunjon, Korea. This was a bitter pill for the veterans to swallow. They did not want to accept Truman's policy of limited war. Nevertheless, the President announced December 26,1953 that the United States would pull two military divisions out of Korea.

<u>United States Casualties</u>

Service personnel including all branches	5,764,143
The total deaths	36,914
The wounded (not mortal)	103,284

There are no good wars. Nearly every community in America lost one or more of its young men. The 474th did not have any men killed in action. Most of us returned home and went to work or to school and started families. There wasn't much to talk about. The Korean War became known as the "Forgotten War". There was no clamoring for a War Memorial in Washington, D.C. or any special privileges. Most of us had friends or knew someone who was killed or wounded in the war. Lt. Werner W. Meyer was killed when his plane crashed soon after he had re-enlisted for another tour of duty.

In time, the General M.C. Meigs became a surplus ship. It broke from the tug that was towing it to San Francisco during a storm. It broke in two and washed ashore south of Cape Flattery, Washington on January 8, 1972.

Several of the 474th veterans re-enlisted and eventually retired after twenty or more years in the army. Captain John Leddon, Howard Coil, Ervin Easterling, Foy Walker, Roy Walker, Billy Bracewell, and Norman Dutrisac were among those who stayed in the Army. The twins, Roy and Foy Walker, were only 37 years of age when they retired. Foy Walker was awarded the Silver Star and a Purple Heart for his valor and wounds on the DMZ in Viet Nam.

Perhaps most of the men joined the VFW or the American Legion. Richard Hovorka was elected State Commander of the American Legion for South Dakota in 1992.

The 474th Signal Aviation Construction Company Reunion Association

A number of the men who served with the 474th stayed in touch for years after their tour of duty were completed. Most had married. Nearly all had moved once or twice – some for great distances. Dick and Marianne Wakefield had continued to exchange Christmas cards with Curtis and Barbara Clendenin over the years. Eventually, the Clendenin's stopped at the Wakefield home in Iowa on their way home from a trip. A few months later they invited the Wakefield's to visit them at Mount Vernon, Illinois. Loren Bacon and Kenny Jones and their spouses were also living in the area and were invited over for dinner. This unintentional mini-reunion was a great success.

Perhaps another ten years passed. Loren Bacon phoned Wakefield on January 1, 1991 with New Year greetings and both resolved at that time to make their dream of a reunion into a reality. Dick Wakefield took charge of getting things started. Locating 474th veterans after more than 38 years wasn't easy, but he was persistent. He checked his old orders; placed notices in the VFW and American Legion magazines; bought phone discs for his computer; and used the Department of Veteran's Administration to locate people.

The first reunion was held August 8 – 11, 1991 at Centerville, Iowa at the home of Dick and Marianne Wakefield. Dick had not yet located very many of the veterans, but fifteen adults and four children were able to attend. They were: Bill & Mary Henley and two grandsons, Herbert & Winnie Spain, Jim & Helen Seeders and two daughters, Alfred & Becky Coleman, Loren & Barbara Bacon, Arvard McNeal, Dick & Marianne Wakefield, and Colonel John W. Leddon, former Commanding Officer of the Company, with his wife Dee.

At this meeting, Col. Leddon presented the little group of 474th veterans with the red campaign streamer, inscribed "KOREA", in token of the Meritorious Unit Citation. The Colonel had kept it in his personal possession through the years after the war to safeguard it. It is now in the possession of the 474th Reunion Association.

This first reunion was so pleasant and successful that the participants decided to have another reunion the following year. The second reunion was held at the home of Loren and Barbara Bacon September 10 – 13,

1992 at West Frankfort, Illinois. It was at this meeting that the Reunion Association was formed and officers were elected. They were: Loren Bacon, President; Alfred Coleman, Vice-President; Herbert Spain, Chaplain; and Dick Wakefield, Secretary-Treasurer.

By the third reunion Dick Wakefield had located 45 veterans of the 474th and discovered eight were deceased. The third reunion was hosted by Becky and Alfred (Crick) Coleman in the Lynchburg, Virginia area from September 16–19, 1993. Colonel John Leddon provided a draft of by-laws for the 474th Association, which were approved at the business meeting. New officers elected were: Alfred Coleman, President; Foy Walker, Vice-President; Albertus Young, Chaplain; and Dick Wakefield, Secretary-Treasurer. A video filmed by Don McArthur was shown.

The fourth annual reunion was held in the Ellaville, Georgia area and was hosted by LaVerne and Foy Walker from September 15-18, 1994. Thirty-five veterans and spouses attended. Richard Hovorka showed a film he made in Japan. Officers elected were: Foy Walker, President; Howard Coil, Vice-President; Albertus Young, Chaplain; and Dick Wakefield, Secretary- Treasurer.

Verna and Howard Coil hosted the fifth annual reunion in Colorado Springs, Colorado September 14-17, 1995. The number of veterans and spouses attending had increased to 43. A decision was made at the business meeting to accept an offer from Raymond Self to produce a video about the 474th. Upon completion it was named "The 474th Signal Company Story". Officers elected for the coming year were: Howard Coil, President; Arvard McNeal, Vice-President; Albertus Young, Chaplain; and Dick Wakefield, Secretary-Treasurer.

The sixth annual reunion was held in the Windsor Locks, Connecticut area and was hosted by Arvard McNeal September 12-15, 1996. The visitors toured the Aquarium and Mystic Seaport. Some visited the Air Museum at Windsor Locks or the Basketball Hall of Fame in Springfield, Maine. The elected officers were; Arvard McNeal, President; Eugene Green, Vice-President; Albertus Young; and Dick Wakefield, Secretary-Treasurer.

Curtis Clendenin had passed away, but he and Barbara had been instrumental in getting the 474th reunions started. Barbara requested to host the seventh reunion at Marion, Illinois from September 11-14, 1997. She, her sons and their families organized and entertained sixty-six people, the largest reunion so far. Officers elected were: Arvard McNeal, President; Eugene Green, Vice-President; Albertus Young, Chaplain; and Dick Wakefield, Secretary-Treasurer.

Sixty-three people attended the eighth reunion in Charleston, South Carolina from September 10-13, 1998. Eugene and Helen Green hosted this event. Several first-time attendees were present. Tours included the historical city and other significant landmarks in the area. Eugene Green was elected President; Gerald Pires, Vice-President; Albertus Young, Chaplain; and Dick Wakefield, Secretary-Treasurer.

The ninth reunion was held at Gresham, Oregon from September 8-12, 1999. Gerald Pires was the host for the occasion. Tours were provided to the Mt. St. Helens National Monument; to the Pacific Ocean coastal area; and the Mt Hood loop ending at Multnomah Falls. The elected officers for the coming year were: Gerald Pires, President; Arvard McNeal, Vice-President; Albertus Young, Chaplain; and Dick Wakefield, Secretary-Treasurer.

Dick and Marianne Wakefield volunteered to host the tenth reunion at Branson, Missouri on September 12 & 13 with the main reunion site at the Ozark Folk Center in Mountain View, Arkansas from September 14-17, 2000. The Folk Center was actually a state park with lodges and a variety of activities. The Blanchard Springs Caverns was only a short distance away. At the business meeting, Arvard McNeal moved up as President; Foy Walker was elected Vice President: and Dick Wakefield continued as Secretary-Treasurer. Our Chaplain, Albertus Young, passed away earlier. Jim Perdue filled in temporarily.

LaVerne and Foy Walker hosted the eleventh reunion in Columbus, Georgia. It ran from September 19-23, 2001. The group had the opportunity to visit The Infantry Museum at Ft. Benning; to tour Warm Springs and The Little White House (F.D.R.'s only home); the Callaway Gardens; the Columbus Museum of Art; and the beautiful Riverwalk along the Chattahoochee River. Fifty-three people were in attendance. Foy Walker was elected President; Alfred Coleman, Vice-President; Jim Perdue, Chaplain; and Dick Wakefield, Secretary-Treasurer.

APPENDIX I

More Men of the 474th Signal Aviation Construction Company, 1954

James A. Alford	Rt. # 1 Brosely, Mo.
Thomas W. Amsler	Knox, Pa.
Willie A. Bell	Sewellton, Ky.
Doyle C. Benefield	1614 Garvin St. Orlando, Fla.
Robert J. Blackburn	3327 H St. Philadelphia, Pa.
Charles Blackwell, Jr.	Rt. # 1 Duncan, S.C.
James C. Blankenship, Jr.	3715 Grace Ave. Chattanooga, Tenn.
William M. Blocker	92 Benning St. Dayton, Ohio
Irving Bowden	605 E. 169th St. Bronx, N.Y.
Ronald L. Brooks	St Albans, Vt.
Adolphus A. Bryant, Jr.	Hinesville, Ga.
Melvin W. Buckles	Rt. # 7 Elizabethtown, Tenn.
James A. Bunn	1004 Shellbanks Rd. Baltimore, Md.
John Cambra	514 Berkley St. Berkley, Mass.
Teddie R. Clark	Oakton, Ky.
Harrison L. Crothers	Whitcomb Ave. Littleton, Mass.
Euwana Daniels	Lakewood, Fla.
Robert E. Downs	Safety Harbor, Fla.
Norman E. Dutrisac	346 West St. Keene, N.H.
James Eason	Rt. # 1 Screven, Ga.
Clayton W. Filler	1207 Funston St. Stockton, Calif.
Walter P. Gallegos	San Luis, Colo.
Eugene E. Green	30 Sasfield St. Boston, Mass.

David Grier, Jr.	113 E. 49th St.Chicago, Ill.
Alvin L. Hall	Rt. # 1 Benton, Tenn.
Johnie E. Head	Pocahontas, Tenn.
Faustino R. Hernandes	1252 E. 66th St. Los Angeles, Calif.
Samuel Hill, Jr.	511, E. 1st St. Los Angeles, Calif.
Edward A. Hopson	1851 Division St. St. Louis, Mo.
William G. Johnson	442 S. Wagner Stockton, Calif.
Vernon Y. King	Florence St. Boston, Mass.
Gordon O. Kinney	5312 El Cagon Blvd. San Diego, CA
Maurice E. Lebel	3 Dutton St. Lowell, Mass.
James F. Little	Rt. # 1 Smithfield, W. Va.
LeRoy A. Malinowski	3509 Wellington St. Philadelphia, Pa.
Ernest Marrow	8911 Church Hill Rd. N. Bergen, N.J.
Joseph J McCrea, Jr.	W. Woodstock, Conn.
Edward H. McGill	1016 Goochland St. Richmond, Va.
Arvard D. McNeal	8510 S Burnham Ave. Chicago, Ill.
Landon A. McQuinn	244 Sumner Ave. Brooklyn, N.Y.
Robert G. Olsen	78 N. Main St. Penacook, N.H.
Talmadge Pittman	315 Line St. Chattanooga, Tenn.
Walter Pollack	122 N. Ashland St. Chicago, Ill.
Louis V. Russell	233 E. Division St. Sparta, Mich.
John Sanford, Jr.	236 S. Louis St. Montgomery, Ala.
Mariano F. Sauro	330 New Freedom Rd. Berlin, N.J.
John N Schenkelberg	Marriottsville, Md.
Henry L. Sharpe	Lexington, S.C.
Joe W. Shaw	Rt. # 1 Dubberly, La.
John C. Short	4224 Broadhead Rd. Aliquippa, Pa.
Clyde P. Smith	922 W. Walnut St. Columbus, Ohio
Roland S. Stapleton	92 St. Nicholas Ave. New York, N.Y.
Gentry C. Stepp	Hamlet, Ind.

Collin R. Stilwell   Rt. # 1 Sylvatus, Va.

George Trujillo   2525 Union St. Tampa, Fla.
Arthur L. Tucker   58 William St. Glassboro, N.J.
Lester Turner   Rt. # 2 Pink Hill, N.C.
Richard D. Tyler   1740 Trenton Denver, Colo.

Arnold L. Wansley   Decatur, Miss.
Charlie G. Wiley   5211 Fifteenth Ave. Columbus, Ga.
Eugene H. Williams   1705 N. Newstead Ave. St. Louis, Mo.
Francis C. Wittkop   Freeburg, Mo.
Abraham Wright   San Antonio, Tex.

Peter H. Zagwyn, Jr.   57A West St. Newton, Mass.

APPENDIX II

Full Roster as of November 1, 2001

Men who served with the 474th Signal Aviation Construction Company August 30, 1946 – January 18, 1954

James S. Adamski — 239 E. Myrtle St. Duluth, MN 55811
James R. Alford — RR 4 Poplar Bluff, MO 63901
Tom Amsler — P.O. Box 180 Knox, PA 16232
Ethan E. Anderson — 1118 N. 7th Tacoma, WA 98403
George J. Anthony — 1475-27 Jerusalem Ave. Mernch, NY 11566
Marshall Aquillard — 148 22nd St. Okeechobee, FL 34974
LeRoy Arnette — 2601 Billings Road Hephzibah GA 30815

Kemper Bacon — 4202 W. Van Buren Phoenix, AZ 85009
Loren Bacon — 204 N. Ida West Frankfort, IL 62896
Gene Bart — PO Box 916 Battle Creek, MI 49016
Thurman T. Baughman — 7512 Allegheny Road Manassas, VA 20111
Willie A. Bell — 6399 S Hwy 127 Jamestown, KY 42629
Leo A. Birch — 430 Village Rd Longwood, FL 32779
James C. Blankenship — 402 McClure Chattanooga, TN 37415
Joseph C. Blumel — 9580 Melnore Dr. SW Portland, OR 97225
Walter Bolin — PO Box 144 Ezel, KY 41425
Clifford Boothby — 1147 E. 4th St. Casa Grand, AZ 85222-4234
Billy Bracewell — 439 Benning Dr. Destin, FL 32541
Thomas W. Bradford — 7961 Thouron Ave. Philadelphia, PA 19150
Adolphous Bryant — 2352 Jackson St. Waycross, GA 31503
Billy P. Bryant — 1316 Township Rd. Ashland, Ohio 44805
Melvin Buckles — 843 Hwy 91 Elizabethton, TN 37643
Harold G Bullo — 38976 Claremont Ct. Sterling Heights, MI 48310
C.C. Burr — 404 Burns St. Wadesboro, NC 28170

John Cambra	522 Berkley St. Berkley, MA 02779
Tony Carnemolla	2665 Lunada Lane Alamo, CA 94507
Thomas Carr	306 Broad Ave. Susquehanna, Pa.
Ralph Caruso	RR 2, PO Box 2422 Grove City, PA 16127
Wilson J. Christian	19441 Tracey St. Detroit, MI 48235
Raymond O. Chryst	325 NE 121st Terrace Miami, FL 33161
Teddy R. Clark	106 Maple Cove Martin, TN 38237
Thomas A. Clark	RR 2, PO box 19B Gladstone, VA 24553
Park A. Close	298 Podunk Road Trumansburg, NY 14886
Howard Coil	1055 Red Brook Drive Colorado Springs, CO 80911
Alfred B. Coleman	2358 Elon Rd. Madison Heights, VA 24572
Horace A. Creary	11804 Marsden St. Long Island, NY 11434
Ray Daniels	421 Lake of the Woods Dr. Venus, FL 34293
Bennie Davis	RR 3, 22 Cliffwood Longview, TX 75603
Gilman A. DeMars	8844 Kathlyn Berkeley, MO 63134
Valentino DeVaca	716 Kathryn Ave. Santa Fe, NM 87501
Angelo J. DiFrancesco	901 Twining Road Dresher, PA 19025
Everett Donegan	100 Alex Place, Apt B11 Livingston, AL 35470
Onist R. Doss	PO Box 44089 Lemon Cove, CA 03244
Calvin Dowell	3040 Old Brownsville Rd. Ripley, TN 38063
Dewey Dowell	3040 Old Brownsville Rd. Ripley, TN 38063
Norman E. Dutrisac	514 Apple St. Ashdown, AR 71822
James Eason	561 East 56th Jacksonville, FL 32208
Ervin Easterling	1111 W. White Dove St. Azle, TX 76020
Anthony Esposeta	21 Faun Drive Chesire, CT 06410
Thomas Finney	1190 Grange Rd. Westcosville, PA 18106
Merwin R. Flagg	1201 Kingston Way Gardnerville, NV 89410
Jimmie Fowlks	6214 Longview Dr. Murray, UT 84107
Glen J. Francis	1397 Kewaunee St. OshKosh, WI 54904
Donald R. Francois	63 Roaring Brook Prospect, CT 06712
Walter Gallegos	PO Box 423 San Luis, CO 81152
Paul W. Gammon	217 W. 15th St. Bowling Green, KY 42101
Richard S. Gardner	1506 Beaver Rd. Sewickley, PA 15143
Slaton E. Gile	10305 Middleground Rd. Savannah, GA 31419
Ezekiel Gilmore, Jr.	12418 Oberlin Dr. Dallas, TX 75243

Ernest L. Giordano   124 Countryside Dr. Basking Ridge, NJ 07920
Eugene E. Green   1184 Maple Ave. Denmark, SC 29042
William Grubbs   2193 Alfred Dr. Flint, MI 48507
Reuben E. Gunn   886 Verna Lee Blvd. Harker Heights, TX 76548

Richard Haberkamp   6 N. 188 Riverside Dr. St. Charles, IL 60174
Leo Harris   1899 Grinan Dr. San Jose, CA 95122
Lynwood L. Harris   818 Belafonte Dr. Augusta, GA 30901
John E. Head   134 Bunch St. Selmer, TN 38375
George T. Hearn   665 W. Oak Dr. Hurst, TX 76053
Bill Henley   315 S. Arthur Pierre,SD 57501
John W. Hercules   PO Box 2031 Elm Grove, WV 26003
Faustino R. Hernandez   8457 Poinsettia Dr. Buena Park, CA 90620
Jack Hess   12724 Hunters ChaseFoley, AL 36535
Richard D. Hovorka   42058 307th St. Tabor, SD 57063-6002
Charles Hughes   21 S. Wright Ave. Dayton, Ohio 45403
Robert S. Hull   218 W. 4th St. Weston, WV 26452
Howard R. Humphrey   831 Wolf Trail Casselberry, FL 32707

Peter J. Inzero   108 Blacks Rd. Cheshire, CT 06410

Frank JonesPO Box   113Elk Garden, WV 26717
Kenneth Jones   RR 2 Cartersville, IL 62918

Thomas W. Kelley   PO Box 114 Ebony, VA 23845-0114
Vernon King   66 Clifford St. Roxbury, MA 02119

John W. Leddon, Col.(USA ret)
                          PO Box 118 Lovettsville, VA 20180
Lonnie Lovern   8570 Possum Hollow Rd. Fort Sills, SC 29715

LeRoy A. Malinowski   8745 S. Escanaba Ave. Chicago, IL 60617-3116
Will Mathis   633 Pinebrow Trail Chattanooga, TN 37421
Walter P. Matulis   23 North St. Upton, MA 01568
Donald D. McArthur   1600 Rainer St. Aberdeen WA 98520
Charles McCain   1310 Cleveland Ave. Palatka, FL 32177
James McCoy   7206 Idlewild St. Pittsburg, PA 15208
Obie McDonald   336 Glendora Ave. Louisville, KY 40212
Daniel H. McDowell   PO Box 694 East Pepperell, MA 01463
Robert N. McEldowney   3417 Waterford Ct. NE Grand Rapids, MI 49505

Robert Z. McGlumphy   PO Box 183 Lost Creek, WV 26385
Avard D. McNeal   15 Laurel Rd. Windsor Locks, CT 06096
Henry McNeal   1449 Laudeen Dr. Memphis, TN 38116
Gordon A. Meesuen   461 RR 146, Apt.305 Gilderland Center, NY
                      12085
Jack Miles   8 Sullivan St. Lexington, MA 02173
Zenon Mocarski   42 Lobsterback Rd. Trumbull, CT 06611
Marvin Morrow   608 N. Grace Ave. Grand Island, NE 68803
David Myers   704 Saybrook Circle Wadesboro, NC 28170

Frank Noles   PO Box 1164 LaGrange, GA 30241-1164

Robert Oquita   PO Box 725 Douglas, AZ 85608-0725
Clovis A. Owens   19910 Santa Barbara Dr. Detroit, MI 48201
Robert L. Owens   4000 Strong Highway El Dorado, AK 71730

James S. Paramore   1013 E. 6th St. Washington, NC 27889
Gerald E. Parrott   24335 Chippendale Ave. W.Farmington, MN
                      55024
Roger S. Paulsen   7509 Columbus Ave. Richfield, MN 55423
Vernice Peeple   1208 Rhue Road Winston Salem, NC 27107
Frank E. Penn   502 E. Poplar St. Normal, IL 61761-1744
James Perdue   PO Box 97 Alamo, GA 30411
E. Gerald Pires   39707 SE Wildcat Mtn. Dr. Eagle Creek, OR
                      97022
Talmadge Pittman   6014 Hancock Rd. Chattanooga, TN 37421
Romeo J. Potelle   PO Box 204 China, Maine 04926
Vincent C. Priola

Henry Rahm   4124 NE Minnesota St. Bartlesville, OK 74006
Charles V. Rece   2499 Pebble Creek Ct. Lincolnton, NC 28092-
                      6115
Arlie W. Redburn   1506 McArtor Rd. Dodge City, Kansas 67801
Clement Riha   2884 Hwy V18 Elberon, IA 52225
George Rinehart   1437 State Route 603 W Shiloh, OH 44878
Louis V. Russell   12710 Heintzelman Rd. Cedar Springs, MI
                      49319

John Schenkelberg	7421 Marriottsville Rd. Marriotttsville, MD 21104
Roland Schexnayder	205 E. 31 St. Reserve, LA 70084-5037
Richard P. Scott	4532 N. Forestview Chicago, IL 60656
Carl J. Scozzaro	10283 Green Trail Dr. N Boynton Beach, FL 33436
James E. Seeders	HC-86 Box 43 Springfield, WV 26763-9511
Henry L. Sharpe	1901 Parliament Rd. Cayce, SC 29033
William M. Shelby	6954 Cario-Lies Rd. Henderson, KY 42420
Harry Shimokawa	2576A Kekuanoni St. Honolulu, HI 96813
George Sipos	313 Mountain View Manor Cresson, PA 16630
Renford W. Skeens	PO Box 85South Webster, OH 45682
L. J. Small	203 N. Forest Ave. Tyler, TX 75702
Edward Speights	14 3rd Ave. South Birmingham,AL 35205
Ronald Stapleton	No Address
Gentry C. Stepp	78 Sharon Rd. Chillicothe, OH 45601
Paul K. Sweeney	1140 Audubon Rd. North Augusta, SC 29841
Robert J Sweeney	9 Colonial Rd. Brookside, NJ 07926
Elias B. Swire	156 Devall Rd. Hackberry, LA 70645
Arthur C. Thearling	13172 Commonwealth Southgate, MI 48195
George Trujillo	1711 Ferris Drive Tampa, FL 33603
Lester Turner	PO Box 362 Pink Hill, NC 28572
Richard D. Tyler	PO Box 151 Encampment,WY 82325
Richard Wakefield	205 E. Fair, RR 3 Centerville, IA 52544
Foy Walker	RR 2, PO Box 39 Ellaville, GA 31806
Roy Walker	641 Oakdale Dr. Belvedere, SC 29841
William Weissborn	4108 Academy Dr. Metairie, LA 70003
Edmond L. Whitmire	24346 Condon St. Oak Park, MI 48237
Thomas L. Williams	407 E. Locust St. Vincennes, IN 47591
Morris Wingo	95 Levels Rd. Empire, AL 35063
Frances C. Wittkop	426 Christopher Pl. Jefferson City, MO 65101
Harry Wittlin	25 Sutton Place South New York, NY 10022
Pete Zagwyn	PO Box 1455North Eastham, MA 02651
James Zurn	5824 N. 94th St. Milwaukee, WI 53225-2606

Roster of Deceased 474th Veterans as of November 1, 2001

Willie Aiken

Israel Alperin

Pryor Ancrum

Paul L. Anderson

Bobby Atkins

Jesse J. Baden

Clarence E. Bailey

Freddie Baker

Ralph W. Banks

Ronald Bartley

Morris W. Beal

Anthony Bell

Donald Bengston

Robert Berger

Robert J. Blackburn

Charles Blackwell, Jr.

Richard Bolig

William Borrelli

James Bowden

Johnny Bradford

David Brancato

Gaylon Brittain

Clarence C. Brooks

Hue L. Browder, Sr.

Randolph W.Browdus

Richard C. Brown

Venon F. Brown

Blount J. Bunn

James Bunn

Stanley C. Bush

Thomas Butler

Raymond T. Capalbo

Thomas Carroll
Willey E. Cathey
Daniel S. Caudle
Gordon Chambers
Joseph Cirino
Rondal Clemons
Curtis Clendenin
Herbert E. Cole
Keith Conley
Charles Coston
Harrison Crothers
Ralph Curtis
Frank Daniels
LeRoy David
Alvin Davis
James E. Davis
John M. Davis
William Davis
Joseph Day
Earl W. Deel
Louis Dixon
Lesley Dooley
Willie D. Edwards
Albert Equils
Jack E. Erickson
Earl L. Faircloth
Louis G. Flores
George Frame
.Millard Fullmore
Lester Gant
Frank W. Gantz
Marion Gentkowski
Richard E. Gruden
Alvin L. Hall
William Harris

William F. Harrison
.James V. Hart
Thomas Harvey
Grant Hayes, Jr.
John Hendrickson
George Hinton
Jeremiah Hobson
Thomas Holcomb
William B. Holmes
Neal H. Hoover
Edward A. Hopson
Fritz Huffine
William J. Humber
Buford L. Hunt
Herman R. Jacks
Donald T. Jefferson
Carl Jeffries
David A. Johnson
Robert D. Johnson
Jesse Jones
Alfred D. Julian
Alpheus Kearney
Gleason Kent
Eugene Kielek
Herman Kimbrell
Gordon O. Kinney
Tommy Klassen
Stanley J. Kozenko
Saint C. Lambson
Maurice E. Lebel
Edward Lenortavage
Jimmie E. Little
George R. Macholl
Lornie Mallory

Glover D. Manning
John T. Maron
Royster Matthews
Delmar McCall
J.J. McCrear, Jr.
Edward McGill
Earl E. McGinnis
Ambrose McKim
Landon McQuinn
Jessie E. Mersier, Jr.
Roy E. Montrell
Donald Mooney
Floyd Morris
Lyman L. Murphy
.William L. Murray
Lloyd Nickerson
LeRoy Palmer
Kay J. Pearson
Clem Perkins
Louis C. Perry
James Peters
Curtis Pierce
Walter Pollack
James O. Powers, Jr.
John Pupplo
Andrew Raney
Lloyd Reed
Martin Reed
Samuel Reynolds
Edward A. Roberts
Clayton C. Robinson, Jr.
Napoleon P. Roderick
Mariano Frank Sauro
Ronald Searcy

Raymond D. Self
Joe W. Shaw
George D. Sherwin
William R. Shons
John C. Short
Jack Shrewsbury
Charles E. Smith
Clyde P. Smith
Armstead C. Sneed, Jr.
Herbert Spain
Raymond Spivey
Collen Stillwell
Douglas Taylor
Franklin D. Taylor
Clarence W. Thomas
.Clyde E. Thomas
Gilbert Thornton
James W. Trapp
Arnold L. Wansley
William E. Waters
George A. Webb
Dale E. Wendtlandt
Harry L. Wheat
Bruce White
Charles C. Wiley
Donald R. Williams
Eugene Williams
Donald R. Williamson
Johnnie Willis
Herbert Wilson
Abraham W. Wright
George C. Wright
Albertus Young

Printed in the United States
6040

Associate Members and Friends

Alperin, Mrs. Israel
Berger, Linda (Mrs. Robert)
Blackburn, Kim (Mrs. Robert)
Bunn, Dorothy (Mrs. James)
Clemons, Mrs Rondal
Clendenin, Barbara (Mrs. Curt)
Davis, Mrs. James E.
Frame, Mrs. George
Gentkowski, Kathleen (Mrs. Marion)
Holcomb, Mrs. Thomas
Hunt, Mrs. Beuford
Hurt, Dan and Donna
Jacks, Mrs. Herman R.
Kent, Barbara (Mrs.Gleason)
Kozenko, Stephanie (Mrs. Stanley)
Lenortavage, Dorothy (Mrs. Edward)
Murray, Mrs.Bill
Reynolds, Dennis & Velinda
Self, Ann (Mrs. Ray)
Spain, Winnie (Mrs. Herbert)
White, Mrs. Bruce
Young, Alvestus (Mrs. Albertus)